Flyfisher's Guide to™

Yellowstone
National Park

Including Grand Teton National Park and Jackson Hole

Fishing Titles Available from Wilderness Adventures Press, Inc.™

Flyfishers Guide to™

Flyfisher's Guide to Alaska

Flyfisher's Guide to Arizona

Flyfisher's Guide to the Big Apple

Flyfisher's Guide to Chesapeake Bay

Flyfisher's Guide to Colorado

Flyfisher's Guide to the Florida Keys

Flyfisher's Guide to Freshwater Florida

Flyfisher's Guide to Idaho

Flyfisher's Guide to Montana

Flyfisher's Guide to Michigan

Flyfisher's Guide to Minnesota

Flyfisher's Guide to Missouri & Arkansas

Flyfisher's Guide to Nevada

Flyfisher's Guide to the New England Coast

Flyfisher's Guide to New Mexico

Flyfisher's Guide to New York

Flyfisher's Guide to the Northeast Coast

Flyfisher's Guide to Northern California

Flyfisher's Guide to Northern New England

Flyfisher's Guide to Oregon

Flyfisher's Guide to Pennsylvania

Flyfisher's Guide to Saltwater Florida

Flyfisher's Guide to Texas

Flyfisher's Guide to the Texas Gulf Coast

Flyfisher's Guide to Utah

Flyfisher's Guide to Virginia

Flyfisher's Guide to Washington

Flyfisher's Guide to Wisconsin & Iowa

Flyfisher's Guide to Wyoming

Flyfisher's Guide to Yellowstone National Park

On the Fly Guide to™

On the Fly Guide to the Northwest

On the Fly Guide to the Northern Rockies

Anglers Guide to™

Angler's Guide to the West Coast

Complete Anglers Guide to Oregon

Saltwater Angler's Guide to the Southeast

Saltwater Angler's Guide to Southern California

Best Fishing Waters™

California's Best Fishing Waters

Colorado's Best Fishing Waters

Idaho's Best Fishing Waters

Montana's Best Fishing Waters

Oregon's Best Fishing Waters

Washington's Best Fishing Waters

Field Guide to™

Field Guide to Fishing Knots

Fly Tying

Go-To Flies™

Flyfishing Adventures™

Montana

Flyfisher's Guide to™

Yellowstone National Park

Including Grand Teton National Park and Jackson Hole

Ken Retallic

Flyfisher's Guide to™ Series

Wilderness
Adventures
Press, Inc.™

Belgrade, Montana

Flyfisher's Guide to™ Series

Published by Wilderness Adventures Press, Inc.™
45 Buckskin Road
Belgrade, MT 59714
866-400-2012
Website: www.wildadvpress.com
email: books@wildadvpress.com

Second Edition 2009, 2011

Printed in the United States of America.

ISBN 978 -1-932098-14-3 (1-932098-14-3)

Dedication

Dedicated with heartfelt affection to Michael Retallick and Eugene Knapik, kindred souls on the stream, zealous travelers ever ready to test the best of the West, and conversant campfire companions.

Table of Contents

Acknowledgments

Over three decades in the West, those who have mentored my endeavors and understanding of fly fishing Yellowstone's waters are legion. Among the most influential are Michael Graham, Bernie Kuntz, Dale Whitington, Bob Messerol, Rob Thornberry, Rocky Barker, Bruce Staples, Jerry Painter, Jimmy Gabettas Sr., Jimmy Gabettas Jr., Steve Ellis, Mark Gablin, Jack Parker, Ron Howard, Mike Lawson, Renee Harrop, Jimmie Green, Ron Jones, Lynn Kaeding, Dan Mahony, Bob Jacklin, Rob Gibson, Jim Jones, Ed Michael, Bob Dunnagan, Loren Albright, Troy Tvrdy, Scott Yates, Ben Collins, Willy Cook, Eugene Knapik, and Mike Retallick.

Tips on Using This Book

In the hub city listings for each park we have tried to provide accurate, affordable choices, but it's always a good idea to call ahead before your arrival. Many of the motel and hotel listings for each park are followed by dollar signs to indicate the general cost for accommodations.

Hotel cost key: $—inexpensive $$—moderate $$$—moderate to expensive

Preface

Yellowstone is a magical place, special in its geology, geography, and history—one of the most visually rewarding and awe-inspiring sites in North America. Once seen, never forgotten. Once experienced, always to return.

I first answered its siren call more than 30 years ago as a neophyte flyfisher. And in my mind's eye I can still see the first wild, native trout that fell to a mayfly pattern I'd tied myself. Yet, those three decades of flashbacks are not just about cutthroat caught or lost, they are also sprinkled with the memories of family and friends who've joined me in savoring the park's myriad wonders.

To me, Yellowstone is all about sharing and appreciating the gift our forebears so insightfully protected and preserved in the world's first national park over a century ago. Enjoy its wonderful fishing waters, and work to maintain its treasures for the next generation.

Old Faithful.

Yellowstone National Park

Yellowstone National Park was "dedicated and set apart as a public park or pleasuring ground for the benefit and enjoyment of the people" and "for the preservation, from injury or spoilation, of all timber, mineral deposits, natural curiosities, or wonders... and their retention in their natural condition," by Congress on March 1, 1872.

Yellowstone is the oldest national park in the world. The commanding features that initially attracted interest and led to its preservation are the geological wonders. There are more geysers and hot springs in the park than in the rest of the world combined. The colorful Grand Canyon of the Yellowstone River, fossil forests, and the size and elevation of Yellowstone Lake also make it unique.

Today, the park is famous for its unique concentrations of wildlife, including elk, bison, moose, deer, grizzly bears, black bears, wolves, coyotes, trumpeter swans, and bald eagles. The park's native trout, the Yellowstone cutthroat, is a prime attraction to both wildlife watchers and anglers. Ninety-nine percent of the park's 3,400 square miles (2.2 million acres) remain undeveloped, providing a wide range of habitat types. Yellowstone is a true wilderness, one of the few large, natural areas remaining in the Lower 48 States.

Cultural sites dating back 12,000 years are evidence of the park's human history. More recent history can be seen in structures and sites that represent the various periods of park administration and visitor facilities development. Visitors meet nature here on its own terms. Park regulations exist for visitor safety and for the protection of natural and cultural resources. Please obey all park rules and regulations.

Summer temperatures are in the seventies and eighties, with cool nights in the forties, and thunderstorms are common. Mild to cool temperatures linger through September and October. Rain gear is recommended during spring, summer, and fall. The first heavy snows fall by November 1 and continue through March, with snow and frost possible during any month.

COPING WITH THE CROWDS

More than 3 million tourists visit Yellowstone annually, primarily between Memorial Day and September 30, but it's almost always crowded when roads are open. Traffic through the park's loop roads is slow and delays occur regularly, often the result of animal sightings close to the road, which prompt tourists to stop their cars en masse, or construction projects. Anticipate these delays and don't expect to arrive at planned destinations at highway speeds.

The five entrances to the park are reached from the following gateway communities: North Entrance—Gardiner, Montana; Northeast Entrance—Cooke City, Montana; East Entrance—Cody, Wyoming; South Entrance—Jackson Hole, Wyoming; and West Entrance—West Yellowstone, Montana. In addition, the park's southwest corner—Cascade Corner, home of the Fall and Bechler River drainages—can be accessed from Ashton, Idaho, although there are no connecting roads directly into the rest of the park.

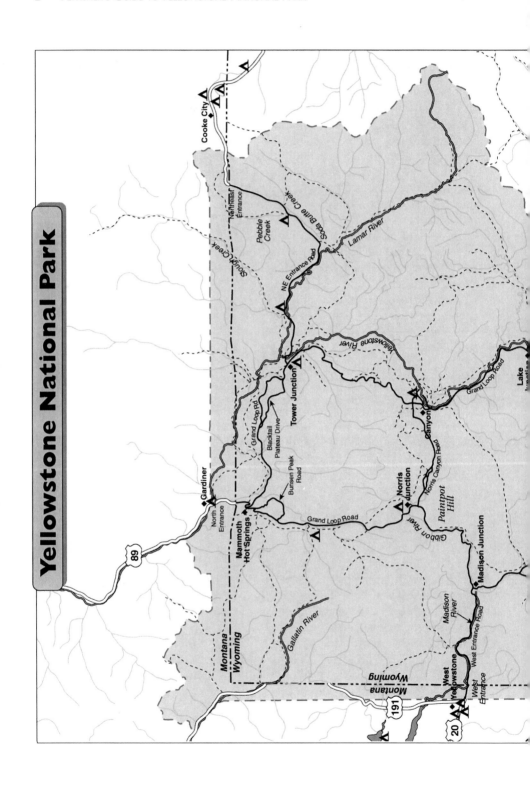

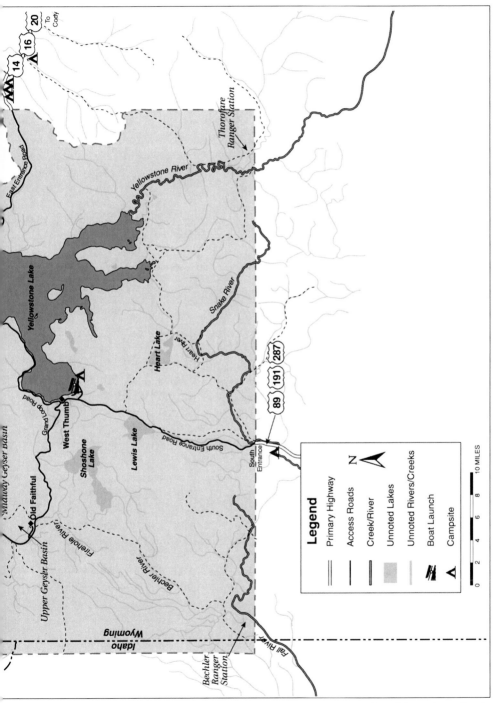

Legend

	Primary Highway
	Access Roads
	Creek/River
	Unnoted Lakes
	Unnoted Rivers/Creeks
	Boat Launch
	Campsite

N

0 2 4 6 8 10 MILES

Park roads typically open in May, as early as conditions permit, and close after the first Sunday in November. The only stretch of road open year-round is from Gardiner, Montana, to the Northeast Entrance near Cooke City, Montana.

A visit to Yellowstone requires advance planning and timing. During the summer season, lodging and camping facilities in the park, and in gateway communities, generally fill by early afternoon. Reservations are essential for peak-season stays at the park's lodges and inns. Some reservations must be made as much as a year in advance.

All reservations for accommodations and designated campgrounds in the park are handled by Xanterra Parks & Resorts, which operates lodges in Yellowstone and other parks. The phone number for Yellowstone is 307-344-7311, and the company offers free reservations at www.xanterra.com. The official concessionaires for all national parks can be found at www.nps.com.

Accommodations are available on a seasonal basis at the following locations:
- Mammoth Hot Springs: Mammoth Hot Springs Hotel and cabins
- Tower Junction: Roosevelt Lodge and cabins
- Canyon Village: Canyon Village Lodge
- Lake Village: Lake Hotel and cabins, Lake Lodge and cabins
- Grant Village: Grant Village Motel
- Old Faithful Village: Old Faithful Inn, Old Faithful Lodge, Snow Lodge

Camping in the park opens May 1 and ends November 3, except at Mammoth, which is open year-round. Seasonal campground reservations can be made for the following sites in the southern half of the park: Bridge Bay, Canyon Village, Fishing Bridge recreational vehicle area (hard-sided vehicles only), Grant Village, and Madison Junction.

Park campgrounds available only on a first-come, first-served basis are located at Mammoth, Norris, Indian Creek, Slough Creek, Pebble Creek, and Tower Falls in the northern half of the park, and at Lewis Lake Campground near the South Entrance. They frequently fill by noon. Arrive early, plan carefully, and seek information at visitor centers.

Yellowstone's headquarters are located at Mammoth Hot Springs, and visitor centers are located at each of the villages on the park's loop road. Shaped like a figureeight, the loop road parallels most of the park's major rivers.

A permit is required to fish in Yellowstone's waters, and the park has its own set of fishing regulations (see Yellowstone's Fishing Rules). Advance reservations are required for backcountry campsites. Other activities such as boating, canoeing, and snowmobiling also require registration, permits, or licenses. Special regulations may apply, so take the time to become informed at any visitor center or ranger station.

For more information write, Yellowstone National Park, Attn: Visitor's Service,
P.O. Box 168, Yellowstone National Park, Wyoming 82190-0168; or call
307-344-7381 or 307-344-2386; or go online at www.nps.gov/yell/.

Yellowstone Quick Facts

Size

- 3,472 square miles, 2,219,823 acres
- 63 miles north to south, 54 miles east to west; larger than Rhode Island and Delaware combined, with 91 percent located in Wyoming, 7.6 percent in Montana, and 1.4 percent in Idaho

Topography

- Highest point: Eagle Peak at 11,358 feet
- Lowest point: Reese Creek at 5,282 feet
- Tallest waterfall: Lower Falls of the Yellowstone River at 308 feet
- Approximately 5 percent is covered by water, 15 percent is meadow and grassland, and 80 percent is forested.

Weather

- Precipitation ranges from 10 inches at north boundary to 80 inches in the southwest corner. Temperatures range from 10 degrees F (–12 degrees C) mean in January, to 55 degrees F (13 degrees C) mean in July at Lake Yellowstone in the center of the park.

Flora

- 8 species of conifers, with approximately 80 percent of the forests comprised of lodgepole pine. Approximately 1,050 species of native vascular plants and 168 species of exotic (non-native) plants.

Wildlife

- Largest concentration of free-roaming wildlife in the Lower 48 States and the global temperate zone. There are 7 species of native ungulates (hoofed mammals); 2 species of bears; approximately 50 species of other mammals, including the gray wolf, which was reintroduced in 1995; 290 species of birds; 18 species of fish (5 nonnative); 6 species of reptiles; and 4 species of amphibians. Five species are protected as threatened or endangered.

Ecology

- Approximately 10,000 thermal features and approximately 200 to 250 active geysers. The park has one of the world's largest calderas (volcanic explosion crater), measuring 28 miles by 47 miles.

Yellowstone Lake

- 136 square miles surface area, 110 miles of shoreline, 20 miles north to south, and 14 miles east to west. Average depth is 139 feet, and maximum depth is 390 feet.

Roads and Trails

- 370 miles of paved roads and approximately 1,200 miles of trails, with 97 trailheads. There are 300 backcountry campsites.

Legends and Follies:
A Century of Fishing in Yellowstone

One of Yellowstone National Park's most attractive hallmarks is its legendary fishing. Everyone has a favorite Yellowstone fishing story. Mine is the day swarms of deerflies drove a horde of faint-hearted flyfishers out of Slough Creek's first meadow. A 23-inch cutthroat was a handsome reward for the painful insect bites.

The pas de deux between angler and trout is performed on a stage of stunning beauty and dramatic variety. Majestic backdrops feature fountain-spewing geysers and sulfurous mud pots, snowcapped mountains and rainbow-colored canyons. Crystalline streams and emerald green lakes host cutthroat, rainbow, brown, brook, and lake trout, as well as grayling and whitefish. Quick to steal a scene are elk, deer, moose, grizzly bears, black bears, coyotes, wolves, eagles, ospreys, and pelicans.

As early as 1903, tourism promotions for the park, like this Northern Pacific Railroad poster, extolled the park's fishing paradise, comprised of five different species of trout. Prior to 1889 there was only one species, the native cutthroat.

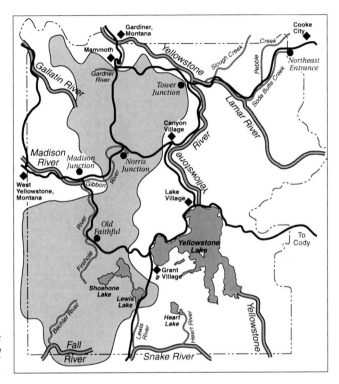

Shaded area shows region in park that had no fish prior to 1889.

Today's campfire yarns and endless magazine articles rival the tall tales of early explorers and tourists. Sooner or later there comes a time in Yellowstone "when a dry fly fisherman thinks he's died and gone to heaven," says Tim Wade of North Fork Anglers in Cody.

Slough Creek in the upper Lamar Valley is a popular wilderness getaway in late summer and autumn. Even with overcrowding, it's still possible to find some solitude in the stream's alpine meadows. Surrounded by the Absaroka Mountains' volcanic ramparts, the meandering flows of First Meadow are a comfortable hike from the campground road. Second and Third Meadows are just up the trail.

Former President Jimmy Carter hiked to First Meadows in 1993. Unlike VIPs of the past, he fished the park without fanfare. His Volunteer Angler Report details the bounty of a pristine stream. In three days, Carter caught and released 25 Yellowstone cutthroat. Four were 10 to 12 inches; two, 12 to 14 inches; three, 14 to 16 inches; seven, 16 to 18 inches; eight, 18 to 20 inches, and one over 20 inches.

"Fished caddis hatch size 16–18. Tricorythodes size 22–24, and size 12 Muddlers and hoppers," Carter noted in his report.

Albert McClane, author of McClane's Game Fish of North America, was captivated by Slough Creek's scenery and the marvel of 30-fish days. "However, it's not the quality of the angling that is so compelling as the feeling, I suppose, of being transposed to a valley that was chronologically bypassed."

The allure of wilderness retreats also draws anglers to the headwaters of the Yellowstone River, Bechler Meadows, the upper Lamar River, Heart Lake, and Shoshone Lake.

Owen Wister, author of The Virginian, marveled in an 1887 journal entry that he could look back across the broad expanse of Yellowstone Lake and see the distant Grand Teton and its sister peaks looming above the Continental Divide. A less traveled trail, even today, is into the Grand Canyon of the Yellowstone, where the river's rumbling flows drown all sounds of civilization. Wister couldn't resist its depths. "The canyon seems so deep that the sky comes close to the tops of the trees," he wrote.

But Wister's diary notations were more prosaic a short four years later.

"We came down the [Yellowstone] river and camped on an island near the mud geysers where we had originally intended to ford. Good fishing, but some of the trout wormy. Lots of outfits and people passing on the road and children screaming," he wrote on August 11, 1891. "This park is an immense thing for the American bourgeoisie. Popper takes mommer and children in a very big wagon with two mules and their kitchen and beds, and forth they march hundreds of miles and summer in the park. Nothing like this ever existed before, I think."

Grumbling about crowds is easy to appreciate today. Harder to fathom was the incredible abundance of 19th-century Yellowstone's cutthroat trout—or the gluttony of park visitors. Living off the land was the order of the day. Give a boy a fishing rod, and he could help feed a party of 40 dignitaries and cavalry troopers.

At age 15, Edward Hewitt fulfilled his camp duty with single-minded zeal in 1877. He landed 50 or more cutthroat a day from the mouth of Yellowstone Lake. On the party's way out of the park, an officer enlisted the youth to help feed another, even larger cavalry troop. In a single afternoon, Hewitt said he hooked 450 to 500 pounds of cutthroat from a stream he called Boulder Creek. From his description, it must be the South Fork of the Madison River.

Impossible? Not if you can picture Rocky Mountain flying fish. General W. F. Strong described the technique in an 1887 diary entry. Stout poles and heavy lines were used so that when fish were hooked, they "could be immediately jerked clear of the moving water and flung to men waiting on the grassy banks."

Hewitt returned to the park in 1914. In his book, A Trout and Salmon Fisherman for 75 Years, he bragged about a fishing duel on the Madison River. The contest was between his dry flies and a commercial fisherman's wet flies. Hewitt lost 165 to 162 fish, but said he was way ahead until high winds hindered his fly casting.

More noteworthy than his embellishments is Hewitt's notation that his catch was composed mostly of browns and a few rainbows.

The brown trout, a European fish, was introduced into the Madison in 1890, and in less than a quarter century it was a dominant species. Rainbow and brook trout also made their way into the river. Native westslope cutthroat trout and fluvial Arctic grayling of the Madison drainage have been struggling for survival ever since. It's a story that's been repeated throughout the West.

Fortunately, this didn't happen in the park's Yellowstone drainage. The star player in Yellowstone's legendary fishing is still a cutthroat. In the last citadel of the intermountain West native trout, the Yellowstone cutthroat still reigns, albeit struggling from modern-day threats in Yellowstone Lake and the Yellowstone River.

The park's fishery, despite overcoming its bumpy ride through more than a century of abuse and tinkering, confronts perhaps its greatest threats today in three devastating invasions from the outside.

The park's Yellowstone cutthroat stronghold is drastically threatened by the unauthorized introduction of predatory lake trout into Yellowstone Lake and the invasion of park waters by two exotic species: Myxobolus cerebralis, the parasite that causes whirling disease in trout, and the New Zealand mudsnail, a gastropod that has the potential to displace virtually all other bottom-dwelling invertebrates in a stream.

THE JOHNNY APPLESEED ERA

Early explorers found nearly 40 percent of Yellowstone's waters barren of fish. In streams of the Lower Geyser and Norris Geyser Basins, the absence of fish was attributed to thermally heated and chemically impregnated waters. But waterfalls were actually the most common barriers to upstream migration.

Barren streams included the upper Firehole and Gibbon Rivers in the Madison drainage; the Gardner River in the Yellowstone drainage; and the Bechler, Fall, and Lewis Rivers in the Snake drainage. Only 17 of the park's 150 lakes were known to hold fish. Lewis and Shoshone Lakes were not among them.

The first formal survey of park waters was conducted in 1889. David Starr Jordan found 11 native fish. Four were game fish: Yellowstone cutthroat, westslope cutthroat, fluvial Arctic grayling, and whitefish. Seven suckers and minnows and the mottled sculpin are also natives.

Today, biologists note that Snake River finespotted cutthroat occur in small numbers in the upper Snake. Also, while it is genetically the same as Yellowstone cutthroat, park biologists say the Heart Lake cutthroat has different characteristics, including predatory instincts. A small, isolated population of Sedge Creek cutthroat is considered to be on the evolutionary fast track to subspecies status.

But even as Jordan conducted his survey, early fishery biologists rushed in to fill vacant waters under the park's original mandate "for the benefit and enjoyment of the people." The fledgling U.S. Fish Commission was eager to take the job because it needed "a proper outdoor laboratory in which to exercise its science," according to park historian Aubrey L. Haines in The Yellowstone Story. The park offered "an opportunity to broaden the commission's activities...[to include] the development of a sport fishery in what was then the only area of wild land under federal management."

This "grand experiment" left an indelible imprint on Yellowstone's lakes and streams.

In 1889, brook trout were introduced into the upper Firehole and Gardner Rivers, as well as Glenn Creek. The upper Gardner also received Yellowstone cutthroat, and the upper Firehole received brown trout. Rainbows were planted in the upper Gibbon River. The following year, lake and brown trout were introduced into Shoshone and

Park Ranger DuPuir and two other helpers plant fish in a small lake in Yellowstone National Park in 1922. (NPS photo/YNP)

Lewis Lakes. Brown trout were stocked in the Madison River, and mountain whitefish were planted in the Yellowstone River above its falls. Only the whitefish did not take.

Rainbows stocked in tributaries of Shoshone Lake in 1893 also did not survive, but the brook trout planted in 1895 did.

Yellowstone has no warmwater game fish, but not for lack of trying. In 1895, black bass were planted in the Gibbon River and several lakes with outlets to the Firehole River in Lower Geyser Basin. None survived.

Rainbows were planted in the Yellowstone River above the falls in 1902. They disappeared, presumably genetically swamped by the dominant Yellowstone cutthroat.

Five years later, park officials began to display mixed feelings about the Johnny Appleseed philosophies of the U.S. Fish Commission.

David C. Booth, a fisheries employee, was reprimanded in 1907 for an unauthorized stocking of rainbow into Yellowstone Lake. The next year, transplants of landlocked Atlantic salmon were sanctioned in Yellowstone and Duck Lakes, but a request to plant smelt in Yellowstone and Shoshone Lakes was rejected. The rainbows and salmon did not survive.

A lake-dwelling subspecies of Montana grayling was transplanted to Grebe Lake, headwaters of the Gibbon River, in 1921. Not until 1936 was stocking of non-native fish in native fish waters banned by the National Park Service. However, yellow perch in Goose Lake had to be poisoned in 1938. No one knows how they got there. In 1967, brown trout were poisoned in Duck Lake. Brook trout discovered in Arnica Creek, a tributary of Yellowstone Lake, were poisoned in 1985.

One of the park's worst nightmares appeared in 1994 when lake trout were officially recorded in Yellowstone Lake. Former Superintendent Bob Barbee called illegal stocking of the voracious predator in the lake "environmental vandalism." Yellowstone declared a war of attrition against the threat to the last refuge of inland cutthroat.

Another perspective on the transplantation debate, according to John Varley, chief of Yellowstone research, and others, is that some park waters contain "museum quality" trout from single or limited plants in the past. Lake trout eggs collected from Lewis Lake were used to establish brood stocks to replenish Lake Michigan, where lake trout were decimated by the sea lamprey and pollution. Isolated populations of rainbow may one day provide answers to the whirling disease threat that has descended on numerous western streams—perhaps even a future brood stock.

THE HATCHERY ERA

Turn-of-the-century efforts to improve nature did not stop with importing game fish to the park. During its 50-year hatchery period, starting in 1901, Yellowstone Lake became the largest exporter of inland cutthroat eggs to the world. Its hatcheries also stocked several park waters and, supposedly, made more cutthroat available for Yellowstone Lake's sport fishery.

In 1921, a rainbow hatchery was established on Trout Lake to maintain stocks of "catchable size" fish in park streams, including the Firehole, Madison, Gallatin, Gardner, Bechler, Snake, lower Yellowstone, and lower Lamar. Internal and external grayling exports were added to the park's cottage industry in 1931 with a hatchery at Grebe Lake.

Most of the park's small lakes also were stocked with a variety of trout. Many did not take, but the number of lakes with fish increased from 17 in the past to 40 today. Two of the latter include Wolf and Cascade Lakes, which accepted grayling transplants.

Of the park's hatcheries, only the one for grayling appears to have had redeeming value. Today, "most western grayling stocks can be traced back there," states Mary Anne Franke in "A Grand Experiment: 100 Years of Fisheries Management in Yellowstone" in Yellowstone Science. But no amount of spin-doctoring can obscure the sins of the past. Most manipulations of Yellowstone cutthroat populations were misguided and decidedly unprofitable.

"Between 1903 and 1953, 818 million trout eggs were exported from Yellowstone," Franke wrote. "All together, more than 50 federal, state, and private hatcheries received eggs from Yellowstone.... The Yellowstone cutthroat has survived in seven western states and two Canadian provinces in which it was planted..."

The more pernicious impact of the Yellowstone cutthroat follies occurred on the mother lake. The abstract of a 1988 report to an American Fisheries Society symposium is succinct but revealing:

"Although egg-taking and hatchery operations [on Yellowstone Lake] were terminated over 30 years ago, it is now apparent egg removal, genetic mixing, and greatly reduced natural spawner escapement led to a gradual reduction in reproductive potential and undermined the complex mosaic of reproduction and recruitment. Angler harvest also had a negative impact as it became excessive," according to John Varley and Robert Gresswell, a former U.S. Fish and Wildlife Service researcher.

CORRECTING PAST SINS, CONFRONTING NEW THREATS

A native son of the West, the cutthroat trout is a colorful fish. It has evolved into as many as 15 subspecies, including the three present in the Greater Yellowstone ecosystem. In a trout fishing contest, the cutthroat would win the Miss Congeniality title.

Park rangers drove a truck to the bank of the Bechler River to stock fish in the secluded stream in 1936. Proposals in 1920 and 1926 to dam the Bechler to create an irrigation reservoir were rejected by park officials. (NPS photo/YNP)

During the last Ice Age, cutthroat took the lead in migrations up the Columbia River system. They beat out their Pacific Coast cousin, the rainbow, and became the only native trout in the vast intermountain interior of the West. Cutthroat even managed to cross the Continental Divide; however, later barriers, such as Shoshone Falls on the Snake River in Idaho, halted the rainbow's upstream migrations.

To share the limited resources and make the best of short growing seasons, accommodation became the cutthroat's forte. This species doesn't compete well with introduced trout. Also, when hybridization with rainbows occurs, rainbow characteristics usually become dominant.

"The cutthroat trout appears to be more social and less territorial than the introduced salmonids," reports John Varley, chief of park research. "In unexploited or lightly exploited streams, pools seem to have cutthroat of various sizes schooled together which exhibit no territorial or antagonistic behavior towards each other."

They also are highly susceptible to overharvest. In a catch-and-release fishing experiment, "wild cutthroat trout were twice as catchable as wild brook trout and 18 times more vulnerable than wild brown trout," Varley said.

Yet, it wasn't until after Yellowstone celebrated its centennial that the park's cutthroat were first protected under no-kill regulations. In 1973, cutthroat were declared catch and release only on almost all park streams. At the same time, the creel limit on Yellowstone Lake and its tributaries was set at two fish under 13 inches. Fishing Bridge was closed. The upper river and the mouths of the lake's creeks were declared off-limits until July 15 each year, when spawning runs were assumed to have ended.

Then, at the turn of the 20th century, all the park's native game fish gained full protection. Former Superintendent Michael Finley changed fishing regulations in 2001 to place all native fish under catch-and-release rules, including Yellowstone, Snake River finespotted and westslope cutthroat, grayling, and mountain whitefish.

Then and now, anglers have readily accepted the regulations. Most are proponents of catch-and-release fishing for all trout. An Idaho State University study in 1980 showed that, on average, each cutthroat in the upper Yellowstone River was caught nearly 10 times during its short fishing season. The catch-and-release mortality rate was estimated at 3 percent.

In another study of the upper river, "85 percent of the fishermen catch one or more wild cutthroat trout in an average daily trip," Varley said in the late 1990s. "Excellent fishing is provided despite enormous pressure, in the recent annual range of 2,800 anglers per stream mile.... The fishery remains excellent only because all cutthroats caught are returned alive to the stream to be caught again." It is perhaps the park's greatest success story, Varley said at a fisheries managers' conference in Jackson, Wyoming.

Under the first set of stricter regulations, cutthroat numbers in Yellowstone Lake and the upper river bounced back to historical levels in the late 1980s to mid 1990s. Fish size increased dramatically and age distributions reflected natural, preexploitation population levels.

But a rapid reversal occurred as the park passed into the 21st century. Dramatic population losses caused first by predatory lake trout illegally introduced into Yellowstone Lake and later by the debilitating effects of whirling disease became progressively more apparent. "Non-native lake trout, whirling disease, and the ongoing drought (1998–2004) have pushed the population down to levels not seen since the 1950s, when cutthroat were heavily fished and eggs were removed for hatcheries," noted Mike Stark in a 2004 Billings Gazette article titled "Yellowstone Cutthroat Trout in Trouble: But There is Hope."

While the jury is still out on how devastating the invasions will ultimately be on the park's cutthroat, Varley remained optimistic. "The Yellowstone cutthroat, especially those at Yellowstone Lake, was ill-adapted for many of these kinds of changes that it's seeing. But I'm not going to count them out," Varley told Stark.

Some of his colleagues weren't so sanguine, however.

"Two significant threats to the native Yellowstone cutthroat trout, discovered [in Yellowstone Lake] over a five-year period during the 1990s, irreversibly altered the future of this thriving and diverse ecosystem," states the Yellowstone Fisheries & Aquatic Sciences Annual Report 2002. "Without swift and continuing action, negative effects on this trout population—a keystone energy source for at least 42 species of mammals and birds and a recreational focus for visitors—have the potential to produce ecosystem-wide consequences. Predatory, non-native lake trout, illegally introduced to the lake at least 20 years ago and not discovered until 1994, can each consume over 40 Yellowstone cutthroat trout annually. They have the potential to decimate the Yellowstone Lake fishery in our lifetime without heightened and maintained management efforts.

"Whirling disease, a parasite that attacks the developing cartilage of young fish resulting in skeletal deformity, whirling behavior, abnormal feeding, and increased vulnerability to predation, was first detected in Yellowstone Lake in 1998 and in the Firehole River in 2000," the report continues. "This devastating disease further threatens already declining Yellowstone cutthroat trout populations. Although whirling disease is currently believed to be concentrated in the northern regions of the Yellowstone Lake watershed, several other tributaries have already been identified as high risk."

On the other hand, fishing pressure in the park has changed over the decades, primarily since the introduction in 1994 of a fee for a fishing permit. Triple-digit angler numbers dropped dramatically once the pay system was installed.

A total of 136,300 angler permits were recorded in 1975, the first year records were kept, and numbers waxed and waned to a high of 161,000 in 1991. Numbers then dropped approximately 40 percent to 88,300 in 1994, and by almost 50 percent to 65,990 by the 2000 season. On the other hand, the park has been attracting more sophisticated anglers who now stay longer. These fishermen are more in tune with modern conservation principles protecting native trout and naturally reproducing introduced species (i.e., wild trout). The average angler spent less than two days fishing in the park in the 1970s. This number grew to three days by 1994, and increased to four days by the 2004 season.

Also, despite the exotic species threats confronting the fisheries—as well as a prolonged drought at the turn of the century that may or may not be a growing factor due to global warming—angler satisfaction has remained high.

According to the *Yellowstone Fisheries & Aquatic Sciences Annual Report 2003*: "The more than 3 million visitors to Yellowstone National Park in 2003 represented another all-time high. Angling remains a popular visitor pastime; over 54,000 specialuse fishing permits were issued in 2003. A volunteer angler response (VAR) card is provided with each fishing permit, providing anglers the opportunity to report where they fish, the species and size of fish caught, and their satisfaction with the fishing experience. There has been a response rate of almost 4,000 angler outings per year in recent years from the VAR cards.

Early day–tourists flocked to Fishing Bridge over the Yellowstone River at the mouth of the lake. On a single day in June 1954, U.S. Fish and Wildlife Service biologists recorded more than 700 cutthroat creeled by anglers on the bridge. It was closed to fishing in 1973, and cutthroat were restricted to catch-and-release fishing on the majority of park streams. (NPS photo/YNP)

"Park fisheries managers use the information provided by VAR cards to get an overview of fish population dynamics and angler attitudes toward the fisheries resource throughout the waters of Yellowstone National Park. Data from 2001 and 2002 indicate that anglers fished 2.75 hours per day during typical fishing trips in the park. Single-day anglers reported catching at least one fish 78% of the time, and on average landed almost one (0.89) fish per each hour of fishing. Native cutthroat trout remained the most sought-after and caught fish species, making up 59% of the total catch, followed distantly by rainbow trout at 15%, brown trout at 9%, brook trout at 8%, whitefish and lake trout each at 4%, and grayling at 1%. The majority of anglers were satisfied with their overall fishing experience (75%), the numbers of fish caught (62%), and the size of the fish caught (68%). Anglers typically reported on many fishable waters in the park; their observations can be the first line of information toward identifying potential fisheries-related problems.

"Yellowstone Lake remains the most popular destination for anglers that come to the park; an estimated 13,685 anglers fished Yellowstone Lake in 2002.

"The angler catch per effort for cutthroat trout in Yellowstone Lake has decreased for the past four years, and is now at its lowest level (0.8 fish per hour in 2003 compared to 2 fish per hour in 1999) since summaries of VAR cards were compiled in 1979. Average total length has increased annually for seven years and is also at an extreme, its highest level since 1979. These changes to the fishery coincide with the discovery and subsequent expansion of lake trout since the mid-1990s (and the apparent loss of young, smaller cutthroat year classes over a period of years).

"Angler catch per effort of lake trout was at its all-time high in 2002; however, lake trout are still caught at a much lower rate than cutthroat trout."

FISHERIES MANAGEMENT TIMELINE

Yellowstone has been the proving ground for numerous transitions in wildlife management, including the "natural regulation" concept. Pivotal events in protection of the park's trout include:

- 1908: First angler creel limit set at 20 fish per day; decreased to 10 fish in 1921, to 5 fish in 1949, to 3 fish in 1954, and to 2 fish in 1973.
- 1919: Commercial fishing banned.
- 1936: Introduction of non-native fish in native fish waters banned.
- 1950: Madison, Firehole, and lower Gibbon Rivers restricted to fly fishing only.
- 1953: Cutthroat hatcheries closed; grayling and rainbow hatcheries closed in 1956.
- 1968: National Park Service implemented natural regulation of wildlife, including fish.
- 1969: Bait fishing banned in park.
- 1973: Cutthroat restricted to catch-and-release angling, except in Yellowstone Lake and the river above the lake.
- 1994: First year a fee was charged for a fishing permit.

- 1994: Declared war on non-native lake trout in Yellowstone Lake; park begins massive gillnetting program to limit the predator's threat to cutthroat. Anglers required to kill all lake trout caught in Yellowstone Lake and its tributaries.
- 1997: Native Fish Restoration Plan submitted for public review.
- 1998: Yellowstone Lake opened to fishing June 1 to give anglers a better chance to take more lake trout.
- 2001: All native sport fish species—Yellowstone, Snake River finespotted and westslope cutthroat, grayling, and mountain whitefish—placed under catch-and-release regulations.
- 2001: Opening of Yellowstone Lake returned to traditional June 15 opener because anglers were catching more cutthroat than lake trout.
- 2004: Fishing in Pelican Creek, a primary cutthroat spawning tributary on the north shore of Yellowstone Lake, was closed until further notice due to the devastating loss of the fishery from impacts of whirling disease.
- 2006: Park announced increase in daily bag limit of non-native fish in cutthroat streams to five per day and established a sport fishery in non-cutthroat waters like the Madison, Firehole, and lower Gibbon that prohibits harvest of fish.

Curse of the Aliens: Guardians Still Tinkering with Paradise

Few believed more than a century ago that there was a lake in the Rocky Mountains where a fisherman could easily catch a trout, turn around, and cook it on the line in the boiling waters of a geyser—all without moving a foot.

Today, this erstwhile highlight of fishing trips to Yellowstone Lake is preserved only on grainy photographs and faded postcards. Casting to cruising trout from Fishing Cone in West Thumb Geyser Basin is verboten. Fishing Cone is symbolic of the transitions in attitudes and policies during Yellowstone National Park's history, now spanning three different centuries of thought.

Millions of tourists view the geyser basin as just another geological marvel to squeeze into their whirlwind tours. Those who read the boardwalk sign at Fishing Cone see it as a historical footnote. Most anglers view it differently. Its off-limits status reflects more than a lost opportunity. Fishing in Yellowstone is no longer a novelty. It is serious business.

Once the primary exporter of cutthroat eggs to the world, the park is now the strongest proponent for conservation of inland cutthroat. The only native trout in the intermountain West presently occurs in only 10 to 15 percent of its historic range. Ninety percent of the Yellowstone cutthroat's current range is within the park's boundaries. Westslope cutthroat are virtually gone from the Madison drainage, and struggling to hang on in only a few tributaries in the Gallatin drainage.

In 1900, a U.S. Cavalry trooper demonstrates the unique practice of catching a Yellowstone cutthroat trout from Yellowstone Lake and cooking it on the spot at Fishing Cone in West Thumb Geyser Basin. Current park rules prohibit fishing from the cone or from shore in this area. (NPS postcard/YNP)

But changes in management perceptions and goals were slow to come following the casual introductions of exotic, or non-native, game fish into the park's lakes and streams in the late 1880s and early 1900s. Not until 1936 was stocking of non-native fish banned in the home waters of cutthroat trout and fluvial (river-dwelling) Arctic grayling. The hatcheries were closed in the late 1950s, and put-and-take stocking of fish ended. Stricter fishing regulations imposed in the 1970s and mid-1990s were directed at restoring Yellowstone cutthroat populations to historic levels, first in Yellowstone Lake and later in the lower river's tributaries. But it was not until the turn of the century that all native fish gained full protection under catch-and-release rules imposed in 2001.

Both cutthroat and anglers reaped tremendous benefits from the stricter regulations of the late 20th century. But even as fisheries managers patted themselves on the back, another storm cloud spilled over the Continental Divide into Yellowstone Lake. In 1994, the park declared a take-no-prisoners war against illegally transplanted lake trout threatening the largest bastion of Yellowstone cutthroat.

The following year, to assess the seriousness of lake trout establishment in Yellowstone Lake, the Park Service convened a panel of experts from throughout the United States and Canada. Their task was to determine if the situation was as dire as first perceived and to provide strategies for elimination or control of this large predator in Yellowstone Lake. A large majority of the biologists agreed that without some type of intervention, a 70 percent or greater reduction in cutthroat trout abundance was highly probable within 50 to 100 years. However, a concerted gillnetting effort to destroy lake trout, combined with angler harvest, might reduce cutthroat losses to less than 30 percent of the existing population.

To date, a massive gillnetting effort has been the park's primary assault against the lake trout invasion. In its 2003 "Protection of Native Yellowstone Cutthroat Trout in Yellowstone Lake" update, biologists reported that "since 1995 more than 75,000 lake trout have been removed from Yellowstone Lake via gillnetting. The majority of these fish have come from West Thumb and Breeze Channel where most of the gillnetting effort is concentrated. Catch rates, total numbers, numbers and sizes of spawning adults caught in fall sets all appear to be declining. Increased resources, including nets and staffing, have allowed better lake coverage; total catch and catch rate continue to decline. Bioenergetics modeling (estimates of how many cutthroat trout a lake trout potentially consumes) suggests that a mature lake trout can eat between 50 to 90 cutthroat trout per year. Thus, the lake trout control project has saved a large number of cutthroat trout from predation by lake trout."

While most believe the illegal transfer of lake trout to Yellowstone Lake was misguided, at best, the introduction of two other alien species to park waters probably was inevitable.

Exotic "aquatic hitchhikers"—most likely carried in on the fishing gear of anglers and the equipment and watercraft of boaters—known to have invaded Yellowstone waters include the New Zealand mudsnail, a pernicious gastropod that drives out other invertebrates, first recorded in the Firehole River in 1997, and Myxobolus cerebralis, the parasite that causes whirling disease in trout, discovered in Yellowstone Lake in 1998.

The snail has the ability to reproduce quickly and can become as dense as 500,000 snails per square meter. The snail can have an impact on the food chain of native trout and may alter the physical characteristics of streams. Studies into the mudsnail's growing presence in Yellowstone were initiated just a few years ago. Reports up through 2002 indicated that the pest was most prevalent in the Firehole River drainage and trickling downstream into the Madison River. Other "hot spots" included the Gardner River's Boiling River hot springs area and Polecat Creek in the Snake River drainage.

But if ever there could be a doubt about the pernicious outcome of an alien species taking hold in a new environment, Yellowstone offers an almost classic example of the devastating threat of whirling disease, which has plagued the West since the early 1980s. Park officials announced in 2004 that the Pelican Creek cutthroat fishery had been virtually wiped out by the parasite inadvertently imported from Europe and spread throughout western waters.

Pelican Creek is the second largest tributary of Yellowstone Lake and as recently as the early 1980s hosted an annual spawning migration of nearly 30,000 Yellowstone cutthroat trout. "The outbreak of whirling disease, combined with the invasion of non-native lake trout, has sent Yellowstone Lake cutthroat plummetin to their lowest numbers since population surveys began in 1969," according to the Greater Yellowstone Coalition's Summer 2004 Report. "Because there is no known cure for whirling disease and Pelican Creek is already in a pristine condition, there is little biologists can do except monitor the situation and hope that some cutthroat eventually develop a resistance to the disease."

So, at the outset of the 2004 fishing season, Yellowstone National Park Superintendent Suzanne Lewis announced that fishing was no longer permitted in the Pelican Creek drainage. She noted that the closure likely would continue for additional years as biologists monitor the severity of the disease and the status of the cutthroat trout population until improvement warrants reopening this stream system for enjoyment by future anglers.

"Our objectives are to protect the remaining cutthroat trout in Pelican Creek from stress and prevent potential movement of the destructive whirling disease parasite from Pelican Creek to other streams of Yellowstone," stated Supervisory Fisheries Biologist Todd Koel. He said it is likely that Pelican Creek's warm water and relatively muddy bottom make it a good habitat for the tubifex worm, the secondary host for the whirling disease parasite. Cooler and rockier streams are less hospitable for the species.

Biologists hold out hope that the lake's southern tributaries and its south arms will prove to be less vulnerable to whirling disease incursions. Another bonus may be that the lake trout threat seems to be less threatening in the south arms because of their shallow waters.

Current Park Service policies reflect another morality play driving modern fisheries management. Natural regulation concepts stress protection of native fish where they still remain and encourage their return to vacated waters. In Yellowstone, the emphasis is on restoring westslope cutthroat and fluvial grayling to the Madison and Gallatin drainages. However, due to the intense needs of the battle against lake trout in Yellowstone Lake, as well as the invasion of mudsnails and whirling disease, this program and several others received limited attention until 2004, when the park increased fees for its fishing permits.

Funds raised by the fee increase will be directed toward restoration of native species, stream monitoring and restoration, water-quality monitoring, and the volunteer angling program. Park officials hope to raise approximately $700,000 a year with the fishing permits.

Koel said native fisheries restoration would again focus on westslope cutthroat in the Gallatin drainage, but also include work on bringing grayling back to the Madison drainage. Ultimately, the westslope program could lead to removing non-native fish and restocking native cutthroat. But the last time non-native fish removal was proposed it did not sit well in certain quarters around the park.

Yellowstone's lightning rod in the politically charged debate in the mid-1990s was former Superintendent Michael Finley. In addition to two highly publicized quandaries—finding a way to halt the slaughter of migrating bison and justifying the reintroduction of gray wolves—he tried to smooth troubled waters on the fishing front.

In a 1996 report to the Federation of Fly Fishers (FFF), he made key commitments to preserving Yellowstone's fishing traditions. Moreover, he acknowledged Park

Service mandates to restore native fish "is not practical in all waters" in Yellowstone.

"At the same time, we have no plans to change the way we manage fish in waters that were originally fishless but where non-natives have been stocked," Finley stated, citing Shoshone and Lewis Lakes as examples. "Our goal during the next few years is to move cautiously toward protecting, enhancing, and restoring native fish and mitigating the effect of non-natives on natives while continuing to provide recreational angling."

Finley said the park's primary goal was to suppress the lake trout threat to cutthroat in Yellowstone Lake. Heart Lake's lake trout were added to the list of enemies to be consistent with the concept of protecting "native fish in waters where they are clearly threatened by non-natives." Anglers are obliged to join the battle. All lake trout caught in Yellowstone Lake must be killed, and there is no limit on the number of lake trout that can be taken out of Heart Lake.

"Our second priority is to mitigate the effects of non-native fish in waters where they are suppressing native fish [such as brook trout in several cutthroat drainages], and to protect native species where they exist currently without threats from nonnatives [such as the cutthroat in the upper Yellowstone River]," Finley said.

Finley's report to the 1996 FFF conclave went almost unnoticed. Not until the park formally announced a native species restoration proposal the following January did some anglers hoist storm warning flags.

So far, the park has had a checkered track record in restoration efforts. Canyon Creek was poisoned in 1976 in an attempt to reintroduce grayling. The fish didn't take. A manmade barrier prevented upstream migration of rainbows and browns, but the grayling slipped downstream. Also, grayling in Cougar Creek, a Madison River tributary, struggled after being stocked between 1993 and 1996.

"The fluvial grayling don't seem to be very fond of Cougar Creek," said John Varley in Yellowstone Science. "They're a big river fish. But we'll probably get them back in the park someday."

Adding confusion to this part of the restoration debate are well-established populations of grayling in Grebe, Wolf, and Cascade Lakes. They are a lake-dwelling Montana subspecies, but in high-water years, grayling often make their way into the Gibbon and Madison Rivers. The state of Montana also has stocked grayling in the Gallatin River beyond the park border.

But the vagueness of the stream restoration proposal is the biggest concern of outfitters and anglers. They are skeptical it won't have downstream impacts on the brown and rainbow fisheries in the Madison and Gallatin Rivers. It also is seen by some as the opening salvo in a future war of attrition against all non-native fish in the park.

The plan endangers two of the park's best fisheries, said Bob Jacklin, a wellknown West Yellowstone, Montana, outfitter. He feels brown, rainbow, and brook trout deserve naturalized citizenship. Their roles in Yellowstone's legendary fishing cover nearly a century, too.

Jacklin is not opposed to saving westslope cutthroat and fluvial grayling from extinction, "but not at the expense of killing all non-native, or 'exotic,' salmonids." He favors nonlethal measures to remove exotics from native fish refuges established in

Yellowstone's backcountry. A majority of other comments on the plan also stress that restoration efforts should be confined to headwater tributaries.

"Introduced species such as the brook, brown, lake, and rainbow trout have, in fact, become 'native' and are self-propagating, and I might add a very large reason why Yellowstone has become the mecca and home of quality trout fishing in the United States," Jacklin said in a letter to Finley. "Yellowstone, like no other place in the world, shares this unique title."

In 2010, a native fish conservation plan was proposed, with the following goals for managing fisheries over the next two decades:

- Reduction in the long-term extinction risk for fluvial Arctic grayling, westslope cutthroat trout, and Yellowstone cutthroat trout;
- Restoration and maintenance of the important ecological role of native fishes;
- Creation of sustainable native fish angling and viewing opportunities.

The plan proposes to accomplish the following objectives within the Yellowstone Lake ecosystem:

- Increase large-scale suppression of lake trout to reduce the population by 25 percent each year.
- Maintain surface water access for spawning cutthroat trout in at least 45 of the 59 known, historical spawning tributaries.
- Recover yellowstone cutthroat trout abundance to the average observed during the five years following lake trout discovery (1995–1999; average of 12,800 spawning Yellowstone cutthroat trout at Clear Creek).

And in other park streams, rivers, and lakes:

- Preserve and/or restore genetically unaltered Yellowstone cutthroat trout to maintain their current spatial extent in streams (3,300 km, which is 75 percent of the 4,400 km that historically contained Yellowstone cutts).
- Restore genetically unaltered westslope cutthroat trout until they occupy at least 200 km (20 percent of 1,000-km historical westslope cutthroat distribution).
- Restore fluvial grayling until they occupy at least 200 km (20 percent of 1,000-km historical arctic grayling distribution).

HELP PREVENT THE SPREAD OF EXOTIC SPECIES

Yellowstone National Park officials are asking visiting anglers and boaters to make sure all equipment is clean and free of exotic species prior to entering the park. Biologist warn that the potential for movement of exotic aquatic "hitchhikers" as anglers and boaters move among waters within and outside the park is very high.

If it's not rule No. 1 in every angler's mind by now, it should be: Never release fish or any other living creature into any water it did not originate in.

"At present, there are more than 250 exotic aquatic species in the United States," notes Supervisory Fisheries Biologist Todd Koel. Exotic species are those that originated on another continent and have been introduced to North America. In most cases, the exotic invaders displace native species and have the potential to cause disruption at the ecosystem level.

"Boats and trailers are a primary mode of transport for these harmful species," Koel said. "We need to do everything we can to prevent the introduction of any new exotic species to Yellowstone and other waters in the region."

In addition to the New Zealand mudsnail and the parasite that causes whirling disease already present, the zebra mussel and Eurasian watermilfoil are examples of invasive species that are approaching the park. And there are others, often so small they are difficult to see.

"Of particular concern are species such as the spiny water flea and other tiny exotics that can be transported in water within a boat bilge or livewell," said Koel. The larvae of these animals can also live in mud, dirt, sand, and on plant fragments.

A complete inspection of all boats and trailers should be made prior to movement among different bodies of water. Water should be drained from holding areas, and all vegetation, mud, and debris should be completely removed from the boat hull and trailer prior to leaving any site. Boats and trailers should be cleaned with hot highpressure water more than 140 degrees in temperature, including the bilge and livewell areas. Engine cooling systems also should be flushed. Since some exotic aquatic species cannot survive without water, allowing the boat and other equipment to dry in the sun for at least five days after cleaning would also be helpful. However, many of these species, including zebra mussels, can survive out of water for several weeks.

Additional information regarding aquatic invasive species can be found on several websites, including "Stop Aquatic Hitchhikers" at www.protectyourwaters. net; "100th Meridian Initiative" at www.100thmeridian.org; "U.S. Geological Survey" at http://nas.er.usgs.gov/; and the "National Sea Grant College Program" at www. sgnis.org. The Montana Department of Fish, Wildlife & Parks also has information available in the West Yellowstone area; tune your radio to AM 1600.

Sanitize Fishing Gear

The rapid spread of New Zealand mudsnails has prompted state and federal fisheries managers throughout the West to set up wader and wading boot cleaning stations at popular fishing sites. If one is not available, anglers are asked to consider using one of the following methods to sanitize their gear before moving to new waters:

- Field-rinse and clean waders, boots, nets, float tubes, boats, and other equipment after exiting the water to remove all river mud and debris.
- Later, immerse equipment in a bucket or sink with 130-degree water (under running, hot tap water) for five minutes. Be sure to soak all crevices.
- Or kill them with dry heat: Let waders, boots, nets, and other gear dry completely in the hot sun and at low humidity for several hours.
- Or kill them with extreme cold: Freeze equipment for 6 hours or longer.
- Or kill them chemically: Immersing your equipment in either of the following solutions for five minutes has been proven effective (spraying on these solutions is not a reliable substitute): a 10-percent solution of bleach (can degrade cotton or rubberized materials); grapefruit seed extract (two teaspoons per gallon of water). GSE is available from health stores and feed suppliers. It is organic, biodegradable, non-persistent, virtually nontoxic, and won't degrade equipment. It's only effective in solutions above 45 degrees.

Yellowstone's Fishing Rules

To reduce competition, predation and hybridization stress on native fishes, Yellowstone increased harvest limits of rainbow and brown trout in waters where they co-exist with cutthroat trout and fluvial arctic grayling. Two areas with differing fishing regulations now exist: the Native Trout Conservation Area and the Wild Trout Enhancement Area.

Yellowstone also enforces a barbless hook rule to reduce handling time and injury, and improve the overall condition and appearance of fishes, especially in heavily fished waters. In addition, there is a no lead rule for all terminal tackle, including weighted flies, lures and jigs, sinkers, split shot and lead-ribbon wraps on leader tippets.

The season begins the Saturday of Memorial Day weekend (usually the last weekend in May) and extends through the first Sunday in November. Later opening dates for specific waters are listed below under stream and lake exceptions, and in the park's fishing regulations brochure. Obtain a copy when purchasing fishing permits.

In drought conditions, and super hot summers, some streams may be temporarily closed to protect fish populations due to low water levels that lead to high water temperatures.

Anglers must be in possession of a valid Yellowstone National Park fishing permit to fish in the park. A fee-paid permit is required for anglers 16 years of age or older. Anglers 15 years of age or younger have two options: Children 15 or younger may fish without a permit if they are fishing under the direct supervision of an adult who has a valid park fishing permit. Or, children 15 or younger may obtain a free permit that must be signed by a responsible adult; with this permit, a child can fish without direct adult supervision.

All types of vessels—including float tubes—require a fee-paid boat permit. No boats, canoes or kick-boats are permitted on any park river or stream. Float tubes are not allowed on certain lakes or on any river or stream in Yellowstone except the Lewis River channel between Lewis and Shoshone lakes.

Be sure to sign your fishing permit and read all the park's regulations before fishing.

Again, a key rule to remember is that Yellowstone was among the first to enforce a nontoxic fishing policy. Fishing tackle, such as lead split shot or sinkers, weighted jigs (lead molded to a hook), and soft, lead-weighted ribbon for nymphs are not allowed. The rule that only nontoxic alternatives, such as tungsten split shot, are permitted as fishing weights is equally important to prevent lead poisoning of waterfowl.

Anglers are required to use barbless hooks when catching fish, in part, to reduce injury to native species like the Yellowstone cutthroat and arctic grayling.

The rule went into effect in 2006, after years of fish sampling by Yellowstone biologists and a year-long public comment period. More than 90 percent of public comment respondents supported the change, Todd Koel, the park's supervisory fisheries biologist, said in a Bozeman Chronicle report.

Biologically, there aren't any studies proving that barbless hooks affect fish mortality rates, but that's not the reason behind the change.

"From a mortality standpoint, we can't justify the change," Koel said. "But from an aesthetic and visitors point of view, barbless hooks do help."

People come from all over the world to fish in a protected ecosystem like Yellowstone, and deformed-looking fish caused by overfishing can negatively affect that experience, he said.

"And we just don't like to see injured fish," Koel said. "Barbless hooks, of course, will help that. There's less handling time and they are easier to remove. All we're asking is to bend or crimp your barbs."

Penalties for breaking the barbless hooks and no lead weights rules can include fines and loss of fishing rods.

Native Trout Conservation Area

This area conserves native trout in their remaining drainages, including:
- Gallatin, Yellowstone, Shoshone, Snake, and Falls rivers, tributaries and associated lakes
- Hebgen Lake tributaries and associated lakes, including Cougar Creek, Duck Creek and Grayling Creek systems.
- This area does not include the Lewis River system above Lewis River Falls (Lewis and Shoshone lakes and tributaries).

Possession and length limits:

- Catch and release all native species.
- Possession limit: 5 combined non-native fish any size per day.
- All lake trout from Yellowstone Lake must be killed.
- No possession limit on lake trout in Heart Lake.

Wild Trout Enhancement Area

This area conserves native trout and some non-native trout. It includes:

- Firehole River, Gibbon River below Gibbon Falls, and Madison River, including its tributaries and associated lakes (but not including streams and associated lakes tributary to Hebgen Lake)
- Lewis River system above the Lewis River Falls, including Lewis and Shoshone Lakes and their tributaries

Possession and length limits:

- Catch and release all native species.
- Catch and release all rainbow trout and brown trout.
- Possession limit: 5 combined brook trout or lake trout. Exception: In the Lewis River system above the Lewis River Falls, this combination may include two brown trout.

- Above Lewis River Falls, only one fish more than 20″; all fish in possession must remain whole.

Exceptions to General Regulations

Madison and Gallatin River Drainages (including Firehole and Gibbon rivers and tributaries):

- Closed to fishing: Firehole River from road bridge 1/2 mile upstream of Old Faithful to road bridge at Biscuit Basin; Firehole River 200 yards either side of Midway footbridge; Madison River from Seven Mile Bridge upstream 250 yards .
- Flyfishing only: Madison River, Firehole River, Gibbon River below Gibbon Falls (not including their tributaries). Use only artificial flies regardless of the type of rod or line.

Snake River Drainage (Snake and Lewis rivers and tributaries):

- Heart Lake opens to fishing July 1 due to bear activity.
- No size or possession limit on lake trout caught in Heart Lake.
- Above Lewis River Falls, only one fish more than 20″; all fish in possession must remain whole.

Lower Yellowstone River Drainage (Yellowstone and Lamar Rivers & tributaries between North Park Boundary and Chittenden Bridge near Canyon):

- Agate and Cottonwood creeks, and portions of the Yellowstone River within 100 yards of these creeks, open to fishing July 15.
- Gardner River, Obsidian, Indian, and Panther creeks, and Joffe Lake: Children 11 years of age or younger may fish with worms as bait.
- Slough Creek upper meadows have been invaded by rainbow trout. If you are positive of your fish identification, please harvest rainbow trout here to help conserve cutthroat trout.
- Trout, Shrimp, and Buck lakes, and connecting waters, open to fishing June 15. The stream and inlet area that drains into Trout Lake opens to fishing July 15.
- Closed to fishing: Yellowstone River, from Chittenden Bridge downstream through the Grand Canyon of the Yellowstone to a point directly below Silver Cord Cascade.

Middle Yellowstone River Drainage (between Chittenden Bridge near Canyon and Yellowstone Lake)

- Fishing season opens July 15.
- Permanently closed to fishing:
    - i. Fishing Bridge and an area one mile downstream (toward Canyon) and one-quarter mile upstream (toward Yellowstone Lake) from the bridge.

ii . The Yellowstone River for 100 yards up- and downstream of LeHardys Rapids.

iii . The entire west channel of the Yellowstone River near the road at Nez Perce Ford (a.k.a. Buffalo Ford).

iv . The Yellowstone River and its tributaries through Hayden Valley from the confluence of Alum Creek upstream (toward Yellowstone Lake) to Sulphur Caldron.

Yellowstone Lake and Upper Yellowstone River Drainage (Lake and tributaries):

- Fishing season on Yellowstone Lake opens June 15.
- Streams flowing into Yellowstone Lake (its tributaries) and areas within 100 yards of each stream's outlet open July 15.
- Clear and Cub creeks open August 11 due to bear activity .
- Sylvan and Eleanor lakes open to fishing July 15. Boats and float tubes are prohibited.
- Permanently closed to fishing:
    i . Pelican Creek and its tributaries.
    ii . The shoreline of Yellowstone Lake from West Thumb Geyser basin to Little Thumb Creek (to protect fragile thermal resources).
    iii . Bridge Bay Marina/Harbor & Grant Village Marina/Harbor and their channels to the lake.
- All lake trout caught in Yellowstone Lake, its tributaries and the Yellowstone River must be killed. If you do not want to keep the fish, puncture the air bladder and drop it into water as deep as possible.

Fish Species Regulations and Descriptions

It is the angler's responsibility to distinguish one fish species from another.

Native species

Cutthroat Trout—CT

- Two subspecies of Yellowstone cutthroat (large spotted form and finespotted form, aka Snake River finespotted cutthroat) and Westslope cutthroat (numerous smaller spots along back and rear of body).
- Only species with red slash under jaw; few spots on head; dark spots on body, yellowish/brownish background; never has white on edges on fins. All fish with red slash under jaw are considered cutthroat.
- Yellowstone cutthroat are native to Yellowstone and Snake River drainages; Snake River finespotted cutthroat to Snake River and Heart Lake; Westslope cutthroat to Madison and Gallatin drainages.

- Catch & Release only. If it has a red slash, put it back. (Exception: In upper meadows of Slough Creek, anglers are requested to take hybrid cutthroat-rainbow trout, aka "cuttbows" as well as rainbow to help efforts to preserve this critical cutthroat fishery.)

Arctic Grayling—GY

- Gray-silver blue body; large, sail-like dorsal fin; large scales; dark spots on front half of body; forked tail.
- Distributed in Grebe Lake and throughout Gibbon River, sometimes in Madison and Firehole rivers.
- Catch & Release only.

Mountain Whitefish—MW

- Gray-metallic white body with large scales and no spots; small dorsal fin; small mouth with "lips," no teeth; forked tail.
- Distributed throughout Snake River and Lewis River below falls; Yellowstone River below Upper Falls; Gardner River below Osprey Falls; Madison and Gallatin drainages.
- Catch & Release only.

Non-native species

Brown Trout—BN

- Brown-to-dark tan upper body; yellowish lower flanks and belly; pale haloes around black spots.
- Distributed in Gallatin, Gibbon, Firehole, Madison, Lewis, Snake and Gardner rivers, and the Yellowstone River below Knowles Falls.
- Native Trout conservation Area: 5 fish any size in combination with other species
- Wild Trout Enhancement Area: Catch and Release only in Madison and Firehole Rivers and Gibbon River below falls; two fish (only one fish of any species over 20"), all fish in possession must remain whole in Lewis River system (Lewis Lake, Lewis Channel and Shoshone Lake and tributaries).

Rainbow Trout—RT

- Dark green-to-greenish black back; light red-to-crimson band along flanks; numerous spots on head; numerous black fleck-like spots along upper body; often white edges on fins.
- Distributed throughout Madison and Gallatin drainages, Falls River drainage, and Yellowstone River below the Upper Falls and its tributaries.
- Native Trout conservation Area: 5 fish any size in combination
- **Wild Trout Enhancement Area: Catch and Release only**

A note about hybridized (genetically impure) cutthroat Trout:

- In cutthroat trout waters where rainbow trout have been introduced--either by intentional, historic stocking or by invasion from a downstream source--the result has been a serious degradation of the cutthroat trout population through interbreeding of the two species. Presently, hybridized cutthroat trout exist throughout the Bechler, Falls, Gallatin, Gardner and Lamar rivers, Slough Creek, and the Yellowstone River below the Upper Falls.
- Cutthroat/rainbow trout hybrids will have characteristics (coloration and spotting patterns) that are consistent with the two species, making identification often difficult. In all cases, hybridized cutthroat trout that have any indication of a red/orange jaw slash are fully protected by catch- and-release regulation. "If it has a red slash, put it back."
- Exception: Slough Creek upper meadows have been invaded by rainbow trout. If you are positive of your fish identification, anglers are requested to harvest rainbow trout here to help conserve this cutthroat trout stronghold.

Brook Trout—BK

- Very colorful: worm-like lighter markings on bronze-to-green-black back; red spots and light spots on dark background; black and white edges on fin:
- Widely distributed due to historic stocking, however, brook trout do not exist in Yellowstone Lake,
- Yellowstone River above the Upper Falls, or the Gallatin River.
- Native Trout conservation Area: 5 fish any size in combination
- Wild Trout Enhancement Area: 5 fish any size in combination

Lake Trout—LT

- Numerous spots on head; white spots, dark gray background on body; often white edges on fins; large mouth; deeply forked tail.
- Distributed in Heart, Lewis, Shoshone and Yellowstone Lakes.
- Lake trout illegally introduced into Yellowstone Lake in the 1980s have destroyed its native Yellowstone cutthroat population. Coupled with the devastating effects of whirling disease and drought, a fraction of Yellowstone Lake's historic cutthroat population struggles to maintain a presence in its former stronghold. Cutthroat spawning runs into the upper and lower Yellowstone River and other lake tributaries are mere remnants of their glory days.
  1. Yellowstone Lake, its tributaries, and the Yellowstone River: All lake trout caught must be killed. If you do not want to keep the fish, puncture the air bladder and drop it into water as deep as possible.
  Anglers are allowed to use special gear to fish for lake trout, such as lead-core line and heavy downrigger weights (> 4 lb.) to allow targeting lake trout deep within Yellowstone Lake. If you accidentally hook a cutthroat trout at great depths and bring it to the surface, handle it quickly and release it carefully, so it won't die.

2. Heart Lake: No size or possession limit. Do not discard lake trout carcasses along lake shore as they will attract bears.
3. Lewis Lake, Lewis channel, and Shoshone Lake and their tributaries: five fish in combination (either lake trout or brown trout); only one fish of any species over 20"; all fish in possession must remain whole).

Always Remember: You're in Bear Country

Yellowstone is bear country, and there is no guarantee of your safety. Bears often utilize trails, streams, and lakeshores. Entry into some areas may be restricted; check with a ranger for specific bear management information. Traveling alone in bear country is not recommended. Create enough noise to make your presence known to bears. Carefully read all bear country guidelines and regulations and be prepared for any situation.

GARBAGE DISPOSAL AND FISH CLEANING

Please pick up all trash, including items such as monofilament fishing line and six-pack holders, which may cause injury to wildlife, and properly dispose in trash receptacles.

When fish cleaning and disposal areas are not provided, dispose of fish entrails by puncturing the air bladder and dropping them into deep water. Do not clean fish in backcountry campsites.

BE CAUTIOUS THROUGHOUT THE PARK

Visitors are encouraged to be alert for signs of bear activity and remain cautious when hiking and viewing bears and other wildlife. Do not approach a bear under any circumstances. It is unlawful to approach within 100 yards of bears, within 25 yards of other wildlife and nesting birds, or any distance that causes disturbance or displacement of wildlife—if wildlife reacts to your presence, you are too close.

Be alert for tracks, do not approach carcasses, and avoid surprising bears in any location or situation. If you encounter a bear, do not drop your pack and do not run. Running may elicit an attack from an otherwise non-aggressive bear. If a bear is unaware of your presence, keep out of sight and detour behind and downwind of the bear. If a bear is aware of you and is nearby but has not acted aggressively, slowly back away. Some bears will bluff their way out of a threatening situation by charging, then veering off or stopping abruptly. Bear experts generally recommend standing still until the bear stops and then slowly backing away. If a bear attacks, lie face down and completely flat. Spread your legs and clasp your hands over the back of your neck. If precautionary measures fail and a bear charges, behavioral reactions such as those described above can be used to defuse an encounter in most cases. Bear pepper spray is a good last line of defense that has been effective in most reported cases where it has been used.

The purpose of the Yellowstone National Park bear management policy is to ensure a natural and free-ranging population of black and grizzly bears. One important aspect of the management program is the separation of bears from unnatural food sources. Visitors are reminded that food and odors attract bears. Items such as cooking stoves, utensils, coolers, trash bags, food, and toiletries may not be left outdoors or in tents or tent trailers, unless they are in immediate use. Superintendent Lewis reminds visitors that a bear's conditioning to groceries, garbage, or intentional feeding and habituation to people may lead to their causing human injury and property damage and occasionally requires their destruction. Because of these serious consequences, persons who knowingly violate food storage regulations can expect to receive a citation.

With enforcement of the park's strict food regulations implemented in 1970, the number of bear-related injuries to park visitors has been reduced. Prior to 1970 there were an average of 48 bear-inflicted injuries per year; now there is an average of only one per year.

While driving through the park, visitors should be especially cautious during late evening and early morning hours when it is more difficult to see wildlife on roadways. If wildlife is struck, please report the incident to the nearest ranger station.

Park staff, along with other local, state, and federal agencies in the Greater Yellowstone area constantly strive to protect visitors and the bear population through

Grizzly bears are common throughout the park.

public education, enforcement of regulations for proper food and garbage handling, the relocation of problem bears when appropriate, and seasonal, visitor-use closures.

Park visitors are asked to report to a park ranger at any ranger station or visitor center any sightings of a grizzly bear with a bright yellow collar in or near park campgrounds or developed areas.

Rivers and Streams of Yellowstone

Winter snows in Yellowstone fall on a gargantuan, percolating sponge. The broad plateau crisscrossed by the Continental Divide's wandering course is the fountainhead of the West's two preeminent networks of fly-fishing streams, the Madison and Gallatin River drainages. The Madison and Gallatin exit the park's northwest corner and flow to their confluences with the Jefferson River at Three Forks, Montana, where they all form the Missouri River. The Madison rises at the confluence of the Firehole and Gibbon Rivers, and the Gallatin heads at a small lake on the northwest side of the park.

Carving its ancient course through the park's colossal caldera is the Yellowstone River, the Missouri's largest tributary. The Yellowstone's principal tributaries in the park are the Lamar and Gardner Rivers. The Snake River, largest tributary of the Columbia River, rises in the park's southernmost highlands and flows through western Wyoming into Idaho. Its flows are augmented by the Lewis and Heart Rivers in the park. The Fall River in the southwest corner of the park picks up the Bechler River and exits into Idaho to join the Henry's Fork, or North Fork, of the Snake.

The Yellowstone is the longest free-flowing river in the contiguous United States. But from the park's earliest days, the Yellowstone and other streams were the focus of schemes that would dam them for flood control or divert their flows for irrigation and hydroelectric power. These assaults on its waters were dubbed the "Second Yellowstone War" by park historian Aubrey Haines in The Yellowstone Story. (The first war denied the invasion of Yellowstone by railroads.)

In 1893, an Idaho senator launched a counterattack with a proposal to set aside two unnamed waterfalls to produce power for an electric train loop. A generation later, both the Idaho and Montana congressional delegations attempted to tap the park's bounty in the 1920s: Montana proposed a dam on the Yellowstone 3 miles below the lake and Idaho proposed to dam the Fall and Bechler Rivers. The state of Idaho even tried to have the Bechler Basin removed from the park. The most grandiose resolution was a product of the Dust Bowl drought of the 1930s. Its improbable scheme was to tunnel through the Continental Divide from Yellowstone Lake to Shoshone Lake and through the Pitchstone Plateau to the Fall River to divert irrigation waters to the Henry's Fork.

"Though it was but a war of words, Yellowstone Park stood in grave jeopardy, and with it the integrity of the entire national park system," Haines said. "However, it was a fight in which the park found staunch allies who saved the day."

Yet, like a phoenix, attempts to tame the Yellowstone as a "working river" continued over the years, both in the park and downstream. The most bitterly fought battle was in the 1970s, against plans to dam it south of Livingston, Montana, and flood the beautiful Paradise Valley. Later, a hydropower entrepreneur's filing of a claim to dam the mouth of Yellowstone Lake in the mid-1990s resulted only in a collective rolling of the eyes at his audacity.

Past transgressions in the addition of non-native trout and manipulation of the park's native cutthroat were not considered problematic at the time. However, significant changes in modern fishing attitudes and management practices have revealed the errors, and today managers and anglers work to ameliorate these past sins, as well as confront the rising threat of exotic species already discussed.

"While we can never return to pristine conditions, Yellowstone still sustains one of the least impacted areas of the Lower 48 States," noted John Varley. In a Trout magazine report, Varley and his colleague, Paul Schullery, dispelled concerns about the long-term effects of the devastating forest fires of 1988 on streams and fish. Their short answer that the trout are doing "just fine" was based on 20 years of U.S. Fish and Wildlife Service surveys. Anglers embraced efforts to protect cutthroat, Varley said in another report. "The old campfire meal tradition is now rare, more by angler choice than federal regulations."

Yellowstone cutthroat trout are still the principal quarry in the park's waters, primarily on Yellowstone Lake, the Yellowstone River and its tributaries, the Lamar River, Slough Creek, Soda Butte Creek, and the lower Gardner River. At the opposite end of the park, the Fall River is also an excellent cutthroat stream.

The most crowded fishing area in the park is the Yellowstone River between the lake and its Grand Canyon. This short stretch sees 90 percent of the river's nearly 11,000 annual anglers. Still, U.S. Fish and Wildlife surveys indicate that more than 70 percent of the Yellowstone's one-day anglers land one or more cutthroat. The caveat is that both the cutthroat and the catch rate decline dramatically after August.

If crowds are a concern, dip into the Yellowstone's canyon stretches. And to get completely off the beaten track, explore the river's headwaters above the lake. This corner of the park and the Snake River basin offer the most remote fishing waters in the park. The lower Fall River and Bechler Meadows are also good choices for solitude; trailheads to the basin are accessible by road only from Idaho.

If you find the cutthroat too tame, brown trout in the Gibbon, Firehole, and Madison offer the park's most challenging fishing. Its finest rainbow trout waters are in the Firehole and Bechler Meadows. The rare grayling is present in Cougar Creek, a tributary of the Madison, and is flushed from Grebe Lake into the Gibbon and Madison Rivers in high runoff years.

A treat reserved for children are the brook trout of Panther, Obsidian, and Indian Creeks, as well as in the Gardner River meadows. The Gardner and its upper tributaries are the only park streams open to worm fishing by children 11 years old or younger. Joffe Lake, near Mammoth, also is open to worm fishing by children.

On the other end of the spectrum, the Madison, Firehole, and the Gibbon below its waterfall are all mandated as fly fishing only.

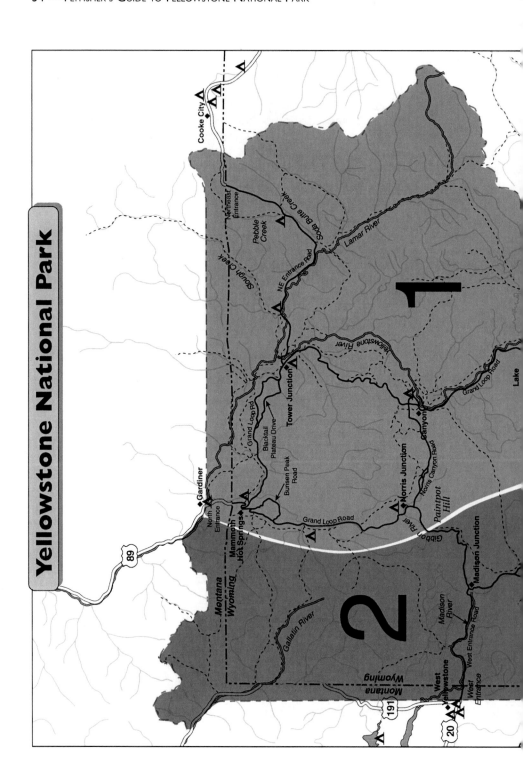

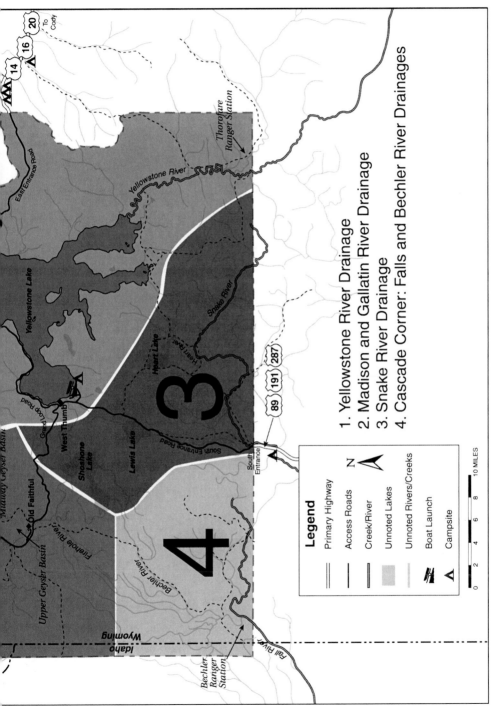

1. Yellowstone River Drainage
2. Madison and Gallatin River Drainage
3. Snake River Drainage
4. Cascade Corner: Falls and Bechler River Drainages

Legend

Primary Highway	
Access Roads	N
Creek/River	
Unnoted Lakes	
Unnoted Rivers/Creeks	
Boat Launch	
Campsite	

0 2 4 6 8 10 MILES

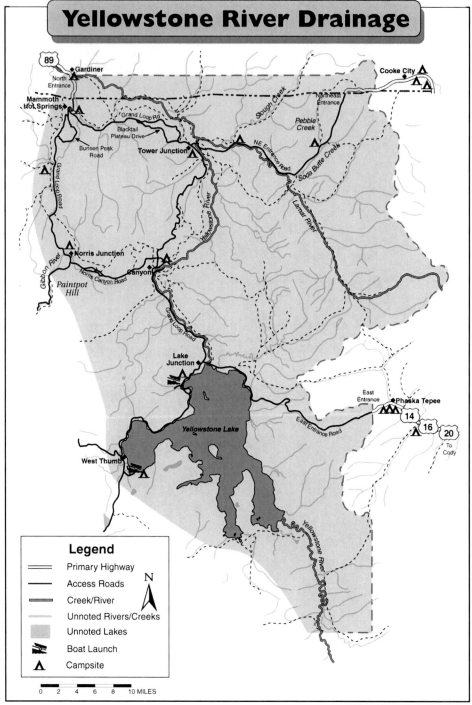

Yellowstone River Drainage

Legend

Primary Highway

Access Roads

Creek/River

Unnoted Rivers/Creeks

Unnoted Lakes

Boat Launch

Campsite

0 2 4 6 8 10 MILES

© 2009 Wilderness Adventures Press, Inc.

The Yellowstone River Drainage

The Yellowstone River drains 60 percent of the park's collected waters. The basin's broad arc extends from the southeastern region to the North Entrance, rigorously eroding two-thirds of the park. Yet prime sections of the river and its tributaries are easily fished along loop roads.

Hardest to reach are the headwaters of the Yellowstone, found in the most remote wilderness left in the Lower 48 States. Hikes or horse-pack trips to fish the Yellowstone delta and Thorofare region above the huge Yellowstone Lake require a minimum of five days, and a week is better. The trip is made easier by a boat shuttle across the lake, but time commitments are about the same.

The loop road closely follows the most heavily fished sections of the river between Fishing Bridge and the Grand Canyon of the Yellowstone. Ventures into the Grand Canyon and Black Canyon are down steep trails with lots of switchbacks.

The two principal tributaries of the Yellowstone, the Lamar and Gardner Rivers, are also closely followed by the loop roads. The Yellowstone and Gardner merge at the park's North Entrance and the gateway community of Gardiner, Montana. Scenic US 89 ascends the Yellowstone from Livingston to Gardiner through Paradise Valley. The loop road then follows the Gardner to Mammoth Hot Springs, the park's headquarters. Soda Butte Creek and the beautiful Lamar Valley are followed by the loop road from the Northeast Entrance at Cooke City, Montana, to Tower Junction.

Two eastern routes to Cooke City traverse some of the most remote and beautiful alpine landscapes in the West. Starting at Red Lodge, Montana, the Beartooth Scenic Highway crosses a 10,950-foot pass via US 212 to Cooke City. The Chief Joseph Scenic Highway, starting about 20 miles north of Cody, Wyoming, follows the Clark's Fork of the Yellowstone through Sunlight Basin to US 212 and Cooke City.

Visitors arriving from Cody by way of Wapiti Valley and the East Entrance first greet the Yellowstone at the famous Fishing Bridge over Yellowstone Lake's outlet. It is also the first view of the river for visitors arriving from Jackson Hole and Grand Teton National Park through the South Entrance.

YELLOWSTONE RIVER

Renowned for its legendary trout fishing, the Yellowstone River ranks among the most famous landmarks on earth. Its sense of place embodies a significance far beyond its role as a river or a name. Yellowstone encompasses the concept of wilderness and is synonymous with the principles of the national park idea that radiated from its environs in 1872.

The earliest known appearance of the name occurred on John Evans's manuscript map of 1797. Evans, a Welshman employed by Spaniards to record the Missouri River drainage, listed a tributary stream as River Yellow Rock. The park's first historian, Hiram Chittenden, considered the name an earlier translation by French explorers of the Minnetaree Indian expression Mi tsi a-da-zi, which means Roches Jaunes, or "Rocks Yellow." In 1798, the French name was anglicized by explorer and geographer David Thompson to "Yellow Stone."

Although Chittenden believed the name Yellowstone originated from the colorful walls of the Grand Canyon of the Yellowstone, most modern historians disagree. They think historic uses of the name referred to the yellowish sandstone bluffs that border the river for about 100 miles near Billings, Montana, as it's unlikely the Minnetaree or early explorers knew of the now famous canyon below Yellowstone Lake.

The Yellowstone rises on the slopes of Yount's Peak, about 20 miles south of the park in the Teton Wilderness. Geologist Arnold Hague traveled to the Absaroka Mountains in 1887 and reported the source of the river "in a long snowbank lying in a large amphitheater on the north side of the peak." The mountain was named for Harry S. Yount, Yellowstone's first gamekeeper, or park ranger.

From its source, the Yellowstone flows 671 miles to the Missouri at Williston, North Dakota. It pauses once—at Yellowstone Lake, the largest natural freshwater lake above 7,000 feet in the Lower 48 States.

On its 115-mile passage through the park, the river meanders through two extensions of the ancient lake, the delta and meadows above the lake, and Hayden Valley above the Upper Falls. Floods from melting glaciers carved the Grand Canyon of the Yellowstone during the last Ice Age, and the river was ultimately redirected by resurgent ice caps into the Missouri and the Atlantic Basin.

In all, four major canyons line its course from the mountains to the plains. The Grand Canyon features the dramatic 109-foot Upper Falls and 308-foot Lower Falls. At its deepest point, the multi-hued cliffs tower 1,200 feet above the river. The canyon is 4,000 feet wide at its broadest point. Downstream, the Black Canyon extends from Tower Junction to Gardiner. North of the park are Yankee Jim Canyon, above the town of Gardiner, and Rock Canyon, closer to Livingston.

Sometime before or after the river carved its exit to the north, Yellowstone cutthroat trout arrived through the basin's back door. Cutthroat began their migration up the Columbia and Snake Rivers about 1 million years ago and crossed the Continental Divide during the last Ice Age. The fish made their way up Pacific Creek to 8,200-foot Two Ocean Pass north of Jackson Hole. From the pass, Atlantic Creek flows northeast to the Yellowstone River.

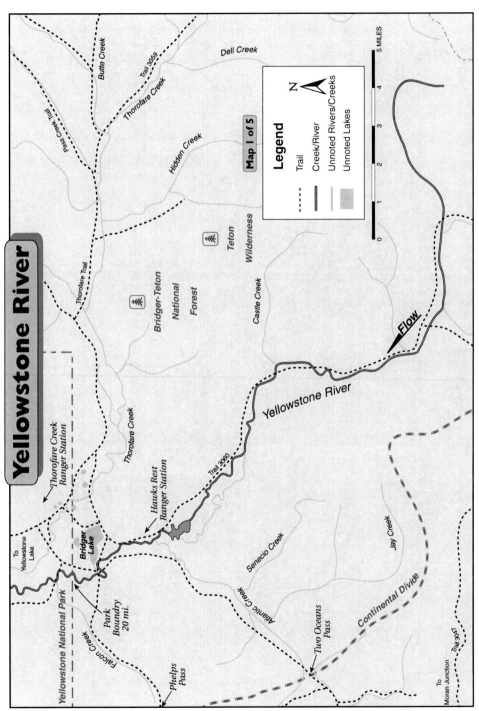

Yellowstone River

Map I of 5

Legend

- - - - - Trail
───── Creek/River
───── Unnoted Rivers/Creeks
░░░░░ Unnoted Lakes

N

0 1 2 3 4 5 MILES

Butte Creek

Dell Creek

Trail 3059

Thorofare Creek

Pass Creek Trail

Hidden Creek

Teton
Wilderness

Thorofare Trail

Bridger-Teton
National
Forest

Castle Creek

Flow

Yellowstone River

Thorofare Creek
Ranger Station

Thorofare Creek

Hawks Rest
Ranger Station

Trail 3060

To
Yellowstone
Lake

Bridger
Lake

Senecio Creek

Jay Creek

Park
Boundry
20 mi.

Atlantic Creek

Two Oceans
Pass

Continental Divide

Yellowstone National Park

Falcon Creek

Phelps
Pass

To
Moran Junction

Trail 3047

© 2009 Wilderness Adventures Press, Inc.

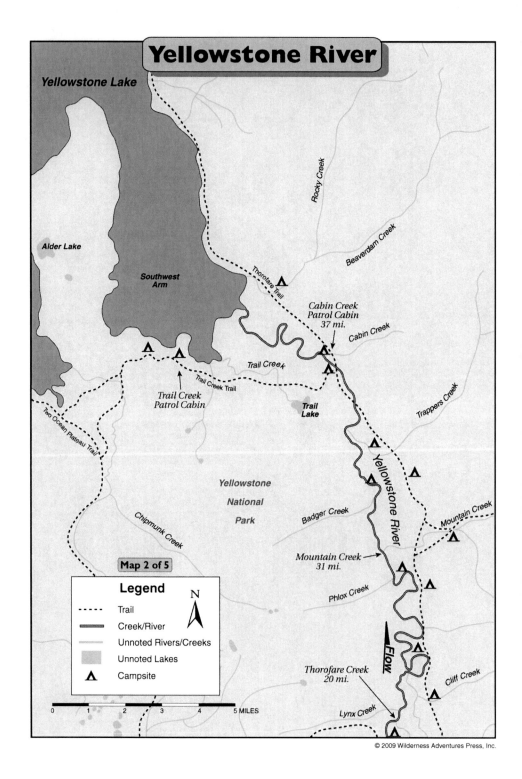

Yellowstone River

Yellowstone Lake

Rocky Creek

Beaverdam Creek

Alder Lake

Southwest Arm

Thorofare Trail

Cabin Creek Patrol Cabin 37 mi.

Cabin Creek

Trappers Creek

Trail Creek

Trail Creek Trail

Trail Creek Patrol Cabin

Trail Lake

Two Ocean Plateau Trail

Yellowstone River

Yellowstone National Park

Badger Creek

Mountain Creek

Chipmunk Creek

Mountain Creek 31 mi.

Map 2 of 5

Phlox Creek

Flow

Legend   N

- - - - Trail

━━━━ Creek/River

         Unnoted Rivers/Creeks

         Unnoted Lakes

⏶   Campsite

Thorofare Creek 20 mi.

Cliff Creek

0   1   2   3   4   5 MILES

Lynx Creek

© 2009 Wilderness Adventures Press, Inc.

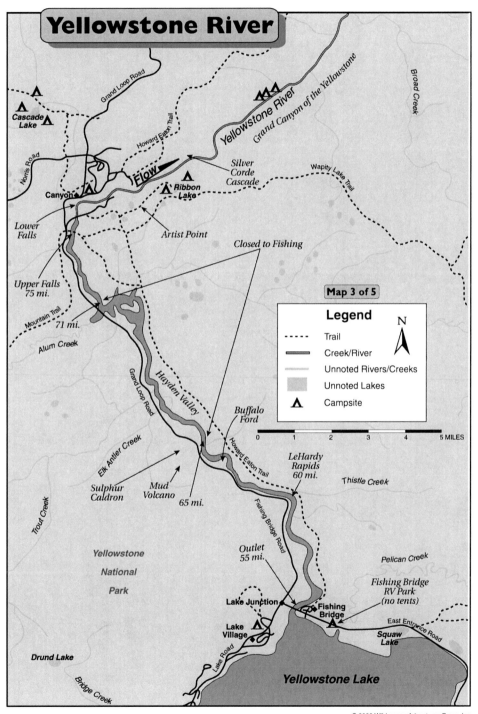

Yellowstone River

Cascade Lake

Grand Loop Road

Howard Eaton Trail

Norris Road

Flow

Canyon

Ribbon Lake

Lower Falls

Artist Point

Silver Corde Cascade

Wapity Lake Trail

Grand Canyon of the Yellowstone

Yellowstone River

Broad Creek

Closed to Fishing

Upper Falls 75 mi.

Mountain Trail

71 mi.

Alum Creek

Grand Loop Road

Hayden Valley

Buffalo Ford

Howard Eaton Trail

LeHardy Rapids 60 mi.

Thistle Creek

Elk Antler Creek

Sulphur Caldron

Mud Volcano 65 mi.

Fishing Bridge Road

Trout Creek

Yellowstone National Park

Outlet 55 mi.

Pelican Creek

Fishing Bridge RV Park (no tents)

Lake Junction

Fishing Bridge

Lake Village

East Entrance Road

Squaw Lake

Drund Lake

Bridge Creek

Lake Road

Yellowstone Lake

Map 3 of 5

Legend

N

- - - - Trail

——— Creek/River

——— Unnoted Rivers/Creeks

▨ Unnoted Lakes

⛰ Campsite

0   1   2   3   4   5 MILES

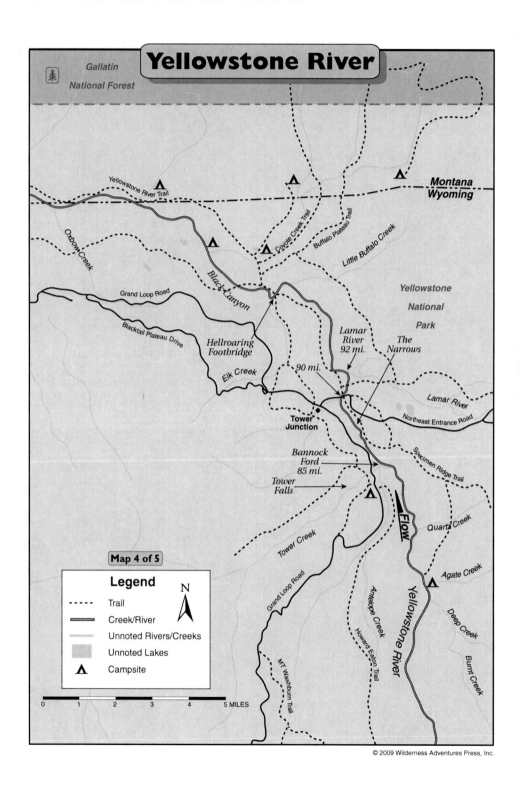

Yellowstone River

Gallatin

National Forest

Yellowstone River Trail

Oxbow Creek

Grand Loop Road

Blacktail Plateau Drive

Black Canyon

Hellroaring
Footbridge

Elk Creek

Coyote Creek Trail

Buffalo Plateau Trail

Little Buffalo Creek

Montana
Wyoming

Yellowstone

National

Park

Lamar
River
92 mi.

The
Narrows

90 mi.

Lamar River

Northeast Entrance Road

Tower
Junction

Bannock
Ford
85 mi.

Tower
Falls

Tower Creek

Grand Loop Road

MT Washburn Trail

Howard Eaton Trail

Antelope Creek

Specimen Ridge Trail

Flow

Quartz Creek

Agate Creek

Yellowstone River

Deep Creek

Burnt Creek

Map 4 of 5

Legend

N

- - - - Trail

——— Creek/River

——— Unnoted Rivers/Creeks

Unnoted Lakes

▲ Campsite

0   1   2   3   4   5 MILES

© 2009 Wilderness Adventures Press, Inc.

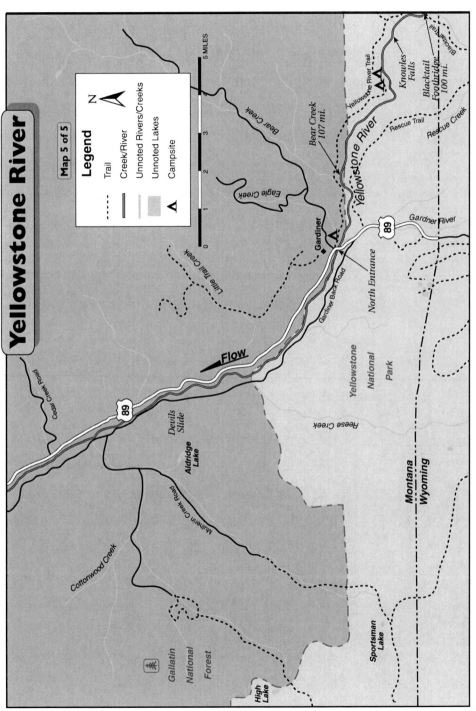

Yellowstone River

Map 5 of 5

Legend

- Trail
- Creek/River
- Unnoted Rivers/Creeks
- Unnoted Lakes
- Campsite

N

5 MILES
0 1 2 3 4 5

Bear Creek

Eagle Creek

Little Trail Creek

Bear Creek 107 mi.

Yellowstone River Trail

Knowles Falls

Blacktail Footbridge 100 mi.

Blacktail Trail

Yellowstone River

Rescue Trail

Rescue Trail

Rescue Creek

Gardiner

89

Gardner River

Gardiner Back Road

North Entrance

Flow

89

Cedar Creek Road

Devils Slide

Aldridge Lake

Mulherin Creek Road

Cottonwood Creek

Reese Creek

Yellowstone National Park

Montana
Wyoming

Sportsman Lake

Gallatin National Forest

High Lake

© 2009 Wilderness Adventures Press, Inc.

Biologists presume that occasional movements of fish across the unique pass occur even today. But until the 19th century, the cutthroat was the only trout on the Atlantic side of the northern Rockies. The Yellowstone cutthroat, which also inhabits eastern Idaho lakes and streams, expanded its range to include the headwaters of the Shoshone, Big Horn, and Tongue Rivers. A subspecies, the westslope cutthroat, crossed the divide by a northern route south of Glacier National Park to reach several western headwaters of the Missouri, including the Madison and Gallatin Rivers.

First planted in the late 1880s in Montana, the rainbow trout is now found in the lower canyon and its tributaries, including the Lamar River. The Yellowstone's Lower Falls prevented upstream migration of rainbows to the upper river and the lake. The 40-foot Knowles Falls, 4 miles east of Gardiner in the Black Canyon, halted the migration of brown trout, another introduced species. Mountain whitefish also are common in the Yellowstone's canyon waters.

Fortunately, attempts to establish non-native game fish in the upper river and lake during the park's early days failed. But these world-famous fisheries face their greatest threat in the illegal introduction of lake trout, a northeastern U.S. and Canadian species, in Yellowstone Lake. Cutthroat anglers will suffer irrevocable losses in both the lake and upper river if the battle against the predatory lake trout is lost. Myxobolus cerebralis, the parasite that causes whirling disease in trout, has also

Opening day at Buffalo Ford on the Yellowstone.

caused dramatic population losses in key spawning tributaries flowing into the lake. For example, 20 years ago Pelican Creek teemed with over 30,000 spawning cutthroat, but today it's virtually devoid of fish.

Flyfishers who flock to Buffalo Ford and other popular stretches of the upper Yellowstone marvel at the size of the cutthroat. Many assume they are year-round residents of this quintessential trout stream, but most are not. Joining the smaller number of resident cutthroat in the river in spring and summer are huge swarms of adults that migrate out of Yellowstone Lake to spawn. The same is true of the headwaters above the lake.

Cutthroat caught in the upper Yellowstone are the same size as those hooked in the lake. Averaging 15 inches in length, they range from 14 to 18 inches, with a few rare trout exceeding 20 inches.

Smaller cutthroat are absent from the river and upper tributaries because they migrate to the lake. For about three years young cutthroat ply its depths, feeding almost exclusively on zooplankton filtered from the water with specially developed gill rackers. At 13 to 14 inches in size they switch to feeding on larger invertebrates and join the schools of adult fish cruising the lakeshore.

The trout make their first migration into the river at 14 to 16 inches in size. Larger trout in the river have survived another two years in the lake to make a second spawning run.

The resurrection of these massive migrations was the park's greatest success story. Today's superb fishing is still the product of a series of strict regulations imposed to reverse previously unsustainable harvests and prevent future exploitation of the cutthroat's "dumb gene."

"The cutthroat is more vulnerable to being caught by anglers than any other species of trout. It exhibits a general lack of wariness and can be readily caught on a wide variety of flies, lures, and baits," notes Albert McClane, author of McClane's Game Fish of North America. "Studies show it can be easily over-exploited by anglers. Even with light fishing pressure, up to half of the legal-sized cutthroat are often caught in a stream. However, it responds well to special regulations, such as size or bag limits, or catch-and-release restrictions."

Before protecting all native fish through catch-and-release regulations in 2001, park guardians initiated several changes in regulations over the last half of the 20th century in hopes of finding the right formula to save the Yellowstone River and Yellowstone Lake fishery. In 1973, a catch-and-release rule protecting cutthroat in the river was imposed and fishing was delayed until July 15 from a mile below Fishing Bridge to the Upper Falls. That same year, Fishing Bridge was closed to anglers and the bag limit was reduced to two cutthroat under 13 inches on Yellowstone Lake. The under-13-inches rule and delayed opening date were extended to the lake's tributary streams, including the Yellowstone delta, in 1978.

A catch-and-release restriction for cutthroat in the lower basin and its tributaries and rainbow trout in all but a few park streams also was imposed in 1987. But in 1996, a two-fish bag limit was reinstated for rainbow trout in the lower Yellowstone drainage. A ban against fishing the 6 miles of river from Sulphur Cauldron to Alum Creek created an additional sanctuary for the cutthroat.

"This prohibition was a good deal for everyone," M. R. Montgomery wrote in Many Rivers to Cross. "The undisturbed spawning beds and loitering pools in the Hayden Valley assure a reservoir of very large fish that will amble upstream and down into fishable waters for the amusement of flyfishers."

Seasons of the Yellowstone

Spring runoff in the Yellowstone drainage is often stupendous, but drought may drastically reduce the river in some years.

In 1997, the perceived end to a decade of drought dramatically demonstrated the full power of the river. Mean flows at Corwin Springs north of Gardiner reached a record high of 22,540 cubic feet per second (cfs) in June of that year. The river's flows were 195 percent of the previous median. It had been above normal in the eight months before spring runoff broke the previous record set in 1996.

Yet, the drought persisted. Increasingly lower flows through the early 21st century caused increased water temperatures that in hotter summers shortened the duration of spawning runs out of the lake, or occasionally caused the cutthroat to retreat to the lake until river temperatures fell enough for the trout to attempt another spawning run.

Throughout this period declining numbers of fish in the river also could be attributed to problems in Yellowstone Lake, including losses to the illegal lake trout invasion and the ravages of whirling disease in key spawning tributaries.

By 2004, U.S. Geological Survey scientists were saying the drought gripping the West could be the biggest in five hundred years, with effects in certain drainages considerably worse than during the Dust Bowl of the 1930s. The Yellowstone River experienced a record low spring runoff that year. Due to a poor snowpack and an early melt, the river crested by the first week of May and fell to a record low of 6,730 cfs downstream at Billings, Montana, by the first week of June. The previous record low flow at Billings was 7,140 cfs.

So the back-to-back record flows in 1996 and 1997 must be viewed as an anomaly. And, until the threat of global warming reared its ugly head, droughts typically have had a cyclical pattern. Either way, it always pays to check on the previous winter's snowpack and late spring conditions before heading to high-elevation rivers like the Yellowstone. A case in point occurred again in 2004 when a string of late-spring storms provided freshets of water to northern Rocky Mountains streams, including the Yellowstone. Spawning runs into the lake's tributaries were reported to be the highest in more than five years.

The Yellowstone's canyons, which open Memorial Day weekend, typically present few fishing opportunities before late June or early July, when the vanguard of the excellent stonefly hatch shows up just as the water begins to clear and drop. It's a great excuse to clamber into the rugged canyons.

LeHardy Rapids.

Runoff above the delta also is problematic around the July opener. It fishes best in August, at least for those who accept the river's biggest commitment in time and effort.

For the majority of the Yellowstone's anglers, the huge lake acts as a buffer to the upper river. Most years it settles into its best fishing by the July 15 opening day. The date is circled on calendars around the world, so expect to share Buffalo Ford and other popular stretches with hordes of flyfishers.

The 9 miles of open river below Fishing Bridge comprise the most heavily fished stream in the park. First-timers need to be aware, however, that the season of plenty is short-lived. After spawning on the spring flood, the cutthroat linger only briefly to rest and feed. They start returning to the lake in August, and by September the river is a whole different ballgame. Autumn trout are scattered, fewer in number, and rarely as accommodating as those in midsummer.

The cutthroat's gullibility results in many anglers catching the same trout over and over. A 1980–1981 Idaho State University study revealed each cutthroat tagged was caught an average of 9.7 times per season above the Upper Falls. Nevertheless, these remarkable trout are not a sure bet against being skunked. Even in the earliest days of a season, they often selectively feed on only one insect species or stage of a hatch. Late summer and autumn anglers are guaranteed challenges to match hatches.

The upper Yellowstone produces the most complex series of overlapping hatches in the park. Summer fly choices range from size 4 stoneflies and size 8 Golden Stones to size 14 Little Yellow Stones and caddis, size 12 or 14 Green Drakes and Flavs, and size 16 or 18 Pale Morning Duns and Blue-Winged Olives. Fly casters also score bonuses with Gray Drake, Pink Lady, and Trico patterns during those sporadic hatches.

Evening spinner falls of mayflies in August at Buffalo Ford can be as exquisite as they are daunting. But on many days caddis outnumber mayflies, and the trout take just about any pattern in the right size during blizzard hatches. An Elk Hair Caddis, small Humpy, or Stimulator is generally the best choice during quiet periods. Grasshoppers and other terrestrials are reliable in drawing up trout, and they linger until the first hard frosts. In September and October, fly choices are mostly restricted to microscopic caddis and tiny fall Baetis—and matched to gossamer leaders and tippets.

Beadheads or nontoxic weights are required to get small nymphs and emergers or moderately sized Woolly Buggers down to bottom lies in summer. Small nymphs and emergers also are effective as dropper flies beneath dries on the surface.

Wear chest waders to fish the Yellowstone, but don't overestimate your strength.

*The much-photographed
Lower Falls.*

Although the upper river runs flat through most of its channels, it is deceptively strong and very difficult to cross. One of the very few places it can be done safely—and only in low water—is above Buffalo Ford. Avoid unstable gravel bars along cutbank channels, and keep an eye out for hidden holes and deep pools. A few braided channels around small islands are more easily managed. Swift powerful riffles run above and below LeHardy Rapids and above Sulphur Cauldron.

Access to the west bank is available at numerous parking lots along the loop road. For your own safety and that of other drivers, use them instead of just pulling off the road. The Howard Eaton Trail follows the river's east bank downstream from Fishing Bridge. It is rarely crowded, but solitary excursions are not recommended since grizzly bears are more common on this side of the stream.

Another wildlife factor to keep in mind is that the bison breeding season peaks in August. Buffalo Ford often lives up to its name. Give all bison a wide berth, particularly bulls escorting cows. A mature bull may weigh up to 1,800 pounds and can run 35 miles per hour.

The open section of river downstream from Alum Creek to the Yellowstone's Grand Canyon runs deeper over a broad, weedy flat. Wading this stretch is difficult, and downright dangerous near the Upper Falls. However, it offers good chances to sight fish for rising trout along the bank. The key hatch to watch for on or around opening day—and to avoid the circus at Buffalo Ford—is the Green Drake.

Forest-lined stretches away from the road offer better chances for solitude at both ends of the upper river.

Canyons of the Yellowstone

Delving into remote sections of the Yellowstone's canyons customarily results in more hiking than fishing, but it is a true wilderness experience. The canyon waters are deep, swift, and milky green in color as the river churns down a boulder-strewn bottom filled with swirling pocket waters and dangerous eddies. Cutthroat range from 10 to 18 inches, with a few going longer. Whitefish join the mix, along with rainbows above Knowles Falls and browns below it. Don't even think about wading; the only safe fishing is from the banks. Leave waders in the car and wear hiking boots.

A wel-documented route to the canyon waters is Seven Mile Trail on the west bank at the top of the Grand Canyon. The first 2 miles of trail are flat and offer great views of Silver Corde Cascade. The next 5 miles drop 1,300 feet to the river, where there is little room to maneuver. The climb out after a long day of fishing is brutal. Think twice before attempting this one, although for the hardy there are reserved campsites at the bottom.

The best route for a day hike is at scenic Tower Falls. A popular trail with easy switchbacks leads to an overlook of the waterfall. Continue the descent to the river, and you will leave the crowds of tourists behind. The broad floodplain and forested banks permit safe fishing for 2 miles or more upstream. The mouth of Tower Creek also offers good fishing.

Downstream at the Tower Junction bridge east of Roosevelt, several footpaths provide access for day hikes into the lower river and to the mouth of the Lamar River. Rock scrambling is required in these areas, so take care along unstable cliffs.

Maintained trails to Black Canyon start at the Hellroaring and Blacktail Deer Creek Trailheads on the Tower–Mammoth Road. Footbridges across the Yellowstone are located at the bottom of the trails. These trails are steep, 5 miles or more in length, and better suited for overnight trips. Hellroaring, Coyote, and Cottonwood Creeks increase the fishing options for smaller cutthroat. Reservations are required for backcountry campsites.

The most exciting fishing in the canyons is during the stonefly hatch in late June or early July. Golden Stones and Little Yellow Stones follow in July. Sofa Pillows, Bird's Stones, and smaller attractor patterns such as Stimulators, Double Humpies, and Yellow Sallies draw full-charge strikes. Throughout the summer, Elk Hair Caddis, Humpies, attractors like Trudes and Wulffs, and grasshoppers are effective in quiet pocket water along current seams.

Pocket waters and holes also can be explored with large dark stone nymphs and Woolly Buggers. Moderate-sized wet flies and streamers are more effective in autumn.

Muddy flows from the Lamar River roil the waters of the Black Canyon after intense summer storms and temporarily shut down the fishing. Check on conditions before heading out.

Yellowstone Headwaters

Flowing out of the Teton Wilderness south of the park, the Yellowstone's Thorofare region above the lake's delta represents the fishing trip of a lifetime. It requires a major commitment since the long hikes in and out take a minimum of four days. Outfitters throughout the region specialize in horseback trips into this pristine area. Many anglers also go in on their own horses, but it still requires about the same amount of time. Reservations are required for backcountry campsites.

Mosquitoes are pesky to fierce all summer in marshy meadows. And the region is prime grizzly country, so it's safer to hike in parties of three or more and absolutely necessary to keep clean camps.

The Thorofare Trail to the delta runs 20 miles along the lake's east shore, starting from Lake Butte Drive. It continues another 20 miles along the river to the park's southern boundary. A footbridge 2 miles south of the park border is the only crossing on the upper river.

The other route to the delta is 35 miles from the South Entrance, starting from the Heart Lake Trailhead and continuing east along the Trail Creek Trail. Crossings the delta east of Trail Creek can be dangerous in high-water years.

Fishing in the Thorofare region of the upper Yellowstone is incredible for trout in the 14- to 18-inch range. It's also great in the many tributaries to the delta and the lake along its east shore. Angling is usually best in August, but runoff varies year to year. Check on current conditions and forecasts before making the trip.

The Yellowstone above the lake is a classic meadow stream, with numerous braided channels, riffles and runs, and large pools. The tributaries, like the highly rated Thorofare Creek, are tumbling mountain streams with pocket waters.

After the spawn, the cutthroat rest in quiet pools and runs of the river and feed throughout the day. Good hatches in early July are Golden Stones, caddis, and Little Yellow Stones. Pale Morning Duns and Green Drakes also are on the water in midJuly and August. The cutthroat readily take generic mayfly and attractor patterns, too, like Adams, Cahills, Stimulators, Renegades, Humpies, and Elk Hair Caddis.

In dry years, anglers who enter the river south of Yellowstone Park's border via Jackson, Wyoming, can fish earlier than the park's July 15 opener. Reservations for designated campsites are not required in the Teton Wilderness.

Trails from Jackson Hole to the Yellowstone's headwaters are up Pacific Creek west of Moose Junction and up the North Fork of Buffalo Fork River from Turpin Meadows east of Moose Junction. Both routes are about 30 miles long, and the trails meet at Two Ocean Pass to continue down Atlantic Creek to the Yellowstone River.

Status of Cutthroat in the Upper Yellowstone

"Although fisheries investigations have been occurring in Yellowstone National Park since just after its creation in the late 1800s, there has never been a survey of the Yellowstone River and its vast array of remote tributaries upstream of Yellowstone

Grand Canyon of the Yellowstone at Tower Falls.

Lake," states the Yellowstone Fisheries & Aquatic Sciences 2003 Annual Report. "With the recent threats of lake trout and whirling disease to cutthroat trout in Yellowstone Lake, determination of cutthroat trout status in this region became crucial for purposes of making future management recommendations regarding this system. In 2003, the Aquatics Section and staff from the Wyoming Game and Fish Department initiated a fisheries assessment of the upper Yellowstone River. The study will determine movements of adult Yellowstone cutthroat trout during their spawning migration in the Yellowstone River and several of its tributaries. We also will determine if any resident populations exist in the drainage.

"Radio transmitters were implanted in 62 adult Yellowstone cutthroat trout in the Yellowstone River and several of its tributaries. Tag life is expected to be two years, with the tags operating for six months of the year (May–November). Tagged fish were monitored with weekly tracking flights and several trips to 'groundtruth' what we were learning from the air. Surveys to locate fish that moved into Yellowstone Lake were conducted via boat.

"Tagged Yellowstone cutthroat trout moved substantial distances through the summer of 2003. Fish as far upstream as Thorofare Creek, south of the park boundary, were found in the mouth of the Yellowstone River at Yellowstone Lake just a few weeks later, a distance of 31.5 stream miles. Signals were also received in Yellowstone Lake at Clear Creek and the Molly Islands, and one fish was captured by an angler at Breeze Point. The majority of fish tagged moved into Yellowstone Lake as the season passed. A few of the fish tagged in the upper reaches of the drainage stayed in the river, but all fish moved downstream from the initial tagging position. There were five known mortalities of tagged fish, including one angler-caused (outside the park boundary), two consumed by white pelicans (tags were recovered on the Molly Islands), and two with cause of mortality unknown. The study is planned to continue for several more years. The final tagging operations will take place [in 2004], with monitoring continuing for a minimum of two field seasons."

Stream Facts: Yellowstone River

Season

- Grand Canyon and Black Canyon: Memorial Day weekend through the first Sunday in November.
- Yellowstone delta and Fishing Bridge to Grand Canyon: July 15 through the first Sunday in November.

Permanently closed to fishing:

- Fishing Bridge and an area one mile downstream (toward Canyon) and one-quarter mile upstream (toward Yellowstone Lake) from the bridge.
- The Yellowstone River for 100 yards up- and downstream of LeHardys Rapids.
- The entire west channel of the Yellowstone River near the road at Nez Perce Ford (a.k.a. Buffalo Ford).

- The Yellowstone River and its tributaries through Hayden Valley from the confluence of Alum Creek upstream (toward Yellowstone Lake) to Sulphur Caldron.
- Yellowstone River, from Chittenden Bridge downstream through the Grand Canyon of the Yellowstone to a point directly below Silver Cord Cascade.

Possession and length limits:

- Catch and release all native species.
- Possession limit: 5 combined non-native fish any size per day.
- All lake trout from Yellowstone Lake must be killed.

Trout

- Cutthroat above and below Yellowstone Lake average 15 inches in length and range from 14 to 18 inches, with a few rare trout exceeding 20 inches. Cutthroat in the canyons range from 10 to 18 inches. A few rainbows and browns are present in the canyons, as are mountain whitefish. Angler report cards give the Yellowstone an 84-percent satisfaction rating for its 0.9-fish-per-hour catch rate for trout averaging 15.3 inches.

Miles

- Mile 20: Park's southeast boundary
- Mile 25: Thorofare Creek confluence
- Mile 31: Trail Creek Trail crossing
- Mile 40: Yellowstone delta
- Mile 55: Yellowstone Lake outlet
- Mile 60: LeHardy Rapids
- Mile 65: Sulphur Cauldron
- Mile 71: Alum Creek
- Mile 75: Upper Falls
- Mile 85: Tower Creek
- Mile 90: Tower Junction bridge
- Mile 92: Confluence of Lamar River
- Mile 95: Hellroaring Creek
- Mile 105: Blacktail Deer Creek
- Mile 110: Knowles Falls
- Mile 115: Gardiner, Montana
- Mile 118: Park's northwest boundary

Character

- The Yellowstone delta and Thorofare region is a high-mountain-meadows run with numerous braided channels, riffles and runs, and cutbank pools.
- Fishing Bridge to Sulphur Cauldron is a long flat run with a pushy current through long meandering glides, riffles and runs, cutbank pools, and a few braided channels. The river below Alum Creek to the lip of the canyon is deep and unsafe to wade.
- Canyon waters are deep and swift as the river churns down a boulder-strewn bottom filled with swirling pocket waters and dangerous eddies. Wear hiking boots and fish from the banks; it is unsafe to wade at any time.

Flows

- The river runs high through June and clears in July in the canyons. Muddy flows from the Lamar River roil the waters of Black Canyon after intense summer storms and temporarily shut down fishing
- Yellowstone Lake acts as a buffer for the upper river, which generally fishes best around its July 15 opener.
- The Yellowstone delta runs high through June and begins to clear in July. It fishes best in August.

Access

- Loop road between Fishing Bridge and Upper Falls bridge.
- Trailheads to the canyons and the Yellowstone delta are located along the loop roads.

Camping

- Canyon Village Campground
- Fishing Bridge RV campground (no tents)
- Mammoth Campground

A Yellowstone cutthroat cruising for food at Buffalo Ford just before opening day.

UPPER YELLOWSTONE RIVER MAJOR HATCHES (ABOVE LAKE)

Insect	A	M	J	J	A	S	O	N	Time	Flies
Golden Stone				█	█				A	Dry: Golden Stone, Yellow or Orange Stimulator, Bird's Stone #6–10; Wet: Bitch Creek Nymph, Montana Stone, Girdlebug, Woolly Bugger #6–10
Little Yellow Stone				█	█				A/E	Yellow Sally, Willow Fly, Blonde Humpy, Yellow Stimulator #10–14
Caddis				█	█	█			A/E	Dry: Tan and Olive Elk Hair Caddis, Goddard Caddis, Renegade, Hemingway Caddis #14–16; Wet: Beadhead Emerger, Soft Hackles, Squirrel Tail #14–16
Baetis					█	█			A/E	Dry: Blue-winged Olive, Blue Dun, Para-Adams, Para-Olive Hare's Ear #16–18; Wet: Pheasant Tail, Baetis Nymph #16–18
Pale Morning Dun				█	█	█			A/ESF	Dry: PMD, PMD Cripple, Yellow Sparkle Dun, Rusty Spinner #14–18; Wet: Hare's Ear Nymph, Pheasant Tail, Beadheads #14–16
Green Drake				█	█				A	Dry: Green Drake, Olive Extended Body Drake, Olive Wulff #10–12; Wet: Ida Mae, Prince Nymph, Zug Bug #10–12
Gray Drake				█	█				A/ESF	Dry: Adams, Gray Wulff, Gray Sparkle Dun, Spinner #10–12; Wet: Hare's Ear Nymph #10–12
Trico					█	█			MSF/A	Black and White, Trico Spinner, Para-Adams #14–18

M=morning; LM=late morning; A=afternoon; E=evening; D=dark; SF=spinner fall; /=continuation through periods

UPPER YELLOWSTONE RIVER MAJOR HATCHES (ABOVE LAKE)

Insect	A	M	J	J	A	S	O	N	Time	Flies
Callibaetis					▮				A/E	Thorax Callibaetis, Crystal Spinner, Para-Adams, Light Cahill, CDC Quill Spinner #14–16
Western March Brown		▮	▮						A	Dry: March Brown Parachute, Light Cahill, Red Quill Parachute, Rusty Spinner #12–14; Wet: March Brown Flymph, March Brown Nymph, Red Quill Soft Hackle #12–14
Brown Drake			▮	▮					E/D	Dry: Brown Wulff, Brown Drake Parachute, CDC Quill Spinner #10–12; Wet: Brown Drake Emerger #10
Terrestrials				▮	▮	▮			M/E	Joe's Hopper, Dave's Hopper, Parachute Hopper #8–14; Foam Beetle, Black Elk Hair Caddis #14–16; Black Ant, Rusty Ant #14–18
Midges					▮	▮			E	Griffith's Gnat, Black and White Midge, Cream Midge, Palomino Midge #18–22

M=morning; LM=late morning; A=afternoon; E=evening; D=dark; SF=spinner fall; /=continuation through periods

LOWER YELLOWSTONE RIVER MAJOR HATCHES (BELOW LAKE)

Insect	A	M	J	J	A	S	O	N	Time	Flies
Stonefly			▮						A	Dry: Sofa Pillow, Bird's Stone, Orange Stimulator, Salmonfly #2–8; Wet: Black Stone Nymphs, Girdlebug, Woolly Bugger #2–6
Golden Stone			▮	▮	▮				A	Dry: Golden Stone, Yellow or Orange Stimulator, Willow Fly #6–8; Wet: Bitch Creek Nymph, Montana Stone, Rubberlegs, Woolly Bugger #6–10
Caddis				▮	▮				A/E	Dry: Olive or Tan Elk Hair Caddis, X-Caddis, Blonde Humpy, Yellow Sally, Stimulators, Renegade, Dark Deer Hair Caddis #14–18; Wet: Beadhead Emerger, Soft Hackles, Squirrel Tail #14–16
Baetis			▮	▮	▮	▮		▮	A/E	Dry: Blue-Winged Olive, Blue Dun, Olive Sparkle Dun, Para-Olive Hare's Ear, Para-Adams #16–22; Wet: Pheasant Tail, Baetis Nymph #18–20
Pale Morning Dun				▮	▮				M/ESF	Dry: PMD, Rusty Spinner, PMD Cripple, Yellow Sparkle Dun, Para-Adams #14–18; Wet: Hare's Ear Nymph, Pheasant Tail, Beadheads #14–16
Green Drake					▮				A	Dry: Green Drake, Olive Extended Body Drake, Olive Wulff, Para-Olive Hare's Ear #10–12; Wet: Ida Mae, Prince Nymph, Zug Bug #10–12
Flav					▮				M/E	Dry: Flav, Para-BWO, Slate Wing Western Drake, Quigley Cripple, Para-Olive Hare's Ear #14–16; Wet: Ida Mae, Prince Nymph, Zug Bug #12–14
Gray Drake			▮	▮		▮			MSF/A	Dry: Adams, Gray Wulff, Gray Sparkle Dun, Spinner, Pink Sparkle Dun, Quigley Cripple, CDC Quill Spinner, Cream Dun #14–16; Wet: Hare's Ear Nymph #10–12
Pink Lady						▮			A/E	Prince Albert, Pink Lady, Pink Cahill #14–18; Pink Lady Spinner #14–16

M=morning; LM=late morning; A=afternoon; E=evening; D=dark; SF=spinner fall; /=continuation through periods

LOWER YELLOWSTONE RIVER MAJOR HATCHES (BELOW LAKE)

Insect	A	M	J	J	A	S	O	N	Time	Flies
Stonefly			▮	▮					A	Dry: Sofa Pillow, Bird's Stone, Orange Stimulator, Salmonfly #2–8; Wet: Black Stone Nymphs, Girdlebug, Woolly Bugger #2–6
Golden Stone			▮	▮	▮		▮		A	Dry: Golden Stone, Yellow or Orange Stimulator, Willow Fly #6–8; Wet: Bitch Creek Nymph, Montana Stone, Rubberlegs, Woolly Bugger #6–10
Caddis				▮	▮	▮	▮		A/E	Dry: Olive or Tan Elk Hair Caddis, X-Caddis, Blonde Humpy, Yellow Sally, Stimulators, Renegade, Dark Deer Hair Caddis #14–18; Wet: Beadhead Emerger, Soft Hackles, Squirrel Tail #14–16
Baetis				▮	▮		▮		A/E	Dry: Blue-Winged Olive, Blue Dun, Olive Sparkle Dun, Para-Olive Hare's Ear, Para-Adams #16–22; Wet: Pheasant Tail, Baetis Nymph #18–20
Pale Morning Dun				▮	▮	▮			M/ESF	Dry: PMD, Rusty Spinner, PMD Cripple, Yellow Sparkle Dun, Para-Adams #14–18; Wet: Hare's Ear Nymph, Pheasant Tail, Beadheads #14–16
Green Drake					▮				A	Dry: Green Drake, Olive Extended Body Drake, Olive Wulff, Para-Olive Hare's Ear #10–12; Wet: Ida Mae, Prince Nymph, Zug Bug #10–12
Flav					▮				M/E	Dry: Flav, Para-BWO, Slate Wing Western Drake, Quigley Cripple, Para-Olive Hare's Ear #14–16; Wet: Ida Mae, Prince Nymph, Zug Bug #12–14
Gray Drake						▮	▮		MSF/A	Dry: Adams, Gray Wulff, Gray Sparkle Dun, Spinner, Pink Sparkle Dun, Quigley Cripple, CDC Quill Spinner, Cream Dun #14–16; Wet: Hare's Ear Nymph #10–12
Pink Lady							▮		A/E	Prince Albert, Pink Lady, Pink Cahill #14–18; Pink Lady Spinner #14–16

M=morning; LM=late morning; A=afternoon; E=evening; D=dark; SF=spinner fall; /=continuation through periods

It's always a good idea to give bison a wide berth.

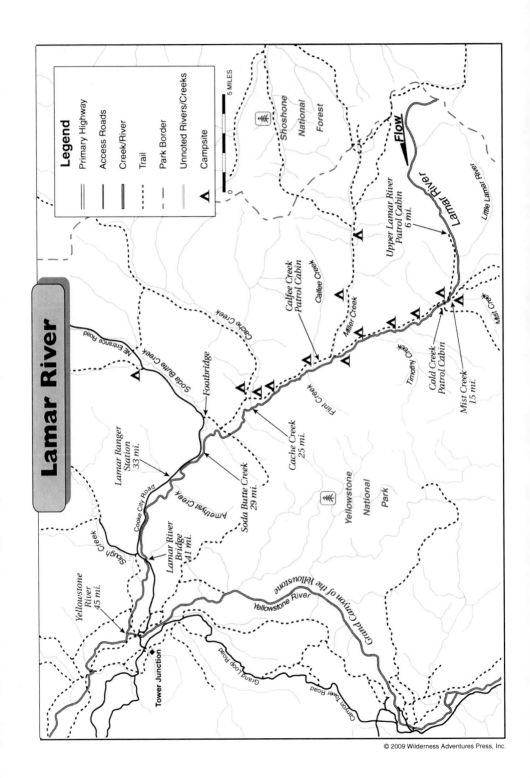

Lamar River

Legend

	Primary Highway
	Access Roads
	Creek/River
	Trail
	Park Border
	Unnoted Rivers/Creeks
▲	Campsite

5 MILES

0

Shoshone National Forest

Flow

Lamar River

Little Lamar River

Upper Lamar River Patrol Cabin 6 mi.

Calfee Creek Patrol Cabin

Calfee Creek

Miller Creek

Cold Creek Patrol Cabin

Timothy Creek

Mist Creek

Mist Creek 15 mi.

Cache Creek

Footbridge

Soda Butte Creek

NE Entrance Road

Lamar Ranger Station 33 mi.

Cooke City Road

Amethyst Creek

Soda Butte Creek 29 mi.

Cache Creek 25 mi.

Flint Creek

Yellowstone National Park

Slough Creek

Lamar River Bridge 41 mi.

Yellowstone River 45 mi.

Grand Canyon of the Yellowstone

Yellowstone River

Tower Junction

Grand Loop Road

Canyon Tower Road

© 2009 Wilderness Adventures Press, Inc.

THE LAMAR RIVER

The Lamar Basin is idyllic and serene through most of its short fishing season, but it no longer offers a solitary experience. The reputations of the Lamar River and Soda Butte Creek for producing large cutthroat trout capture the attention of a growing number of flyfishers each year. And tributary Slough Creek's extraordinary fishing is no longer a secret in Yellowstone. Still, there is plenty of elbowroom, and anglers willing to hike a bit find solitude in secluded valleys and behind gently sloping hills.

The Lamar was named for Lucius Lamar in 1885 when he became Secretary of the Interior for President Grover Cleveland. Lamar is credited with keeping railroads and other developments out of the park. One of the first written descriptions of the beautiful Lamar Valley was 50 years earlier by Osborne Russell. His Journal of a Trapper is filled with intriguing descriptions of the waning days of the mountain men and the matchless wilderness of the Greater Yellowstone region. Awed by the tranquility of the Lamar, Russell called it "Secluded Valley" and hoped its peace would never be disturbed. Earlier maps listed the Lamar as Beaver Creek and East Fork of the Yellowstone.

Today, the big-sky expanses over the broad glacial bowl dwarf huge bison herds grazing on its sagebrush plain. Smaller herds of elk and bands of antelope roam the range, as well. And the rolling hills and mountains of the Lamar once again echo with the howls of gray wolves.

The Mammoth–Tower–Cooke City Road bisecting the Northern Range is the only year-round road in the park.

Geographically, the Lamar Valley extends from Cache Creek to the Lamar Canyon, but most visitors to the basin also embrace the Soda Butte Creek and Slough Creek Valleys.

Soda Butte Creek, largest tributary of the Lamar, is the first stream to tempt flyfishers entering the park through the Northeast Entrance. A smaller version of the Lamar, it parallels the loop road to its confluence with the larger stream at the base of Druid Peak.

One of the few park streams with no road along its banks, Slough Creek's alpine meadows offer scenic backcountry fishing adventures. The legendary Charles Brooks, author of Fishing Yellowstone Waters, encouraged visitors to savor the creek's unique charms: "You are in the most beautiful part of the largest angler's paradise in the world. Take time to enjoy it."

Cutthroat in the Lamar, Soda Butte Creek, Pebble Creek, and Slough Creek are catch and release only. The limit on rainbows in the Lamar drainage is two fish, any size. Cutthroat-rainbow hybrids (cuttbows) also must be released. The limit on brook trout is five fish, any size.

Low-water angling in the Lamar Canyon.

Seasons of the Lamar

The Lamar drains the largest and most rugged mountains in Yellowstone, the Absaroka Range. A rushing torrent in spring, it typically pumps tons of mud and silt into the Yellowstone River long past June. Its runoff surge usually begins to wane by mid-July, but dry fly action often doesn't start in earnest until the end of the month, and sometimes even later.

After the Lamar calms down, much of the broad floodplain dries and the river retreats to its main channel; its numerous side channels are then relatively easy to wade. Still, its summer moods can change as quickly as a flash of lightning. Intense storms periodically muddy the river for days.

The Lamar rises at 8,000 feet in the Hoodoo Basin on the shoulder of Lamar Mountain and flows west and then northwesterly for about 45 miles to the Yellowstone. It tumbles in swift runs down a descent of almost 3,000 feet in 25 miles from the western slopes of the Absarokas to top of the Lamar Valley at Cache Creek.

En route it grows in strength as it picks up the Little Lamar River and Mist Creek near the top, and Miller and Calfee Creeks above Cache Creek. Four miles downstream, it doubles in size as it merges with Soda Butte Creek. From Junction Pool, at the confluence with Soda Butte Creek, the Lamar plays tag with the loop road for more than 6 miles to the mouth of a sheer-walled canyon and another 2 miles to the Lamar Bridge above the confluence with Slough Creek. At the bridge, the river cuts away to the northwest through a shallow canyon for 4 miles to its plunge into the Yellowstone.

The valley, or meadow, run is marked by many serpentine turns through eroded glacial till in long riffles and runs, cutbank pools, and braided channels. Hikes into the river are short and relatively easy, except where the floodplain is marshy. This section receives the most pressure from anglers—for good reason. The canyon run is fast-paced and filled with large boulders, cascades, and pocket waters. Below the bridge, the river is essentially a long continuous riffle, with smaller boulders, pools, and pocket waters.

If you want to get away from the road and most other anglers, try the upper Lamar. The trail to the upper river begins from a footbridge over Soda Butte Creek.

A good day trip is the 4-mile hike to Cache Creek. It has the best fishing of the upper tributaries, and holds small cutthroat that go to 12 inches. Hikes to Calfee and Miller Creeks or to the river's headwaters are better suited for overnight stays. The cutthroat are mostly under 10 inches. Backcountry campsites must be reserved in advance.

Bison in more remote areas of the park are more easily spooked than those seen along the loop roads. Stay alert when a herd comes down to a stream to drink. Grizzly bears are also present in the Lamar Valley, so take the usual precautions.

When the Lamar is clear, the fishing is often hot. Cutthroat in the valley range from 12 to 18 inches, and fish of 20 to 24 inches are occasionally reported. The river also holds a fair number of rainbow and cutthroat-rainbow hybrids. Cutthroat above the confluence of Soda Butte Creek are smaller on average, dropping further in the Lamar's high canyon runs and tributaries.

The Lamar fishes best in August and September, but finding the trout may be more difficult than catching them. They routinely shift holding lies as river conditions and clarity change and flows create or expose secure shelter areas.

Hatches are random and scattered up and down the river, so large attractors and terrestrials are generally the most effective patterns. It is a classic dry fly stream. Some anglers don't even bother to pack nymphs, but they work, too, particularly in the canyon's pocket waters and holes. However, the Lamar is a multi-faceted stream continually changing through the years. In good water years, for example, secluded flat channels may offer technical fishing with hatch-matching flies and careful presentations.

Sporadic stonefly and Golden Stone hatches occur in July, but the river may still be too out of shape to take advantage of the big bugs. Caddis and Little Yellow Stones are better summer options. Pale Morning Duns appear through summer and Baetis linger longest into autumn. The key mayfly hatch to watch for is the Green Drake in late August or September, which is also the prime time for terrestrials. The Lamar is the best grasshopper stream in the park.

Elk Hair Caddis, Stimulators, Humpies, Yellow Sallies, and other high-riding attractor patterns like Renegades, Trudes, and Wulffs work through the season.

Generic mayfly patterns like Blue Duns, Adams, and Light Cahills match most hatch situations, but don't forget a selection of Green Drakes. Grasshopper and beetle patterns should be large and bushy.

If the action remains slow, tie a tag-along fly like an ant or beetle behind a larger terrestrial or attractor pattern. It could be the one the trout hit the hardest.

Searching forays up and down the river are a prerequisite on the Lamar. Ignore shallow riffles and work the logjams, undercut banks, and the holes and deeper runs below side-channel riffles.

Be prepared to buck high winds in these wide-open expanses. They will kick terrestrials onto the water, but fishing with a short lightweight rod is not a good option. Use barbless hooks to avoid going home with an unwanted earring. Wide-brimmed hats and sunglasses also help prevent injury from wind-whipped flies.

When a lightning storm boils over Specimen Ridge south of the valley, head for cover.

Stream Facts: Lamar River

Season

- Memorial Day weekend through the first Sunday in November.

Regulations

- Cutthroat in the Lamar, Soda Butte Creek, Pebble Creek, and Slough Creek are catch and release only. Regulation changes proposed for 2006 would increase the rainbow limit to five fish daily.

Possession and length limits

- Catch and release all native species.
- Possession limit: 5 combined non-native fish, any size per day, including rainbow and brook trout.
- Cutthroat-rainbow hybrids (cuttbows) must be released. (Exception: If you're 100 per cent sure it's a hybrid, anglers are encouraged to keep cuttbows in Slough Creek's upper meadows, above the campground.)

Trout

- Cutthroat in the Lamar Valley range from 12 to 18 inches, and some exceed 20 inches; rainbow and cutthroat-rainbow hybrids are also present in this area. Cutthroat above the confluence of Soda Butte Creek range from 6 to 12 inches. Angler report cards give the Lamar an 81-percent satisfaction rating for its 1.14fish-per-hour catch rate for trout averaging 11.7 inches.

Miles

- Mile 6: Upper Lamar Patrol Cabin
- Mile 15: Mist Creek
- Mile 25: Cache Creek
- Mile 29: Soda Butte Creek
- Mile 33: Lamar Ranger Station
- Mile 41: Lamar Bridge
- Mile 42: Slough Creek
- Mile 45: Confluence with Yellowstone River

Character

- The upper river tumbles down a steep narrow valley to Cache Creek. The valley run is marked by many serpentine turns through eroded glacial till in long riffles and runs, cutbank pools, and braided channels. The canyon run is fast-paced and filled with large boulders, cascades, and pocket waters. Below Lamar Bridge, the river is essentially a long, continuous riffle with smaller boulders, pools, and pocket waters.

Flows

- Spring runoff surges through June and usually begins to wane by mid-July, but the river may not fully clear until the end of the month, and sometimes even later. Periodic summer storms muddy flows for several days.

Access

- Tower–Cooke City Road
- Footbridge across Soda Butte Creek, a mile east of Junction Pool, is the trailhead to the upper river.

Camping

- Slough Creek Campground
- Pebble Creek Campground
- Cooke City
- Gallatin National Forest

LAMAR RIVER/SODA BUTTE CREEK MAJOR HATCHES

Insect	A	M	J	J	A	S	O	N	Time	Flies
Stonefly			■						A	Dry: Sofa Pillow, Salmonfly, Bird's Stone, Orange Stimulator #4–8; Wet: Black Rubberlegs, Woolly Bugger #2–8
Golden Stone			■						A	Dry: Golden Stone, Orange Zonker, Yellow Stimulator #6–10; Wet: Bitch Creek Nymph, Montana Stone, Girdlebug #6–10
Caddis					■	■			A/E	Dry: Tan or Olive Elk Hair Caddis, Blonde Humpy, Goddard Caddis #14–18; Wet: Caddis Emerger, Soft-hackles, Beadheads #14–16; Prince Nymph #16–18
Baetis					■	■			A/E	Dry: Blue Dun, Blue-winged Olive, Para-Adams #14–18; Wet: Pheasant Tail, Baetis Nymph #16–18
Pale Morning Dun			■	■					M/E	Dry: PMD, PMD Cripple, Rusty Spinner, Yellow Sparkle Dun #14–18; Wet: Hare's Ear Nymph, Pheasant Tail, Beadheads #16–18
Green Drake				■					A	Dry: Green Drake, Olive Wulff, Quigley Cripple #10–12; Wet: Prince Nymph, Zug Bug #10–12
Gray Drake					■				A/ESF	Dry: Gray Wulff, Para-Adams, Gray Sparkle Dun, CDC Spinner #10–14; Wet: Hare's Ear Nymph #10–14
Pink Lady					■				A/E	Dry: Pink Albert, Pink Lady, Pink Cahill, Quigley Cripple, Cream Dun #14–16; Wet: Pink Albert Emerger #14
Callibaetis					■				A	Thorax Callibaetis, Crystal Spinner, Para-Adams #14–16
Midges							■		E	Griffith's Gnat, Black and White Midge #18–22
Terrestrials						■	■		M/A	Joe's Hopper, Dave's Hopper, Parachute Hopper #8–14; Foam Beetle, Disc O'Beetle #14–16; Ants #14–18

M=morning; LM=late morning; A=afternoon; E=evening; D=dark; SF=spinner fall; /=continuation through periods

Bighorn sheep are a common sight in the Lamar Valley.

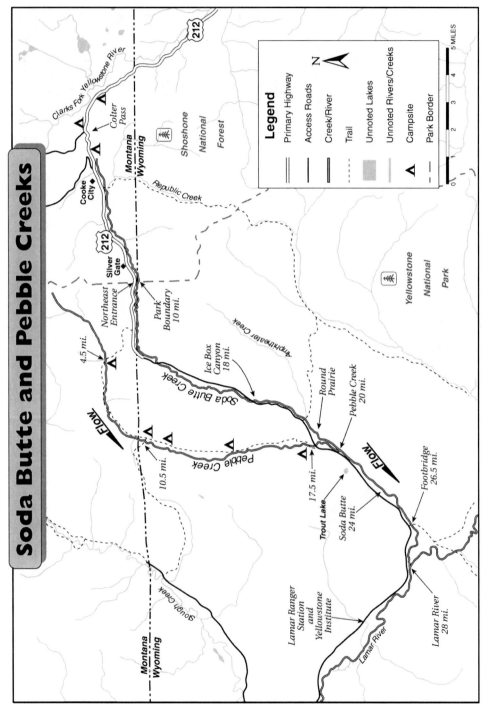

Soda Butte and Pebble Creeks

SODA BUTTE CREEK

Soda Butte Creek, largest of the Lamar River's tributaries, rises in the Beartooth Mountains behind Cooke City, Montana. It skirts the highway as it enters the park near the Northeast Entrance and plays tag with the Tower Junction Road for more than 15 miles en route to its merger with the Lamar. From a small, bubbling brook, Soda Butte grows in strength on its dash through a thickly forested valley, disappears briefly into Icebox Canyon, and bursts into view again at Round Prairie, where it picks up Pebble Creek. After dipping into another short canyon, Soda Butte meanders down a broad, sloping sagebrush plain as it braids into numerous channels and flirts with the road again. Its lower valley run is a smaller mirror image of the beautiful Lamar, which it joins beneath Druid Peak.

Like the Lamar, the creek runs high through June and sometimes is muddied by intense storms in summer. It fishes best from mid-July to October. In fact, Soda Butte Creek boasts the third highest catch rate in the park. Angler report cards give it an 83percent satisfaction rating for landing trout averaging 10.3 inches at a pace of 1.53 fish per hour.

Cutthroat in the 12- to 14-inch range inhabit the riffles and runs, pools, and braided channels of the meadows. But trout going 18 inches or better are occasionally netted from deeper pools and sheltered lies by persistent fly casters who explore sections away from the road. A few rainbows also are found in the creek, and there are reports that brook trout have invaded its headwaters. Cutthroat above Round Prairie average 10 to 12 inches, but, again, occasional surprises are found in the pocket waters and long, deep pools of the forest run and lower end of Icebox Canyon.

The meadows are heavily fished near Soda Butte's confluence with the Lamar and in Round Prairie. To find some solitude, park north of Soda Butte, the travertine core of an extinct hot spring, and hike across the sagebrush flats to the creek. A footbridge crosses the creek about a mile south of Soda Butte.

The stream is easily waded, but a better tactic is to fish from shore. Stalk the banks, channels, and tops of riffle pools in search of rising trout or explore grassy undercuts and logjams with terrestrials or attractors. When necessary, cross the creek at unproductive shallows to avoid disturbing fish downstream.

Hatches mimic those of the Lamar. Baetis, Pale Morning Duns, and caddis make sporadic appearances through summer. Gray Drakes in August and Green Drakes in August and September spur topwater action. The high, semi-arid plain of Soda Butte Valley produces good crops of grasshoppers, beetles, and ants. But the stream also fishes well with attractors and generic mayfly patterns and small nymphs and emergers.

Bison are common in the meadows and should be given the right-of-way to avoid problems. A lucky few might sight wolves at dawn or dusk since the Druid Pack, the most active in the park, has claimed the eastern end of the Northern Range for its home territory. Grizzly bears may be spotted in the upper reaches of the creek. In forested areas, fish with at least two or three partners.

Pebble Creek

Pebble Creek joins Soda Butte Creek at Round Prairie on the Tower-Cooke City Road, about 10 miles southwest of the Northeast Entrance. It's one of the most scenic small streams in Yellowstone and is as popular as a hiking destination as it is for fishing.

The creek's best fishing is in its meadow run through a forested valley near the top of the drainage. Cutthroat averaging 10 inches—with some going 14 to 16 inches—inhabit the run. A few deep pools and numerous logjams shelter the cutthroat in the crystal-clear flows of the upper valley. Trout in the lower half of the 13-mile stream are smaller and very difficult to reach because Pebble Creek tumbles down a narrow rocky canyon. Its last mile is flatter, but it remains swift and quite shallow after spring runoff wanes.

The easiest route for a day hike into Pebble Creek is from the top of its loop trail, which begins at a picnic site about a mile west of the Northeast Entrance. It's a 2-mile hike to the stream. Another trail climbs up and around the canyon starting from the footbridge at the campground above the stream's mouth. It's a steep, 7-mile hike to the creek's upper meadow fishery. All of the half-dozen backcountry campsites along the stream must be reserved in advance.

This also is grizzly bear country, so it's best to explore the region in groups of three or more. Keep a clean camp, both at developed campgrounds and backcountry sites. Pebble Creek Campground often is one of the last ones in the park to fill. It's a good second choice as base camp for anglers who can't find a site at the smaller and more popular Slough Creek Campground.

Upper Soda Butte Creek.

Slough Creek

A hike to Slough Creek's fabled alpine meadows is a rite of passage for many flyfishers new to Yellowstone. For those who return, the trek into the mountains is a pilgrimage of renewal. But both pilgrims and acolytes must anticipate crowds in July and August these days.

Surrounded by the towering Absaroka Mountains, the creek's meandering course through three high meadows is a setting virtually unrivaled for wilderness splendor. But it is the sight of large cutthroat cruising limpid pools as clear as aquariums that most haunts the memories of anglers. Tied for third in sending home happy flyfishers, Slough Creek is given an 89-percent satisfaction rating by those who complete the park's fishing report cards.

In 2003, park biologists "completed a multi-year population assessment of Yellowstone cutthroat trout in Slough Creek, prompted by concerns of perceived damage to riparian areas or the fish population arising from increased angler use," according to the Yellowstone Fisheries & Aquatic Sciences 2003 Annual Report. "In the mid-1990s, annual angler use occasionally exceeded 25,000 angler days per year as Slough Creek became one of the most popular angling areas in the park, particularly in the meadow areas upstream from the campground, even though hourly catch rates were often below one fish per hour. During the drought periods of the past several years, anecdotal information indicated that additional anglers were fishing at Slough Creek as a substitute for other streams that were temporarily closed due to high instream water temperatures. With this information as background, we sampled some of the more heavily used portions of Slough Creek. Our electrofishing results indicated that there is little evidence that the abundance or size structure of the Yellowstone cutthroat trout population has changed since the stream was last sampled in 1989. Although high levels of angler use continued in this popular catchand-release fishery, estimated abundance of adult cutthroat trout longer than 330 mm (13.2 inches) remains at several hundred fish per kilometer. The recent capture (in the upper meadows) of several potentially hybridizing rainbow trout of spawning size in areas of pure Yellowstone cutthroat trout appears to represent a much more serious threat to the long-term persistence of this population than are the current levels of angler use.

"Recent 2001–2003 survey data, when compared to information collected in 1987–1989, suggests that there has been no real change in densities or sizes of fish over this period.... Anglers fishing the upstream section of Slough Creek (in the meadows) catch cutthroat trout at twice the rate of those fishing the downstream section (below the campground). However, the catch rate of fish in the upper section has been on a gradual downward trend. [There was a peak rate of five fish per hour in 1981 compared to two fish per hour in 2003.]

"Anglers reported that rainbow trout are in both sections; however, they were more successful at catching rainbow trout in the downstream section. The length of trout caught in Slough Creek has not changed much in 35 years. Average length of a

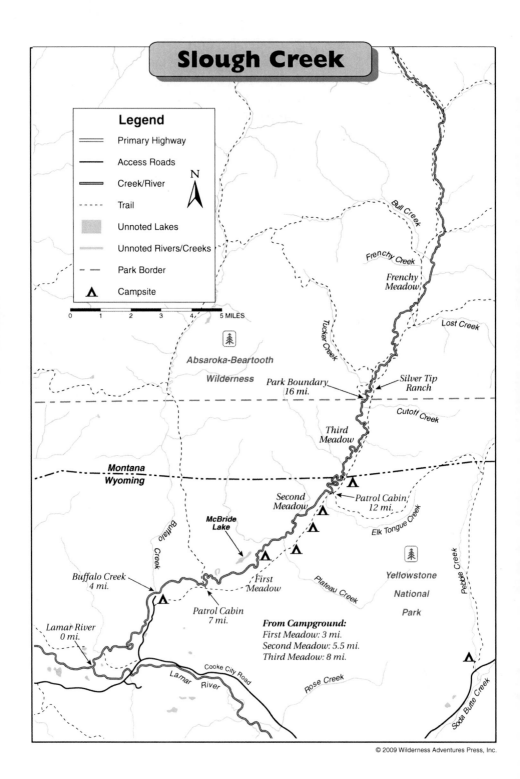

Slough Creek

Legend

═══	Primary Highway
────	Access Roads
────	Creek/River
-----	Trail
▓	Unnoted Lakes
	Unnoted Rivers/Creeks
– –	Park Border
⛺	Campsite

0 1 2 3 4 5 MILES

N

Bull Creek

Frenchy Creek

Frenchy Meadow

Lost Creek

Tucker Creek

Absaroka-Beartooth Wilderness

Park Boundary 16 mi.

Silver Tip Ranch

Cutoff Creek

Third Meadow

Montana Wyoming

Patrol Cabin 12 mi.

Second Meadow

McBride Lake

Elk Tongue Creek

Buffalo Creek

First Meadow

Plateau Creek

Yellowstone National Park

Pebble Creek

Buffalo Creek 4 mi.

Patrol Cabin 7 mi.

From Campground:
First Meadow: 3 mi.
Second Meadow: 5.5 mi.
Third Meadow: 8 mi.

Lamar River 0 mi.

Cooke City Road

Lamar River

Rose Creek

Soda Butte Creek

The author fishing Slough Creek. (Mike Retallick photo)

cutthroat trout caught in Slough Creek during 2002 was 315 mm (12.4 inches), while the average rainbow trout caught was 260 mm (10.3 inches)."

Park officials would like to remove rainbows from Slough Creek and want anglers to help. A proposed regulation change for 2006 would permit harvest of five nonnative fish daily in cutthroat waters.

The cutthroat in all three meadows above the campground are thick-bodied and robust, in contrast to the long, slender cutthroat of the Yellowstone River. Cutthroat in the creek's final meander to the Lamar below the campground are alluring and strapping, too, and a fair number of rainbows and cutthroat-rainbow hybrids up the ante in size classes and dramatic action on the end of a fly line.

Slough Creek is one of the most fertile streams in the park, and its hatches are rich and complex. Fly selections in the meadows range from midges, Blue-Winged Olives, Pale Morning Duns, and caddis, which become progressively smaller as the season advances, to jumbo Gray Drakes and Green Drakes that are available well into September. Grasshoppers, beetles, and ants, including flying ants, are standard fare, as in all meadow fisheries. But low-profile patterns are more productive. Stoneflies, Golden Stones, and Little Golden Stones are early season options in the creek's few large riffles and canyon waters.

Feeding frenzies occur, but just as often the trout key on specific stages of a hatch and are super selective. The gentle flows and clarity of the water give them ample opportunity to window shop. The larger trout cruise at will in long, glassy glides along deeply undercut bends. About the only structure in the meadows is scattered clumps of bank calved into the stream by spring floods. Short, shallow riffles leading into the bends and the inside lies of pools typically hold smaller trout.

Spring creek tactics are required to stalk the trout, and downstream presentations are generally the most effective. As flows diminish through the summer, it becomes even more important to keep a low profile when pursuing rising trout.

There is no need to lug chest waders to the upper meadows; wading boots or hip waders suffice to make stream crossing at the tops of shallow riffles and to get across marshy flats.

Runoff on Slough Creek normally begins to subside by late June, and it fishes best from mid-July through September. But like the rest of the Yellowstone drainage following the end of a protracted drought in 1995, a string of exceptionally high water years has wreaked havoc with fishing agendas. Still, it is often ready earlier than the Lamar and Soda Butte Creek, and clears faster after summer storms.

Slough Creek rises in the Beartooth Mountains near the famous Grasshopper Glacier behind Cooke City. It follows a meandering course down a forested valley

A nice cutthroat from below the Slough campground.

between the Beartooths and Absarokas to Frenchy's Meadow and the Silver Tip Ranch at the Montana border.

The two-track trail from the Slough Creek Campground to the ranch is the only backcountry wagon road in the park. It also is the best route into the stream's three high meadows since the canyon above the campground is virtually impassable.

At the top of Slough Creek's 16-mile run through the park is Third Meadow. It extends about 5 miles to Elk Tongue Creek and the top of Second Meadow. About 2 miles through Second Meadow, the creek dips and romps through a short forestlined stretch of riffles and pocket waters to First Meadow, where it flattens out again. The creek then cuts another long string of meanders for nearly 3 miles to the lip of its steep canyon close to the campground and trailhead.

The trail from the campground below First Meadow climbs about 3 miles up and around the canyon. The first half mile or so is steep, but the rest of the route to First Meadow is relatively flat, with another short drop as the trail returns to the creek. Moose are often seen along this part of the trail.

First Meadow is a comfortable, hour-long hike and is often crowded. Second and Third Meadows are 5.5 and 8 miles from the campground, respectively, and are better suited for overnight visits but close enough for fit hikers seeking solitude in a day trip. Advance reservations are required for the seven backcountry campsites along the creek, as they remain solidly booked throughout the summer season.

The meadows are notorious for their pesky mosquitoes and deerflies. Don't forget bug spray, carry extra water for the hike out, and depart early enough to get back before dark. This last point is particularly important since grizzly bear sightings are very common in this valley. Heed posted warnings, both at the campground and in the backcountry, and don't hike alone. As always, keep a clean camp.

Finding a site at Slough Creek Campground is always tough. High spring runoff may flood out some sites, and the park announced it may move up to 18 sites out of the floodplain to new locations; however, there are no plans to add more sites. The number available will remain a meager 29 after completion of the reconstruction project. Arrive very early in the day to nab one.

The next park campground, about 5 miles east at Pebble Creek, often doesn't fill until late afternoon or early evening. Large public campgrounds are also available a few miles east of Cooke City in the Gallatin National Forest.

Downstream from Slough Creek Campground, the creek meanders through a final meadow for about 3 miles and drops down a short cascade into the Lamar. It has a few brief stretches of pocket water and long deep holes, glassy glides, and oxbows. The trout are especially wary because they get even more pressure than in the high meadows. Rainbow-cutthroat hybrids in this stretch offer line-sizzling battles that may startle the unwary angler. Fly hatches are prolific and mimic those of the Lamar.

A number of turnouts are spaced along the gravel road to the campground. The bottom of the creek also can be reached from the Lamar Bridge on the loop road.

SLOUGH CREEK MAJOR HATCHES

Insect	A	M	J	J	A	S	O	N	Time	Flies
Stonefly			█						A	Dry: Salmonfly, Sofa Pillow, Orange Stimulator #2–8; Wet: Brook's Stone Nymph, Black Rubberlegs, Girdlebug, Woolly Bugger #2–10
Golden Stone				█					A	Dry: Golden Stone, Orange Zonker; Yellow Stimulator, Bird's Stone #6–10; Wet: Bitch Creek Nymph, Montana Stone, Girdlebug #6–10
Little Golden Stone				█	█				A/E	Yellow Sally, Blonde Humpy, Yellow Stimulator, Willow Fly #10–14
Caddis			█	█	█	█			A/E	Dry: Olive or Tan Elk Hair Caddis, X-Caddis, Hemingway Caddis, Partridge Caddis, Renegade #14–20; Wet: Prince Nymph, Soft Hackles, Emergers, Squirrel Tail #14–18
Baetis			█	█	█	█			A/E	Dry: Blue-Winged Olive, Blue Dun, Para-BWO, Flav, Para-Olive Hare's Ear #14–20; Wet: Pheasant Tail #16–18
Pale Morning Dun			█	█	█	█			M/ESF	Dry: PMD, Thorax PMD, PMD Cripple, Sparkle Dun, Rusty Spinner #16–18; Wet: Hare's Ear Nymph, Pheasant Tail #14–18
Green Drake					█				A	Dry: Green Drake, Olive Extended Body Drake, Quigley Cripple, Parachute Olive Drake #10–12; Wet: Olive Sparkle Dun, Prince Nymph #10–14
Flav					█				M/E	Dry: Olive Hare's Ear Parachute, Olive Quill CDC, Green Wulff, Sparkle Dun, CDC Spinner #14–16; Wet: Quigley Cripple, Olive Sparkle Emerger, CDC Cripple #12–16
Gray Drake						█	█		A/ESF	Dry: Para-Adams, Gray Wulff, Gray Sparkle Dun, Spinner #10–12; Wet: Hare's Ear Nymph #10–12
Midges			█	█	█	█	█		E	Griffith's Gnat, Cream Midge, Palomino Midge #18–22; Black and White Midge #16–20
Terrestrials				█	█	█	█		M/A	Joe's Hopper, Dave's Hopper, Parachute Hopper, Foam Beetle, Crystal Beetle, Dave's Cricket #12–14; Flying Ant, Black Ant, Rusty Ant #14–18

M=morning; LM=late morning; A=afternoon; E=evening; D=dark; SF=spinner fall; /=continuation through periods

First Meadow is a popular angling destination, but the crowds thin out the farther in you go.

The canyon mouth below First Meadow.

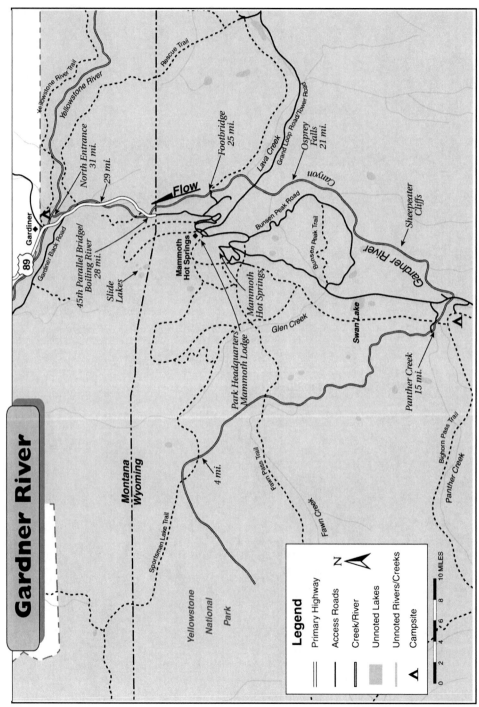

Gardner River

Legend

N

Primary Highway

Access Roads

Creek/River

Unnoted Lakes

Unnoted Rivers/Creeks

Campsite

MILES

0 2 4 6 8 10

© 2009 Wilderness Adventures Press, Inc.

GARDNER RIVER

The Gardner River cuts a steep rocky course on its final sprint to merge with the Yellowstone River before it leaves the park. Joining the Yellowstone in the deep canyon bisecting the gateway community of Gardiner, Montana, the Gardner is the first stream to tempt many visitors who drive through the park's North Entrance.

The river was named for Johnson Gardner, one of the first fur trappers to explore the upper Yellowstone region in the 1830s. Its upper meadow, or "hole," was a favorite mountain man rendezvous site during their heyday.

Divided by a deep impassable canyon, the bottom third of the river holds moderate-sized cutthroat, rainbow, and brown trout, as well as whitefish. Brown spawners running out of the Yellowstone in late fall draw the most attention of anglers. The river's upper mountain meadow run is a haven for small brook trout.

The Gardner River and three of its tributaries, Panther, Obsidian, and Indian Creeks, are the only streams in the park open to worm fishing by children 11 years old or younger. Joffe Lake, a tiny pond east of Mammoth, also can be fished with worms by children.

Cutthroat and mountain whitefish in the river are protected by a catch-andrelease rule. Combined limits on browns, brooks, and rainbow trout is 5 fish, any size.

The fast, shallow Gardner River offers fun fishing.

The upper Gardner near Mammoth.

Seasons of the Gardner

The Gardner rises at 7,500 feet below Cache Lake in the shadows of the park's highest mountain, 10,992-foot Electric Peak, west of Mammoth. It trickles east off the shoulders of the Gallatin Range into a broad bowl and lazily meanders through the marshy Gardner Meadow in a southeasterly direction. At the confluence of its three large tributaries at Indian Creek Campground, it doubles in size. It then swings north, and its pace quickens as it passes the Sheepeater Cliff Picnic Area and plunges into a deep narrow canyon to Osprey Falls.

Emerging from Sheepeater Canyon just above the Mammoth–Tower Road bridge, the river immediately enters the Gardner Canyon and picks up Lava Creek on its remaining 8-mile run to the Yellowstone.

The top 3 miles of the canyon are fairly wide on the south bank as the river cuts a northwesterly course around the barren, sun-baked slopes of Mount Everts. The river descends its narrow channel in a series of riffles and runs, long rock-garden glides, and a few lava chutes. Near the end of this stretch, the steaming waters of the Boiling

River create a hot plume in the Gardner. This is the only hot spring in the park where bathing is permitted.

Just downstream at the 45th Parallel Bridge on the Mammoth–Gardiner Road, the river swings through a short oxbow bend and down a sloping riffle to enter a narrow rapid. The river's final 3 miles is a gallop down a constricted, boulder-strewn channel to its confluence with the Yellowstone.

The Gardner is a torrent of muddy foam-flecked water in May and June. Most years it begins to clear by late June, but in exceptional runoff years it may not fish well with dry flies until mid-July. Summer flows are occasionally clouded by intense storms, but in autumn they are low and crystal clear.

Pan-sized brook trout in the river's headwaters—Gardner Meadow and Panther, Indian, and Obsidian Creeks—offer pleasant diversions for children and adults alike. Visitors staying at the scenic Indian Creek Campground often keep a few of the chubby, brightly colored char for campfire meals.

There are a few small trout in steep, narrow Sheepeater Canyon, but it is too dangerous to pursue them. In the middle of the canyon, the river plunges 150 feet over Osprey Falls.

Resident cutthroat, rainbow, and brown trout in the Gardner Canyon, below the Mammoth–Tower Road bridge, range from 8 to 14 inches, with a few larger browns. Lava Creek, which enters the river just below the bridge, adds more cutthroat to the mix, and both streams hold whitefish. In late fall, big browns run upstream from the Yellowstone to spawn, which makes the Gardner an important nursery stream for its larger sister.

The Gardner Canyon is an excellent dry fly stretch. Effective patterns include high-riding attractors like the Royal Wulff or Coachman Trude, plus Elk Hair Caddis, Humpies, Goddard Caddis, Stimulators, and generic mayflies like the Adams and Light Cahill. Hoppers and beetles draw slashing strikes in late summer. Similar patterns in smaller sizes work on the brookies in the upper meadow and its tributaries.

Stonefly nymphs, beadhead nymphs, caddis emergers, and soft hackles dredge resident trout out of the canyon's pocket waters throughout the season. Larger nymphs, Woolly Buggers, and streamers come into play during the fall migration of browns.

A prolific Dark Stonefly hatch in late June and early July, overlapped by hatches of Golden Stones and Little Yellow Stones, kicks off the dry fly season in Gardner Canyon. Mayfly hatches, primarily Baetis and Pale Morning Duns, are sporadic in the canyon, but summer evening hatches entice the brookies into dimpling the waters of the meadows until after dark. Caddis hatches are good throughout summer into autumn. The milder climate of the park's Northern Range awakens terrestrials early in July and permits them to remain active into October.

Fly fishing is difficult in the narrow canyon below the 45th Parallel riffle due to extremes in water velocity and lack of room to maneuver. Fishing is good upstream to Lava Creek and in the lower end of the tributary's canyon. Only a few small fish are in the river above the Mammoth–Tower Road bridge.

It's a steep scramble down to the river at the bridge. A better route into the top of Gardner Canyon is a trail from the lower Mammoth residence area, east of Mammoth Campground, which starts from behind the elementary school. The parking lot at the 45th Parallel Bridge is often crowded, but the majority of the people using it wear bathing suits, not waders.

A pleasant approach to fishing the canyon is to hike slowly upstream hitting its riffles and runs, pocket waters, and pools with dry flies and attractors. Then, on the way back, search the same waters with nymphs, caddis emergers, or soft hackles. Autumns are often mild in the Gardner Canyon, and fall brown hunters rarely are forced off the river before season's end in November.

The upper meadows are easily reached from the Indian Creek Campground and the Fawn Pass–Electric Peak Trailhead at the top of Swan Lake Flats, where Glen Creek crosses the loop road.

The park's Northern Range is home to one of the largest elk herds in North America. Moose are common in the Gardner's upper meadows and along its tributaries. Bull elk and moose in velvet are fairly docile in summer, but give them a wide berth when they polish their antlers for the fall rut. Also don't get in between a cow moose and her calves.

Black bears and grizzly bears are found in this region, too. Hike in groups when entering the upper meadows, and keep clean camps at both developed campgrounds and backcountry sites.

Stream Facts: Gardner River

Season

- Memorial Day weekend through the first Sunday of November.

Regulations

- Cutthroat and mountain whitefish are catch and release only. Individual limits on browns and rainbows are two fish, any size. Brook trout limit is five fish, any size.
- Children 11 years of age or younger may fish with worms as bait in the Gardner River; Obsidian, Indian, and Panther Creeks; and Joffe Lake.

Possession and length limits

- Catch and release all native species, including cutthroat and white fish.
- Possession limit: 5 combined non-native fish, any size per day, including rainbow, brown and brook trout.
- Cutthroat-rainbow hybrids (cuttbows) must be released.

Trout

- Pan-sized brook trout are found in both the headwaters and meadow run to Sheepeater Canyon. Resident cutthroat, rainbow, and brown trout in the lower canyon range from 8 to 14 inches, with a few larger fish. Large browns run upstream from the Yellowstone River in late fall to spawn. Angler report cards give the Gardner an 85-percent satisfaction rate for its one-fish-per-hour landing rate for trout averaging 8.5 inches.

Miles

- Mile 4: Glen Creek Trail
- Mile 5: Fawn Pass Trail
- Mile 7: Gardner Meadows
- Mile 15: Panther Creek
- Mile 21: Osprey Falls
- Mile 24.5: Mammoth-Tower Road bridge
- Mile 28: Boiling River hot springs
- Mile 29: 45th Parallel Bridge
- Mile 32: Confluence with Yellowstone River

Character

- The top half of the river cuts a narrow winding course across the marshy flats of Gardner Meadows to its confluence with Panther, Indian, and Obsidian Creeks at the Mammoth–Norris Road. About a half mile downstream, it passes under Sheepeater Cliffs and plunges into a steep narrow canyon and over 150-foot Osprey Falls. Sheepeater Canyon is impassable, but the lower canyon below the Mammoth- Tower Road bridge is wider, and its shallow riffles and runs and pocket waters are easily fished. Below the 45th Parallel Bridge on the Mammoth-Gardiner Road, the river gallops down a constricted, boulder-strewn course to its confluence with the Yellowstone River in a deep canyon at the town of Gardiner.

Flows

- The Gardner flows high and muddy through June and starts to clear by late in the month or in early July. Summer flows may be clouded by intense storms, but autumn flows are low and crystal clear.

Access

- Mammoth–Gardiner Road
- Mammoth–Norris Road

Camping

- Mammoth Campground
- Indian Creek Campground
- Gardiner, Montana, and Gallatin National Forest

GARDNER RIVER MAJOR HATCHES

Insect	A	M	J	J	A	S	O	N	Time	Flies
Stonefly			X						A	Dry: Sofa Pillow, Salmonfly, Bird's Stone, Orange Stimulator #2–8; Wet: Black Stone Nymph, Brook's Stone, Girdlebug, Rubberlegs, Woolly Bugger #2–6
Golden Stone				X					A	Dry: Golden Stone, Yellow or Orange Stimulator #6–8; Wet: Bitch Creek Nymph, Montana Stone, Girdlebug, Woolly Bugger #6–10
Little Yellow Stone					X				A/E	Yellow Sally, Willow Fly, Blonde Humpy, Yellow Stimulator #14–16
Caddis						X			A/E	Dry: Elk Hair Caddis (tan, olive, or peacock), Renegade, Yellow or Royal Humpy #10–14; Wet: Caddis Emerger, Soft Hackles, Squirrel Tail #14–16
Baetis							X		A/E	Dry: Blue-winged Olive, Blue Dun, Olive Sparkle Dun #14–18; Adams, Para-Adams #16–18; Wet: Pheasant Tail #16–18
Pale Morning Dun				X					M/ESF	Dry: PMD, Thorax PMD, Yellow Sparkle Dun, PMD Cripple, Rusty Spinner #14–18; Wet: Hare's Ear Nymph, Pheasant Tail, Beadheads #14–18
Terrestrials					X				M/A	Joe's Hopper, Dave's Hopper, Parachute Hopper #8–14; Yellow Humpy, Yellow Trude, Yellow Stimulator #12–14; Madam X #8–10; Disc O'Beetle, Black Elk Hair Caddis #14–16; Ants #14–18

M=morning; LM=late morning; A=afternoon; E=evening; D=dark; SF=spinner fall; /=continuation through periods

Fishing the Madison.

Madison and Gallatin River Drainages

The Madison and Gallatin Rivers drain the northwestern highlands of Yellowstone, exiting the park through separate valleys outlining Montana's Madison Range. Far downstream at the tiny town of Three Forks west of Bozeman, the Madison and Gallatin merge with the Jefferson to form the Missouri River.

Both the Madison and Gallatin run along two scenic highways to the park's West Entrance at the gateway community of West Yellowstone. US 191 follows the Gallatin upstream (south) from I-90 at Bozeman. It's the only major highway that passes through the park, and there are more than 15 miles of direct access to the river.

Scenic US 287 ascends the Madison from I-90 at Three Forks to West Yellowstone. The southern route to the popular resort town is via US 20 through eastern Idaho.

After passing through the West Entrance, anglers find the upper Madison fully accessible for nearly 10 miles of the park's loop road. A gravel side road a half mile inside the entrance provides access to the lower half of the river.

At Madison Junction, the loop road provides the park's next two choices for easily reached fishing waters. The road to the south closely follows the Firehole River to Old Faithful and the Upper Geyser Basin. The road to the north parallels the Gibbon River to Norris Geyser Basin.

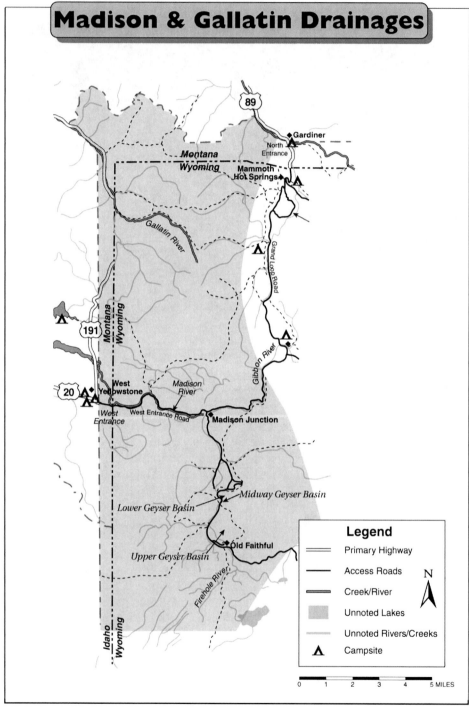

Madison & Gallatin Drainages

MADISON RIVER

The Madison River is the first of Yellowstone's fabled waters seen by the hordes of flyfishers who flock to the gateway community of West Yellowstone. Paralleled by the loop road to Madison Junction, it entices anglers to park, unpack rods, and delve into its mysteries.

The Madison is a moody river, difficult to fish, and gives up its secrets reluctantly. Despite these characteristics, it is the second most renowned river in the park. It's the river Charles Brooks used to research and write his seminal books, Nymph Fishing For Larger Trout, The Living River, and The Trout and the Stream. Classics in fly fishing literature, they are textbooks for complex streams just about anywhere. Brooks claimed the Madison in the park as his home river, but he never said it was easy.

The river has a good mix of moderate-sized brown and rainbow trout, with the browns going to trophy proportions during fall spawning runs out of Hebgen Lake in Montana. It is loaded with whitefish, and a few grayling make their way down from Grebe Lake via the Gibbon River.

One of the largest bison herds in Yellowstone inhabits the Madison Valley. Elk numbers rival bison, especially in autumn. The river is also home to the rare trumpeter swan as well as other waterfowl. Bald eagles and osprey are common.

The Madison is formed by the confluence of the Firehole and Gibbon Rivers at National Park Meadow. The river was named for James Madison, fourth president of the United States.

When the Lewis & Clark Expedition reached Three Forks in 1805 in present-day Montana, the captains found two streams so close in size and appearance that they could not decide which was the real Missouri. "We called the S.W. fork, that which we meant to ascend, Jefferson's River in honor of that illustrious personage [President] Thomas Jefferson. The Middle fork we called Madison's River in honor of James Madison [Secretary of State], and the S.E. Fork we called Gallatin's River in honor of Albert Gallatin [Secretary of the Treasury]," Meriwether Lewis wrote in his journal.

The Madison is restricted to fly fishing only. Rainbow and brown trout, mountain whitefish, and grayling are protected by a catch-and-release rule. The limit on brook trout is 5 fish.

Seasons of the Madison

Winter releases its grasp on the park earlier in the Madison Basin than in other areas of Yellowstone. It offers the best wet fly option for opening-day anglers, although the only guarantee about springtime in the Rockies is that it is capricious.

Runoff on the Madison is dictated by the Firehole and Gibbon Rivers, and most years it is fairly moderate. It peaks by June and begins to clear thereafter. In wet years, the river may run out of its banks and recede more slowly. Muddy flows from the Gibbon occasionally keep it off-color into July.

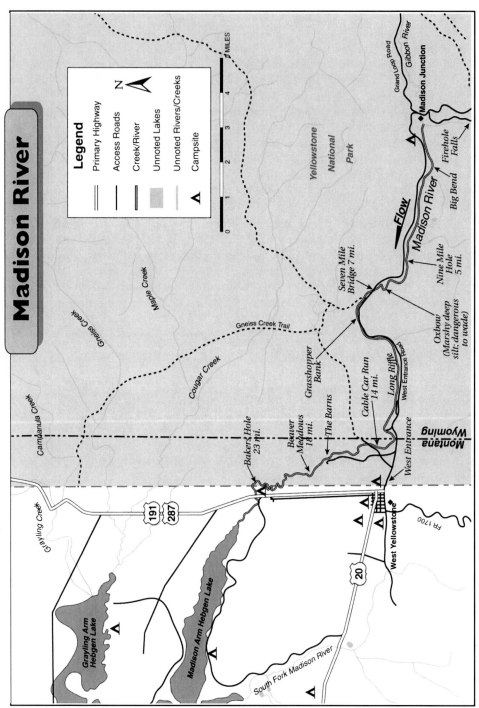

Madison River

Legend
Primary Highway
Access Roads
Creek/River
Unnoted Lakes
Unnoted Rivers/Creeks
Campsite

N

5 MILES
0 1 2 3 4

Yellowstone National Park

Madison Junction
Grand Loop Road
Gibbon River
Firehole Falls
Big Bend
Madison River
Flow

Seven Mile Bridge 7 mi.
Nine Mile Hole 5 mi.
Oxbow! (Marshy deep silt; dangerous to wade)
Grasshopper Bank
Cable Car Run 14 mi.
Long Riffle
West Entrance Road
West Entrance

Gneiss Creek Trail
Maple Creek
Gneiss Creek
Cougar Creek
Campanula Creek

Bakers Hole 23 mi.
Beaver Meadows 18 mi.
The Barns

Montana
Wyoming

Grayling Creek
191 287
20
FR 1700
West Yellowstone

Grayling Arm Hebgen Lake
Madison Arm Hebgen Lake
South Fork Madison River

© 2009 Wilderness Adventures Press, Inc.

The warmer flows of the Firehole cause a summer doldrums on the Madison in low water years. It is less of a factor in cool, wet summers with good flows.

Rainbows and browns are in the 10- to 16-inch range, with a few browns exceeding 20 inches. The larger fish are most often found in the bottom half of the river, away from the loop road.

Late-autumn spawning runs by Hebgen Lake browns extend to the waterfalls on the Gibbon and Firehole, and all three waters are important nursery streams. A good number of the spawners exceed 24 inches. Large rainbows follow the runs upstream from Hebgen to nab eggs drifting out of the brown redds.

The Madison's hatches are not overly complex, but when they occur, they make a difference. Through summer, the river fishes best early and late in the day. Overcast days, and even rainy days, are most productive. Attractor patterns work well in riffle sections of the river.

A stonefly hatch on a few segments of the river draws topwater action from early June into July, although it is difficult to time. The hatch is most productive in the heavier waters above and below Cable Car Run, and sporadic activity occurs near the mouth of the Firehole Canyon. Dark Stone Nymphs, Rubber Legs, and Woolly Buggers are critical to a flyfisher's arsenal throughout the year.

Little Yellow Stones join caddis in June and July, and the caddis outnumber mayflies until late autumn. A short Green Drake hatch mixes with Baetis and Pale Morning Duns in mid-June or early July, but the key mayfly hatch to watch for is the Trico emergence in August and September. The drakes and tiny Tricos are found on quieter stretches of the river.

The Madison's meadow runs make terrestrials important components of fly boxes from early July to the first hard frosts of October. Low-profile hoppers are generally most effective.

Small nymphs, emergers, and beadheads take as many whitefish as trout, and quite often more. Anglers who follow the advice of Brooks in Nymph Fishing for Larger Trout need to remember that Yellowstone is a lead-free zone. Nontoxic materials must be used for weighted flies, split shot, and leader wraps.

The loop road follows the Madison from its birth to about 10 miles downstream, where it cuts away to the northwest to circle behind West Yellowstone. The lower river is reached from a gravel road about a half mile east of the West Entrance. It leads to the famous Cable Car Run and Barns Holes. The trail into the bottom of the Madison's 20-mile run through the park starts from Bakers Hole Campground, a couple of miles north of West Yellowstone. This is the quickest route to Beaver Meadows.

Wading the Madison is tricky in some areas. Its gradient is moderate and currents are subtle, but it flows with the full force of a river. Some channels are deeper than they appear, especially through boulder-filled runs and weed beds and around logjams.

The main place to stay out of is the long meandering bend between Seven Mile Bridge and Nine Mile Hole. It is marshy, and the deep silt in the channel is dangerous. Areas near the bridge may be closed in spring to protect nesting trumpeter swans.

Another set of obstacles to tread lightly around are the "beaver holes" of the lower meadow. These are actually channels cut into streambanks by beavers to reach willows and other shrubs in the marshes. The murky water in the channels hides their depth. Unwary anglers may end up face down in the grass with one leg buried in the muck. Circle above the channels when they are too wide to step across easily.

Collecting the flows of the Firehole and Gibbon, the Madison swings west through Elk Meadow below Madison Campground and rambles though grassy flats past Big Bend down to a wooded run above Nine Mile Hole. The meanders are marked by series of undercut banks, long glides and pools, short swift runs, and weedy channels.

Below Seven Mile Bridge, the river speeds up and swings through a shallow weedy bend to the riffles and runs along Grasshopper Bank. From Riverside Drive, a short byway off the loop road, the river is a long shallow riffle that offers poor fishing until it reaches the Barns Holes and Cable Car Run. This area is a series of rumpled rocky runs, swift riffles above long, deep holes, and intermittent gravel bar channels.

About 3 miles downstream, the river flattens and meanders through the marshy Beaver Meadows in long pool-like glides divided by side channels, broad riffles, and narrow runs. It exits the park just above Bakers Hole Campground in the Gallatin National Forest.

The meadows are prime grizzly bear country, and no tents are permitted in the campground.

In fall, the undercut banks, deeper side channels, and pools of Beaver Meadows are holding areas in the first stage of the brown spawning run out of Hebgen Lake. Browns start showing up in the meadows as early as late August, but most wait until

A beautiful day for fishing the Madison.

autumn storms cool water temperatures in late September or October. The colder the weather, the faster the run surges upstream to Madison Junction and the lower Firehole and Gibbon. And the nastier the weather, the better the fishing.

In cold weather, big weighted nymphs and Woolly Buggers are most effective, along with larger streamers, like Clousers, Spruce Flies, Double Bunnies, and Zonkers. During warmer weather, moderate-sized soft hackles and beadheads such as Prince Nymphs work, and even dry flies occasionally bring up a fish. Egg patterns may nab both rainbows and browns.

The window of opportunity to attack the spawning run is short. The season ends for the winter after the first Sunday in November. Park roads close sooner if early snows are heavy.

Madison Tributaries

Three small tributaries of the Madison flow out of the park north of Beaver Meadows to join the river in the backwaters of Hebgen Lake. A Montana fishing license is needed to fish the creeks west of the park boundary.

The first two, Cougar and Duck Creeks, join just west of US 191, about 8 miles north of West Yellowstone. Short side roads east of the highway lead to parking lots and access to the creeks in the park. The third, Grayling Creek, runs parallel to US 191 for more than 5 miles inside the park before it cuts west to reach the reservoir.

Moose and bison are common in the meadows around Cougar and Duck Creeks, and the region is prime grizzly bear country.

Cougar Creek: Sometimes confused with the Madison by highway travelers, Cougar Creek meanders through a marshy meadow dotted by thick clumps of willows and shrubs and scattered beaver ponds. The turnoff to the park boundary, 7 miles north of West Yellowstone, is a gravel road just south of the highway bridge.

The creek holds rainbow, brown, and brook trout that average about 10 inches, with occasional surprises. There are reports of westslope cutthroat in its higher reaches. Grayling were planted in the creek between 1993 and 1996, but the restoration project has had limited success.

Attractors and generic mayflies work in Cougar Creek, but it fishes best in late summer and fall with terrestrials and streamers. Search carefully for large browns and rainbows in the beaver ponds. They are wary and difficult to hook.

Duck Creek: This challenging mountain meadow fishery flows through a broad, grassy flat with islands of lodgepole pine. The side road to the park boundary, 8 miles north of West Yellowstone, starts at the Highway Department shed south of the junction of US 191 and 287.

Formed by the confluence of Campanula, Richards, and Gneiss Creeks, Duck Creek offers about 3 miles of excellent fishing along its meadow run in the park. Like the Madison, it benefits from spawning runs of rainbows and browns from Hebgen Lake that average 16 inches. Brook trout also are present.

Low-profile, spring creek tactics are required to stalk the wary trout in Duck Creek's open waters. Cautiously presented drag-free drifts of dry flies are critical.

Mayflies in early summer include Pale Morning Duns and Green Drakes, and terrestrials are most effective in late summer and fall. Its grassy undercut banks can be explored with moderate-sized leeches and Woolly Buggers.

Gneiss Creek presents a side-trip option for browns and rainbows averaging 10 inches, and occasional larger fish. Richards and Campanula Creeks hold tiny brookies.

Grayling Creek: A shallow, tumbling mountain stream, Grayling Creek gambols along US 191 in an intermittent series of pocket waters, riffles and runs, cutbanks, and deeper pools. It exits the park at the point US 191 enters it, 11 miles north of West Yellowstone. Anglers can pull over to fish it just about anywhere for the next 6 miles upstream. Northeast of the highway, the creek flows out of a rugged, steep valley not worth the effort to enter.

Grayling Creek holds westslope cutthroat, browns, and rainbows that average about 12 inches. Look for larger trout in deeper pools, sheltered lies, and around logjams.

Spring hatches include Golden Stones, Little Yellow Stones, and caddis; Pale Morning Duns are the predominant mayfly in summer. The creek also fishes well with attractors like Humpies, Stimulators, Irresistibles, Wulffs, and Trudes, and generic mayflies like the Adams and Light Cahill.

Stream Facts: Madison River

Season

- Memorial Day weekend through the first Sunday in November.

Regulations

- The Madison is restricted to fly fishing only. Rainbow and brown trout, mountain whitefish, and grayling are protected by a catch-and-release rule. The limit on brook trout is two fish, any size.

Trout

- Rainbows and browns are in the 10- to 16-inch range, with a few browns exceeding 20 inches. Larger fish are most often found in the bottom half of the river away from the loop road. Late autumn spawning runs by large browns extend to the waterfalls on the Gibbon and Firehole. Large rainbows follow browns out of Hebgen Lake. Whitefish are plentiful, and a few grayling are washed down the Gibbon from Grebe Lake. Angler report cards give the Madison a 62-percent satisfaction rating for its .51-fish-per-hour landing rate for trout averaging 13 inches.

Miles

- Mile 0: Madison Junction
- Mile 5: Nine Mile Hole
- Mile 7: Seven Mile Bridge
- Mile 10: Riverside Drive
- Mile 14: Barns Holes and Cable Car Run
- Mile 18: Beaver Meadows
- Mile 22: Park boundary
- Mile 22.5: Bakers Hole Campground

Character

- The Madison begins at the confluence of the Firehole and Gibbon Rivers. From Elk Meadow below Madison Campground down through Nine Mile Hole, the river twists and turns in long sweeping curves, undercut banks, deeper pools, intermittent riffles and runs, and channels. The marshy area extending above Seven Mile Bridge to Nine Mile hole is hazardous to wade. Flow quickens below the bridge, where a weedy channel descends to the riffles and runs of Grasshopper Bank. At Riverside Drive, the river turns into a long shallow riffle as it veers away from the loop road. Downstream at Barns Holes and Cable Car Run, it flows through a series of rumpled rocky runs, short swift riffles, and long deep pools. The final run flattens and meanders through the marshy Beaver Meadows in long, pool-like glides divided by side channels, broad riffles, and narrow runs to the park's boundary.

Flows

- Spring runoff peaks by June and begins to clear thereafter. In wet years, the river may run out of its banks and recede more slowly. Muddy flows from the Gibbon occasionally keep it off-color into July.

Access

- Madison Junction Road
- Cable Car Road, half mile east of West Yellowstone
- Bakers Hole Campground, north of West Yellowstone

Camping

- Madison Campground
- Bakers Hole Campground
- West Yellowstone
- Gallatin National Forest

MADISON RIVER MAJOR HATCHES

Insect	A	M	J	J	A	S	O	N	Time	Flies
Stonefly			■						A	Dry: Sofa Pillow, Salmonfly, Orange Bucktail, Orange Stimulator #4–8; Wet: Brook's Stone Nymph, Black Rubberlegs, Woolly Bugger #2–6
Little Yellow Stone				■					A/E	Yellow Sally, Yellow Stimulator, Blonde Humpy, Willow Fly #10–14
Caddis						■			A/E	Dry: Tan or Olive Elk Hair Caddis, X-Caddis, Yellow or Royal Humpy, Hemingway Caddis #12–16; Wet: Beadhead Emerger, Soft Hackles, Prince Nymph, Squirrel Tail #14–18
Pale Morning Dun					■				M/ESF	Dry: PMD, PMD Cripple, Sparkle Dun, Rusty Spinner #14–18; Wet: Beadhead Hare's Ear, Pheasant Tail #16–18
Green Drake			■						A	Dry: Green Drake, Olive Wulff, Qui8gley Cripple #10–12; Wet: Ida Mae, Prince Nymph, Zug Bug #10–12
Baetis				■					A/E	Dry: Blue-Winged Olive, Para-BWO, Olive Sparkle Dun, Blue Dun, Para-Adams #14–18; Tiny BWO #18–22; Wet: Pheasant Tail #16–18
Trico						■			MSF/A	Dry: Black and White, Trico Spinner, Para-Adams #18–22; Wet: Pheasant Tail #18–22

M=morning; LM=late morning; A=afternoon; E=evening; D=dark; SF=spinner fall; /=continuation through periods

MADISON RIVER MAJOR HATCHES

Insect	A	M	J	J	A	S	O	N	Time	Flies
Gray Drake			▮						A/ESF	Dry: Gray Wulff, Para-Adams, Gray Sparkle Dun, CDC Spinner #10–14; Wet: Hare's Ear Nymph #10–14
March Brown		▮							A	Dry: March Brown Parachute, Light Cahill, Light Brown Comparadun, Red Quill $14–18; Wet: March Brown Flymph, March Brown Soft Hackle, March Brown Nymph #12–16
Flav					▮				M/E	Dry: Para-Olive Hare's Ear, CDC Olive Quill, Green Wulff, CDC Spinner #14–16; Wet: Quigley Cripple, CDC Cripple, Olive Sparkle Emerger #12–16
Pale Evening Dun				▮					A/E	Dry: PED Thorax, PED Comparadun, PED Parachute, Fluttering Spinner #14–18; Wet: Quigley Cripple, Hare's Ear Nymph, Pheasant Tail #14–18
Western Red Quill					▮				A/E	Dry: Red quill Dun, CDC Red Quill, Rusty Spinner, Pink Cahill #14–18; Wet: Pink Albert Emerger #16
Midges						▮	▮		E	Griffith's Gnat, Para-Adams #18
Terrestrials					▮	▮			M/A	Joe's Hopper, Dave's Hopper, Parachute Hopper, Madam X #8–14; Foam Beetle, Dave's Cricket #14–16; Flying Ant, Black Ant, Rusty Ant #14–18

M=morning; LM=late morning; A=afternoon; E=evening; D=dark; SF=spinner fall; /=continuation through periods

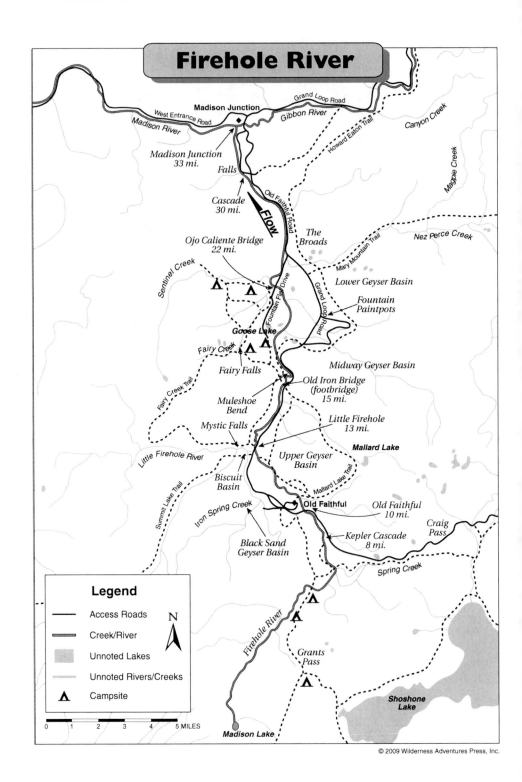

Firehole River

Madison Junction

West Entrance Road

Madison River

Grand Loop Road

Gibbon River

Howard Eaton Trail

Canyon Creek

Magpie Creek

*Madison Junction
33 mi.*

Falls

*Cascade
30 mi.*

Old Faithful Road

Flow

*The
Broads*

Nez Perce Creek

Mary Mountain Trail

*Ojo Caliente Bridge
22 mi.*

Sentinel Creek

Fountain Flat Drive

Lower Geyser Basin

Grand Loop Road

*Fountain
Paintpots*

Goose Lake

Fairy Creek

Fairy Creek Trail

Fairy Falls

Midway Geyser Basin

*Old Iron Bridge
(footbridge)
15 mi.*

*Muleshoe
Bend*

Mystic Falls

*Little Firehole
13 mi.*

Little Firehole River

Mallard Lake

*Upper Geyser
Basin*

Mallard Lake Trail

*Biscuit
Basin*

Summit Lake Trail

Iron Spring Creek

Old Faithful

*Old Faithful
10 mi.*

*Craig
Pass*

*Black Sand
Geyser Basin*

*Kepler Cascade
8 mi.*

Spring Creek

Legend

	Access Roads
	Creek/River
	Unnoted Lakes
	Unnoted Rivers/Creeks
Λ	Campsite

N

Firehole River

*Grants
Pass*

**Shoshone
Lake**

0   1   2   3   4   5 MILES

Madison Lake

© 2009 Wilderness Adventures Press, Inc.

FIREHOLE RIVER

The most exotic trout stream in the world, the Firehole River has mystified and captivated the outside world since its discovery by 19th-century fur trappers.

Its name is often attributed to one of the tall tales of Jim Bridger, the king of the mountain men. However, it more likely derived from first being associated with a nearby valley gutted by a forest fire, and later with its geysers and hot springs. Fur traders and trappers often called open mountain valleys "holes," as in Jackson Hole.

The Firehole's modern fame as an extraordinary dry fly stream springs as much from the wariness of its brown and rainbow trout as from the privilege to cast a line in such a spellbinding amphitheater of nature. Puffs of steam and sulfurous vapors drift on the winds across an arena carpeted with spouting geysers, hissing fumaroles, and bubbling mud pots linked by the most genial of Yellowstone's streams. Lush meadows and verdant pine forests lining its banks harbor large herds of bison and scattered bands of elk, occasionally spooked by roaming coyotes, grizzly bears, and wolves.

The Firehole's character and trout are greatly influenced by voluminous geothermal outflows of the large geyser basins it bisects. While it is commonly assumed that trout cannot live and reproduce in warm waters, they thrive in the Firehole. It is doubly amazing since the river held no fish prior to Yellowstone becoming a park. In 1889, brook trout were introduced into the upper Firehole, and the lower river received brown trout. Rainbows came later, and the river received supplemental plantings until park officials ended its hatchery programs in the mid1950s.

The tiny cold mountain stream rises at an elevation of 8,670 feet from Madison Lake, 17 miles southwest of Old Faithful Village; later, it is dramatically warmed by the Upper Geyser Basin. Continuing to grow in size, it collects the steaming runoffs of Black Sands Geyser Basin and smaller thermal areas. The boiling outwellings of Excelsior Geyser Crater alone increase the temperature of the river by 5 to 7 degrees as it passes the Midway Geyser Basin. By the time it reaches the 40-foot Firehole Falls below the Lower Geyser Basin, the river's temperature has risen almost 27 degrees.

Seasonal temperatures and coldwater tributaries like Iron Spring Creek, the Little Firehole River, and Sentinel and Nez Perce Creeks help moderate the Firehole's temperatures. However, summer flows routinely approach 70 degrees. In hot, dry years they may become lethal to trout as water temperatures approach 80 degrees. Occasionally, to reduce stress on the trout, the park will close the Firehole to fishing in August when water temperatures become extreme.

As temperatures increase in July and August, the trout bail out of the river and into its tributaries. Conversely, in cold, wet summers, larger trout often remain in the river where there is more food and shelter.

The hot, mineralized waters of the geysers and hot springs contribute to winter production of aquatic insects and year-round growth of trout, according to Lynn Kaeding, former Yellowstone research director for the U.S. Fish and Wildlife Service. But summer temperatures are high enough to inhibit brown trout maturity and kill rainbows.

"They grow fast—an 8- or 10-inch fish is only a year or a year and half old, but the high seasonal temperatures may limit growth after that initial burst," Kaeding said. "You'll get some 14 to 16 inches, and even fewer in the 18- to 20-inch range."

A four-year study by Kaeding in the mid-1990s documented the summer trout exodus from the Firehole. "The numbers of fish in tributaries increased exponentially in relation to nearby Firehole River temperatures that ultimately exceeded incipient upper lethal levels for rainbow and brown trout," he stated in his report. But it is not a total evacuation from the river. "Periodic forays from tributaries were made, perhaps in response to food availability and competition for other resources," noted Kaeding. He speculated the trout take advantage of cooler water temperatures at night and in the first hours of daylight to forage in the river. Some trout also linger in cool water plumes below tributaries.

Electroshocking samples by Kaeding's crew found migrating rainbows in the tributaries averaged 10 inches and browns averaged 11.5 inches. The largest rainbow tagged was 19 inches and the largest brown was 22 inches.

Still, Charles Brooks and Ernest Schwiebert, the two deans of fly-fishing literature, often fondly recalled days of yore when the "Queen of Yellowstone" held many more large trout and a richer aquatic insect population. They contended that a series of minor earthquakes in the 1970s raised the Firehole's temperature and flushed toxic silt into the river.

Park biologists, on the other hand, note that significant changes in the river's trout populations occurred after the closure of its hatchery programs. It is now functioning as a wild trout fishery, but it also has had to cope with prolonged droughts.

However, the answer to which view is right might be moot. Kaeding raises an even direr specter. "Rainbow and brown trout in the middle and lower Firehole River in summer live near their upper lethal temperatures, an existence made more tenuous by climate warming," he stated. "As the river warms, use of cool water tributaries will increase, along with agonistic behaviors, predation, disease, and competition among fish in its tributaries. Moreover, the capacity for the cool water tributaries to hold fish could be reduced as ground water, the source of the summer flows in the tributaries, is warmed by climate warming."

A fly-fishing-only stream, the Firehole is closed to fishing in the Upper Geyser Basin. Its rainbows and brown trout are protected by a catch-and-release rule. The limit on brook trout is 5 fish, any size. The same restrictions apply to tributaries.

Seasons of the Firehole

The Firehole sets the pace for Yellowstone's fishing season. Its spring runoff is the earliest in the park, it warms more quickly, and its hatches occur sooner.

Mostly flat along its meandering course through the long valley above its canyon, runoff is usually minor. But when the Firehole runs high and off-color into June, expect the rest of the park's streams to be filled to the brim or even out of their banks.

Generally, the Firehole is at its best in June for all brands of flyfishers. The trout show an interest in a great variety of flies they maddeningly ignore later in the season.

Local flyfishers flock to it in spring, explore other waters in midsummer, and return in autumn for its most challenging dry fly fishing.

Mayflies and caddis are small at the start of the season and truly microscopic as autumn descends into winter. Caddis species outnumber mayflies, but it is not a place for bushy, high-profile flies or attractor patterns. Neither is fair weather a blessing on the Firehole. It fishes best during cool, heavily overcast days.

Try thorax, sidewinder, and parachute patterns for mayflies, along with spinners and Sparkle Duns. The only consistent large mayfly in the river is the Flav, or small western Green Drake. Dark flat-wing caddis patterns and sparsely tied Elk Hair Caddis are most effective. But small Yellow Sallies, Blonde Humpies, and Stimulators work when Little Yellow Stones are on the water. Grasshopper choices rarely exceed size 12 and also require slim silhouettes, like the Parachute Hopper, Jacklin's Hopper, or Joe's Hopper. Tiny ants and small foam or fur beetles round out the terrestrial options.

During spring runoff, small beadhead nymphs or emergers and moderate-sized Woolly Buggers or soft hackles are most effective in exploring the river. They also can be used to prospect for trout after the water clears and topwater action slows through midday. When making quartering casts with wet flies, pause and let the fly dangle at the end of the swing before retrieving it. This tactic often draws slashing strikes.

During hatches, or when using them as dropper flies, nymphs and emergers diminish in sizes like the adult insects as the season progresses.

The Firehole River at Midway Geyser Basin. (Mike Retallick photo)

The Firehole offers a unique angling opportunity.

Early day and evening hatches in June include Baetis (Blue-Winged Olives) and Pale Morning Duns, along with midges on quiet backwaters. PMDs linger the longest into July, and tiny BWOs and midges return in force in late September to close out the season on the upper Firehole. Small Western Green Drakes make their brief appearance around mid-June, and a few Gray Drakes may be encountered on quieter sections of the river about the same time.

Caddis options are good in early season; a few even emerge through the summer doldrums, and a new burst of activity in September and October lasts until hard frosts shut it down. Terrestrial activity is best in late August and September.

The Firehole is easily waded, although it has some deceptively deep channels in its lava-rock floor, around weed beds, and along undercut banks. There also are a few marshy areas that present difficulties in approaching the banks without waders.

But wading usually is a second choice on the Firehole. The larger trout hang tight to the banks, which can have deep undercuts, even along rocky ledges and openings in weed beds. Except when fishing its few braided channels, the outside bends of wide meanders, or channelized weed beds, it is best to stay out of the water as much as possible. Stream crossings should be made at shallow riffles to avoid disturbing trout downstream.

The river is best suited to sneak-and-stalk fishing approaches from the banks, and offers good lessons in spring creek tactics useful on other challenging waters. Precise, delicate casts with good slack in long, light leaders and slender tippets are required to dead-drift flies through the subtle swirls of its currents.

The Firehole's Biscuit Basin Run starts at the loop road bridge just north of the exit to Old Faithful Village. The narrow river loops around the Black Sand Geyser Basin in a series of long slick glides and channels, with deep strong currents, as it gains strength from the flows of Iron Spring Creek and the Little Firehole River.

It then rambles down a narrow rocky channel lined by forests and marshy meadows to the Old Iron Bridge and makes a short rocky turn north to the broad meanders of the famous Muleshoe Bend. This broad S-shaped loop of the Firehole is popular for sight-fishing to rising trout and often is the most crowded section of the river.

Fishing effectively ends as the stream dashes past the Middle Geyser Basin. It picks up again in the meadow and forest runs below Goose Lake in the Fountain Flats. There are some interesting pools and channels in this area, but fishing is often poor in the swift pocket waters above the Ojo Caliente hot spring.

The river then cuts a long loop past the mouth of Sentinel Creek, where there are some deep weedy runs, pools, and long undercut banks through the grassy meadow down to Nez Perce Creek.

From here downstream to the Firehole Cascade, the river rambles down a forestlined flat paralleled by the Madison–Old Faithful Road. This short section, called The Broads, is essentially a long riffle, with weedy channels and braided gravel bars and some deeper pools and pocket waters above the canyon lip.

The pocket waters of the canyon below Firehole Falls receive the most attention in early spring and late autumn, but are worth exploring throughout the park's season. Care should be taken in wading the rough cobble floor of the canyon run, which also requires some rock scrambling.

The middle of the canyon is reached by a one-way spur that begins just south of the loop road bridge below Madison Junction.

This is the one place on the river where big flies come into play. Sporadic hatches of small stoneflies and Golden Stones around mid-June open the canyon's season. Caddis, generic mayfly and attractor patterns, and moderate-sized stonefly nymphs and Woolly Buggers are effective year-round. In late fall the lower canyon is a large nymph and streamer fishery for big brown trout spawners that migrate up the Madison River from Hebgen Lake. Good-sized rainbows tag along to feed on eggs.

Even if your only visit to the park is at the height of summer, don't forego the otherworldly experience of fishing the Firehole. Dawn or dusk visits generally are more productive at this time. The shaded, swift runs through the forests below Biscuit Basin and behind Goose Lake often keep trout active through summer. Trout in the riffles and runs between Nez Perce Creek and the river's canyon may be less picky and continue to feed through summer.

The upper river above Old Faithful presents opportunities for another summer diversion. Rarely crowded, the riffles and runs of its meadow meander below Kepler Cascade hold small brook trout and a few browns.

Remarkable rainbows and browns find refuge in late summer in cooler tributaries like the Little Firehole River, but they are incredibly shy and selective. Crystal-clear flows and tangles of fallen lodgepole pine add to the challenges of netting large, easily startled trout. Nez Perce Creek, the most accommodating of the Firehole's feeder streams, requires a 2-mile hike from the loop road to reach its best fishing in the meadow above the Culex Basin thermal area.

Anglers returning to the Firehole after long absences will find slightly longer hikes to portions of the river. New construction on the Madison–Old Faithful Road turned it away from several portions of the river. Also, the old Fountain Flat Freight Road was closed to motor traffic below the Ojo Caliente Bridge, south of the Nez Perce Picnic Area. The road, which once permitted anglers to drive to Goose Lake and the middle section of the river, is restricted to foot or mountain bike traffic. The southern route into the river above Fountain Flats is the Iron Bridge Trailhead, below Biscuit Basin.

Thermal zones along the river should be approached with caution. Stick to clearly defined footpaths when entering these areas and walking along the banks. Don't attempt to cross chalky, unstable soils around geysers, hot springs, and mud pots.

Some backcountry areas and tributaries of the river, like Fountain Flats south of Ojo Caliente, are periodically closed to entry because of grizzly bear or bison activity. Check on restrictions at local fly shops or the Old Faithful Visitor Center when planning trips into more remote areas.

Stream Facts: Firehole River

Season

- Memorial Day weekend through the first Sunday in November. Upper Geyser Basin, from Old Faithful to Biscuit Basin, is closed to fishing.

Regulations

- The entire river is restricted to fly fishing only. Rainbow and brown trout are catch and release only. The brook trout limit is five fish, any size.

Trout

- Rainbows average 10 inches and browns average 11.5 inches, with fair numbers of both species 14 to 16 inches, and a few in the 18- to 20-inch range. Anglers who fill out the park's report cards give the Firehole a 76-percent satisfaction rating for its 0.8-fish-per-hour landing rate and trout that average 9.7 inches.

Miles

- Mile 0: Madison Lake
- Mile 10: Old Faithful Village
- Mile 13: Little Firehole River
- Mile 15: Old Iron Bridge
- Mile 16: Muleshoe Bend
- Mile 21: Trail from Goose Lake
- Mile 23: Sentinel Creek
- Mile 24.5: Nez Perce Creek
- Mile 31: Firehole Cascade
- Mile 31.5: Firehole Falls
- Mile 34: Confluence with Gibbon

Character

- This is a small mountain stream from its source at Madison Lake on the north slope of the Continental Divide to the Upper Geyser Basin. Below Old Faithful Village, the river drops through riffle-filled runs into the broader, meandering flows of Biscuit Basin and continues to twist and turn through Midway Geyser Basin and behind Fountain Paint Pot Flats to Nez Perce Creek. Serpentine meadow runs hold occasional shallow riffles, numerous cutbanks, deeper pools, and long glides. Below Nez Perce Creek, the river's pace quickens through The Broads, a string of riffles and swift rocky runs above the Firehole Cascade and Firehole Falls. The short canyon is filled with swift channels, pocket waters, and deeper pools above the Firehole's confluence with the Gibbon at Madison Junction.

Flows

- Spring runoff is not a major factor most years, and flows during the remainder of the year are relatively moderate and stable, except in drought years. The Firehole may flow high and off-color through June after exceptionally wet winters.

Access

- The Madison–Old Faithful Road skirts the east bank of the river, with ample pullouts. Trails to the west bank start at Old Iron Bridge, north of Black Sand Geyser Basin, and from Ojo Caliente Bridge, on a dead-end side road south of Nez Perce Creek Picnic Area.

Camping

- Madison Junction Campground
- Gallatin National Forest
- West Yellowstone

FIREHOLE RIVER MAJOR HATCHES

Insect	A	M	J	J	A	S	O	N	Time	Flies
Stonefly			▮						A	Dry: Sofa Pillow, Bird's Stone, Orange Bucktail #4–8; Wet: Brook's Stone Nymph, Black Rubberlegs, Girdlebug, Woolly Bugger #2–8
Golden Stone				▮					A	Dry: Golden Stone, Yellow or Orange Stimulator, Yellow Sally #6–10; Wet: Bitch Creek Nymph, Montana Stone #6–10
Caddis			▮	▮	▮	▮			A/E	Dry: Elk Hair Caddis, Partridge Caddis, X-Caddis, Yellow or Blonde Humpy, Dark Deer Hair Caddis #14–20; Wet: Caddis Emerger, Caddis Pupa, Prince Nymph #14–18
Little Yellow Stone				▮					A/E	Yellow Sally, Yellow Stimulator, Yellow or Lime Trude, Willow Fly #14–16
Baetis			▮			▮			A/E	Blue-Winged Olive, Blue Dun, Blue Quill, Para-Adams #16–22; Tiny BWO #20–24
Pale Morning Dun				▮					M/E	Dry: PMD, Thorax PMD, PMD Cripple, Sparkle Dun, Pale Evening Dun, #16–20; Wet: Hare's Ear Nymph, Pheasant Tail #16–18
Flav				▮					M/E	Para-Olive Hare's Ear, CDC Flav, CDC Quill Comparadun, CDC Cripple, Quigley Cripple #14–16

M=morning; LM=late morning; A=afternoon; E=evening; D=dark; SF=spinner fall; /=continuation through periods

FIREHOLE RIVER MAJOR HATCHES

Insect	A	M	J	J	A	S	O	N	Time	Flies
Gray Drake				X					A	Para-Adams, Gray Drake Sparkle Dun, Parachute Spinner, CDC Comparadun #10–12
Mahogany Dun						X			A	Dry: Mahogany Dun, Mahogany Thorax, Sparkle Dun #14–18; Wet: Mahogany Emerger #14–18
March Brown				X					A	Dry: March Brown Parachute, Light Brown Comparadun, Red Quill, Rusty Spinner #14–16; Wet: March Brown Flymph, Red Quill Soft Hackle, March Brown Nymph #12–16
Pink Lady					X				A/E	Dry: Pink Albert, Pink Lady, Pink Cahill #14–18; Pink Sparkle Dun, CDC Spinner, CDC Emerger, Cream Dun #14–16
Western Red Quill				X					A/E	Dry: Red Quill Dun, CDC Red Quill, Rusty Spinner, Pink Cahill #14–18; Wet: Pink Albert Emerger #16
Midges				X		X			E	Griffith's Gnat, Black and White Midge, Cream Midge #18–22
Terrestrials				X	X				M/A	Parachute Hopper, Jacklin's Hopper, Henry's Fork Hopper #10–14; Flying Ant, Black Ant, Rusty Ant #16–18; Foam Beetle, Disc O'Beetle #14–18

M=morning; LM=late morning; A=afternoon; E=evening; D=dark; SF=spinner fall; /=continuation through periods

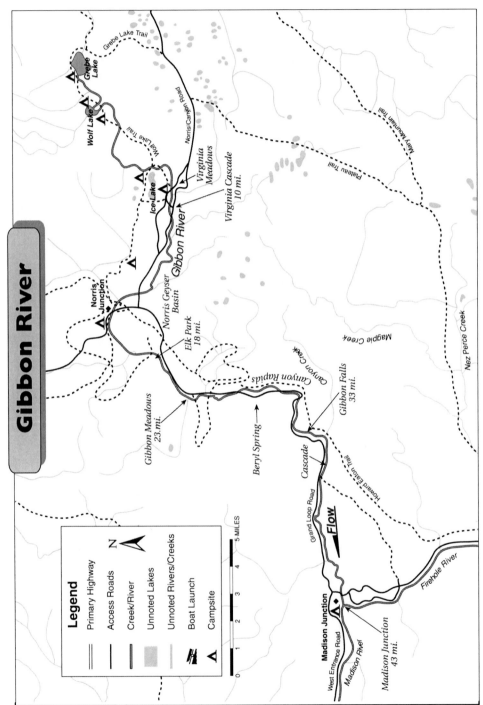

Gibbon River

Grebe Lake Trail

Grebe Lake

Wolf Lake

Wolf Lake Trail

Norris-Canyon Road

Ice Lake

Virginia Meadows

Virginia Cascade

Virginia Cascade 10 mi.

Gibbon River

Mary Mountain Trail

Plateau Trail

Norris Junction

Norris Geyser Basin

Elk Park 18 mi.

Gibbon Meadows 23 mi.

Canyon Rapids

Canyon Creek

Magpie Creek

Nez Perce Creek

Beryl Spring

Gibbon Falls 33 mi.

Cascade

Howard Eaton Trail

Grand Loop Road

Flow

Madison Junction

West Entrance Road

Madison River

Firehole River

Madison Junction 43 mi.

Legend
N
Primary Highway
Access Roads
Creek/River
Unnoted Lakes
Unnoted Rivers/Creeks
Boat Launch
Campsite

0 1 2 3 4 5 MILES

© 2009 Wilderness Adventures Press, Inc.

GIBBON RIVER

The Gibbon River's generous variety of fishing alternatives reflects its transformations in character and trout populations.

Its fish range from pan-sized brook trout in the narrow headwaters and short meadow above Virginia Cascade to small rainbows and browns down through Norris Geyser Basin to large wary browns in the long, meandering glides of Elk Park and Gibbon Meadows to feisty rainbows and more brookies in the cascading, foamflecked pocket waters of its canyon. Grayling in Grebe Lake, the river's source, often are flushed into the Gibbon. Late-fall migrations of brown spawners run up the Madison River from Hebgen Lake to the face of Gibbon Falls.

Following the Gibbon from top to bottom is like opening a textbook on the evolution of a quintessential small mountain stream. Its passage through Norris Geyser Basin adds a uniquely Yellowstone chapter on geothermal dynamics. The 84foot Gibbon Falls in the middle of the canyon is the most photographed waterfall in the park.

The river was originally named Gibbon's Fork of the Madison for General Frank Gibbon, commander of Fort Ellis at present-day Bozeman in 1877. His forces joined the pursuit of northern Idaho's Nez Perce Indians on their ill-fated flight through western Montana and southeastern Idaho en route through Yellowstone to northern Montana. The Gibbon also was briefly known as the East Fork of the Madison and as the Hoppin River.

The Gibbon once had the park's most complex set of regulations, which in many ways reflected the wavering dictates between past and present fisheries management philosophies concerning native fish and introduced species. But that's turned into yet another story for another time ...

Bottom line, the Gibbon's fishing rules were simplified, too, in 2006 when the park was divided into two distinct management regions: Native Trout Conservation Area and Wild Trout Enhancement Area. The Gibbon exists in the latter. Both rainbow and brown trout are protected under catch-and-release, fly-fishing-only rules, along with grayling. Limit on brook trout is five, any size.

Seasons of the Gibbon

Spring comes earlier to the west side of the park, and in normal years flyfishers can look for the Gibbon's runoff to start waning by mid-June. When winter snowpack is exceptionally high, Elk Park and Gibbon Meadows look like small lakes until late in the month.

Matching the hatch is not overly critical on the Gibbon, and generic mayflies, caddis patterns, Stimulators, attractors, and terrestrials often fit the bill on most of its runs. The pocket waters, pools, and riffles and runs above and below the waterfall are perfect for wet fly anglers using beadheads, soft hackles, and small Woolly Buggers. The river's most challenging fishing is for elusive browns in the high meadows.

A Golden Stone hatch in June jump-starts the season in the canyon below Gibbon Falls, and fluttering flights of Little Yellow Stones draw fish to the top in late June and July. Caddis are present throughout the season. A sporadic Gray Drake hatch also occurs in mid-June or early July in the meadow above Madison Junction.

The emergence of Brown Drakes is the principal mayfly hatch local anglers watch for in the upper meadows around the end of June. It is difficult to connect with these Big Mac drakes since both the emergence and spinner fall typically occur after dark. Still, when the weatherman forecasts a dark, heavily overcast day, head for the backwaters of Elk Park or Gibbon Meadows.

Baetis and midges make short appearances in spring, but return in stronger numbers in autumn. Sporadic hatches of Pale Morning Duns occur in July and August, and Mahogany Duns are worth watching for around mid-July.

August and September are the time to fish terrestrials, and hoppers offer the best chances to bring up large browns in the meadows.

Brown spawners, their autumn migration blocked by the waterfall, draw the most concentrated fishing efforts on the Gibbon. Dedicated local anglers routinely brave early winter snowstorms to get a last shot at the lower canyon before the park's roads close for the year. Moderate-sized Woolly Buggers and large nymphs generally work best at this time.

The only reason to journey to the Gibbon's headwaters—and it's a superb one—is to visit Grebe and Wolf Lakes. Among the prettiest backcountry ponds in the park,

Randall Vanhoof fishes the Gibbon Meadows.

both hold the rare grayling and moderate-sized rainbows. Grebe Lake boasts the highest catch rate in Yellowstone, with 1.94 fish per hour, according to angler report cards. Sitting above 8,000 feet on the Solfatara Plateau, the lakes fish best after late June. The hike into Grebe Lake from the Norris Canyon Road is 3.5 miles. Wolf Lake is about a mile west of Grebe.

Fishing starts in earnest on the Gibbon where it exits the forest at the Norris Canyon Road and tumbles into Virginia Meadows. A picnic area offers a good site for family outings and fishing for pan-sized brookies. To reach it, take the byway to the scenic Virginia Cascade and follow the road to the meadow.

Below the cascade, the river loops down to the Norris Junction Picnic Area and passes Norris Campground to circle behind the large geyser basin and enter Elk Park. The pocket waters, pools, and meandering undercut glides between the cascade and the campground harbor more brookies and small to medium rainbows and browns. High-floating generic mayflies, caddis, Stimulators, and attractor patterns are the order of the day on this stretch. It is an excellent place for novices to hone their dry fly skills or to help older children gain confidence and an appreciation of fly fishing.

Elk Park, just south of the impressive Norris Geyser Basin, is where the Gibbon displays its status as a small mountain river. The collected flows of Solfatara Creek and geothermal runoffs from geysers and hot springs add strength and nutrients to the stream. But its long glassy glides and undercut banks resemble a spring creek in nature, and the trout, almost exclusively browns, are correspondingly more wary. The meadow waters also hold a few brookies and rainbows.

A short, quick drop through unproductive pine-lined riffles along the MadisonNorris Road connects Elk Park to the longer Gibbon Meadows and its equally challenging twists and turns across a high grassy plain. The river comes within 100 yards of the road at both meadows, but fishing is better in the interior of the two broad bowls. The water is easily waded, but it is best to cross at shallow runs to avoid disturbing trout downstream.

Browns in the 10- to 16-inch range meet the expectations of most visitors to the meadows, but seasonal reports of trophies exceeding 24 inches haunt the thoughts of serious trout stalkers. Sight-fishing to rising trout requires low-profile approaches to get into casting range. Stalking inside banks helps avoid lining and spooking the trout, and downstream presentations are generally more effective.

Hatches are sporadic and sometimes short-lived. It pays to keep moving in search of rising trout, but tread the banks lightly. Exploring grassy undercuts with hoppers and drifting ants or beetles down the inside lies of channels are often the best options to bring up browns in late summer and early fall.

Few have waxed so eloquently on the challenges of the Gibbon than Howard Back. Author of *The Waters of Yellowstone with Rod and Fly*, he wrote "...your fly must fall like down upon the water, for this is kittle fishing, no work for a novice or a bungler." (Kittle is Scottish for tricky.) Black, who fished the Gibbon in the 1930s, always packed an extra sandwich in his lunch. He knew he would have to apologize to his wife for not returning in time for dinner.

In autumn, the Gibbon's high meadows are hauntingly serene. The fishing is slower, but the days are pleasant and peaceful. Bull elk jealously guard their harems, and their bugling challenges announce the waning days of another season. A few giant bull bison plod stolidly along the river in lonesome forays across the flats. Prowling coyotes freeze in midstep, perk their ears, and nosedive into the amber, sun-cured grasses in pursuit of scampering field mice.

But don't become too beguiled by the wonders of nature unraveling around you. Give each elk bull, his harem, and the bachelors challenging him wide berths.

The Madison-Norris Road closely parallels the Gibbon through its canyon run, and there are several narrow turnoffs to park in while fishing between the meadows and Gibbon Falls. The dramatic forest fires in 1988 generally had little impact on Yellowstone's fisheries, but this is one place where they did. Massive mudslides the following year temporarily blocked the road, and silt smothered some key troutrearing and holding areas.

Still, this is one of the most heavily fished parts of the river simply because it is so visible. Moderate-sized rainbows and brookies are scattered throughout the canyon, so it takes some extra effort to explore pocket waters, deeper pools below rocky riffles, and sheltered lies under logjams. Embark on the search with high-floating attractors, caddis, Humpies and generic mayflies, or small nymphs and Woolly Buggers.

Similar options are presented by the river below the waterfall, where there are longer riffles and runs, grassy cutbanks, and intermittent pocket waters. The channel is less confined than the upper reaches, and short hikes from the road bring you to the water, which is rarely crowded until the browns of October run upstream. The same goes for the short meadow above the Gibbon's confluence with the Firehole, where the Madison is formed. Grasshopper season is a good time to explore its grassy undercut banks, but keep an eye out for bison when entering the lower river.

Brown drake.

Stream Facts: Gibbon River

Season

- Memorial Day weekend through the first Sunday in November.

Regulations

- Rainbow and brown trout and grayling are protected under catch-and-release, fly-fishing-only rules. Limit on brook trout is five, any size.

Trout

- Pan-sized brookies are found in the headwaters and Virginia Meadows. Brookies and 8- to 12-inch rainbows and browns are found above Norris Geyser Basin to Virginia Cascade. In Elk Park and Gibbon Meadows, you'll find mostly 10- to 16inch browns, with a few much larger fish. Brookies and 8- to 12-inch rainbows are found in the canyon runs. Brown spawners migrate up the Madison River to the face of Gibbon Falls in late fall. Grayling are flushed out of Grebe and Wolf Lakes in high runoff years. Angler report cards give the Gibbon a 67-percent satisfaction rating for its 1.02-fish-per-hour catch rate for trout averaging 7.7 inches.

Miles

- Mile 0: Grebe Lake
- Mile 1: Wolf Lake outlet
- Mile 10: Virginia Cascade
- Mile 15: Norris Picnic Area
- Mile 18: Top of Elk Park
- Mile 23: Bottom of Gibbon Meadows
- Mile 33: Gibbon Falls
- Mile 43: Confluence with Firehole River

Character

- A small, narrow, mountain stream to Norris Geyser Basin, where flows increase and the river cuts a shallow meandering course through Elk Park and Gibbon Meadows and enters a steep narrow canyon. It then cascades in swift runs and rocky pocket waters to 84-foot Gibbon Falls and plunges down a wider canyon with longer riffles and runs to a short meadow above Madison Junction.

Flows

- Spring floods normally drop in mid-June, and the river clears by July; runoff may remain high into July after exceptionally wet winters.

Access

- Madison-Norris Road
- Norris Canyon Road

Camping

- Norris Campground
- Madison Junction Campground
- West Yellowstone

A great blue heron on the Gibbon.

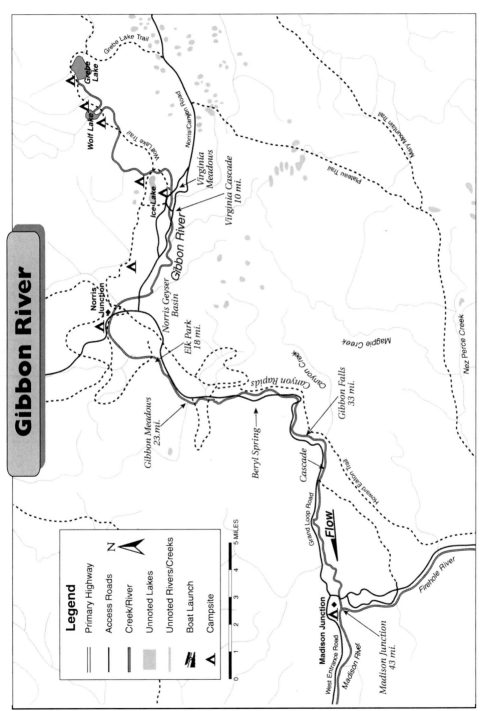

Gibbon River

Legend

N

— Primary Highway
— Access Roads
— Creek/River
▨ Unnoted Lakes
— Unnoted Rivers/Creks
⚓ Boat Launch
▲ Campsite

0 1 2 3 4 5 MILES

Grebe Lake Trail

Grebe Lake

Wolf Lake

Wolf Lake Trail

Norris Canyon Road

Ice Lake

Virginia Meadows

Virginia Cascade
10 mi.

Gibbon River

Mary Mountain Trail

Plateau Trail

Norris Junction

Norris Geyser Basin

Elk Park
18 mi.

Gibbon Meadows
23 mi.

Canyon Rapids

Canyon Creek

Magpie Creek

Beryl Spring

Cascade

Gibbon Falls
33 mi.

Howard Eaton Trail

Nez Perce Creek

Grand Loop Road

Flow

Firehole River

Madison Junction

West Entrance Road

Madison River

Madison Junction
43 mi.

© 2009 Wilderness Adventures Press, Inc.

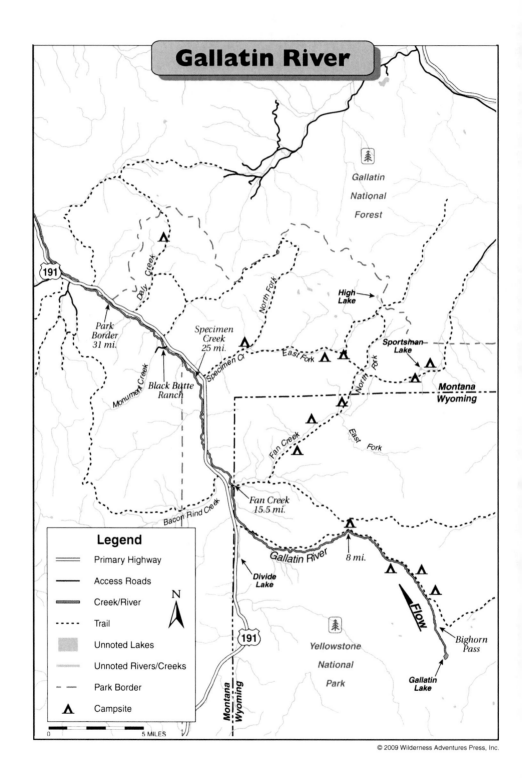

Gallatin River

Gallatin
National
Forest

191

Park
Border
31 mi.

Specimen
Creek
25 mi.

North Fork

High
Lake

Sportsman
Lake

Specimen Cr

East Fork

North Fork

Montana
Wyoming

Monument Creek

Black Butte
Ranch

Fan Creek

East Fork

Bacon Rind Creek

Fan Creek
15.5 mi.

Gallatin River

8 mi.

Flow

Divide
Lake

Bighorn
Pass

Legend

═══	Primary Highway
───	Access Roads
━━━	Creek/River
·····	Trail
▦	Unnoted Lakes
▥	Unnoted Rivers/Creeks
─ ─	Park Border
▲	Campsite

N

191

Yellowstone
National
Park

Gallatin
Lake

Montana
Wyoming

0   5 MILES

GALLATIN RIVER

Coursing down a high mountain valley, the steep incline of the Gallatin River is an evident and lively aspect of its scamper to join the Missouri River. Yet, by western river standards, it is a small and gentle stream over the course of its run through Yellowstone.

The Gallatin is a popular diversion for travelers along US 191, the only major highway through the park. Its best drawing cards are rare westslope cutthroat trout and grayling. It also holds rainbows, cutthroat-rainbow hybrids, and browns, as well as whitefish. Hook-ups on the Gallatin always possess elements of surprise in genial surroundings. Several key tributaries offer interesting side trips into remote, rarely explored waters.

The Gallatin was named for Albert Gallatin, Secretary of State for President Thomas Jefferson. First documented by the Lewis & Clark Expedition, it is the eastern tributary of the three forks that merge to form the Missouri farther north and west in Montana.

Cutthroat and grayling in the park section of the Gallatin are protected by a catchand-release rule. Rainbow and brown trout were added to teh Catch and release rule in 2006. Limit on brook trout is 5, any size.

Seasons of the Gallatin

The upper Gallatin is not a major runoff stream, but it may run high in June and not fully clear until early July. Fishing is good from July into October, except when periodic storms cloud the river and cause temporary doldrums.

Trout in the Gallatin range from 8 to 18 inches and average 11.5 inches. Tributary trout are generally smaller but offer occasional surprises. Grayling were planted in the lower river by the state of Montana and occasionally are found in the park's waters.

Matching hatches usually isn't a problem, even though the river has a good mix of small stoneflies, Golden Stones, caddis, and mayflies to play with when fish are rising. Generic mayflies and high-riding caddis, Stimulators, and attractors answer most situations. Terrestrials are dynamite in late summer and early fall. Caddis are prolific throughout the season. Small Dark Stoneflies and Golden Stones appear in late June and into July, and Little Yellow Stones linger to the end of July.

Green Drakes and Flavs draw topwater action in late June or early July. Baetis and Pale Morning Duns appear through summer, with the Blue-Winged Olives lasting into late fall. Cool, overcast days produce the best mayfly and caddis hatches, which occur progressively later in the day as the season advances.

August and early September are the prime grasshopper periods, but attractors produce on swifter waters from spring to fall. A popular tactic with Montana flyfishers for drawing more strikes is to tie on a tag-along fly, like an ant, beetle, or generic mayfly, behind a larger terrestrial or attractor pattern. When trout start hitting one fly more than the other, it's time to fish in earnest with the hot pattern.

Access to the Gallatin is continuous for about 15 miles north along US 191, from just below the fishless Divide Lake to the park boundary. On the bottom end of the river in the park, anglers must stay within posted boundaries of the Black Butte Ranch on the west bank.

The Gallatin rises from the mouth of fishless Gallatin Lake at 8,500 feet on the north shoulders of Three Rivers Peak in the Gallatin Range. It remains a small trout mountain stream for its first 15 miles, until it gains strength from the flows of Bacon Rind and Fan Creeks two to 3 miles below Divide Lake. The next key tributary is Specimen Creek, about 5 miles down the valley.

Each tributary offers a short interesting hike to less crowded waters, and fishing for smaller but respectable cutthroat and cutthroat-rainbow hybrids in pleasant meadow runs. The scenery is great.

Just off US 191, Fan Creek has its confluence with the Gallatin 22 miles north of West Yellowstone. It has populations of rainbow, cutthroat, and brown trout; some cutthroat in this stream are in the 12-inch range. To reach the fishable stretches of Fan, take the Fawn Pass Trail and then take the Sportsman Lake Trail as it follows the creek.

Bacon Rind Creek is a half mile farther north on US 191. It contains cutthroat and rainbow trout in the 9-inch range, but receives heavy pressure right after snowmelt. Specimen Creek is located 27 miles north of West Yellowstone and offers fishing for cutthroat, rainbows, and cutthroat-rainbow hybrids in the 9-inch range. Fishing is best from the trailhead to the confluence of the East and North Forks 2 miles upstream.

It also should be noted that this is prime bear country. Generally, black bears are more often sighted than grizzlies, but it is always a good idea to travel in groups and keep a clean camp in remote areas.

The Gallatin's romp down the valley along the highway is essentially a continuous riffle, with a few deep pools and braided channels. The trout hold tight to undercut banks and in sheltered lies along current seams.

The river is easily waded and there is no need for chest waders. Narrow channels permit casts from one bank to the other. Its size and basic fly choices make the Gallatin good for beginning flyfishers. Charles Brooks, author of Fishing Yellowstone Waters, saw the Gallatin in the park as "one of the friendliest rivers in the West.... The fish are where you think they are, and you fish it as you think you should. No stream can be more honest."

Downstream of the park, the Gallatin dramatically changes character as it gathers larger tributaries, plunges through a narrow whitewater canyon, and spills onto a high plain for its final run to Three Forks, Montana. A very popular river, it is a great late summer and fall fishery. Its winter fishing ranks among the best in the West.

The Gallatin's wild and free run through the canyon made it the obvious choice as a realistic setting for the popular film *A River Runs Through It*, based on Norman Maclean's classic autobiography.

A father and son explore the Gallatin.

Stream Facts: Gallatin River

Season

- Memorial Day weekend through the first Sunday of November.

Regulations

- Cutthroat and grayling are protected by catch-and-release rule. Limit on brook trout is 5, any size.

Trout

- A mix of trout, mostly cutthroat and fewer rainbows and browns, ranging from 8 to 18 inches and averaging 11.5 inches. Tributary trout are generally smaller but offer occasional surprises. Grayling and whitefish are also present in the river. Angler report cards give the Gallatin a 79-percent satisfaction rating for its .92-fish-perhour catch rate and trout averaging 11.5 inches.

Miles

- Mile 0: Gallatin Lake
- Mile 1.5: Big Horn Pass Trail
- Mile 15.5: US 191

- Mile 19: Bacon Rind Creek
- Mile 25: Specimen Creek
- Mile 27: Black Butte Ranch
- Mile 31: Park boundary

Character

- A gentle mountain meadow stream with swift shallow runs, occasional deep pools and braided channels, and undercut banks along its many twists and turns down a sloping valley. It is easily waded.

Flows

- Spring runoff falls in June, and the river clears by early July. Periodic storms sometimes cloud the river and cause temporary doldrums.

Access

- US 191

Camping

- Gallatin National Forest
- West Yellowstone

GALLATIN RIVER MAJOR HATCHES

Insect	A	M	J	J	A	S	O	N	Time	Flies
Stonefly			▮						A	Dry: Sofa Pillow, Salmonfly, Orange Stimulator #2–8; Wet: Black Rubberlegs, Brook's Stone Nymph, Girdlebug #2–10
Golden Stone			▮	▮					A	Dry: Golden Stone, Yellow or Orange Stimulator #6–8; Wet: Bitch Creek Nymph, Montana Stone, Girdlebug #6–10
Little Yellow Stone				▮	▮				A/E	Yellow Sally, Willow Fly, Blonde Humpy, Yellow Trude, Yellow Wulff #14–16
Caddis			▮	▮	▮	▮	▮		A/E	Dry: Elk Hair Caddis, Goddard Caddis, X-Caddis, Hemingway Caddis, Humpies #14–16; Wet: Beadhead Emergers, Soft Hackles, Squirrel Tail #14–16
Pale Morning Dun				▮	▮	▮			M/E	Dry: PMD, Yellow Sparkle Dun, PMD Cripple #14–18; Wet: Hare's Ear Nymph, Pheasant Tail, Beadheads #14–16
Baetis		▮	▮	▮	▮				A/E	Dry: Blue-Winged Olive, Blue Dun, Olive Sparkle Dun, Para-Adams #14–18; Wet: Pheasant Tail, Baetis Nymph #16–18
Green Drake			▮						A	Dry: Green Drake, Olive Extended Body Drake, Olive Wulff #10–12; Wet: Prince Nymph, Zug Bug #10–12
Flav				▮	▮				A/E	Olive Wulff, CDC Flav, Para-BWO, Para-Olive Hare's Ear, Quigley Cripple #14–16; Lime Trude #12–14
Pink Lady					▮	▮			A/E	Prince Albert, Pink Lady, Pink Cahill #14–18; Pink Lady Spinner, Cream Dun #14–16
Midges						▮	▮		E	Griffith's Gnat, Para-Adams, Black and White Midge #18–22
Terrestrials				▮	▮	▮	▮		M/A	Joe's Hopper, Dave's Hopper, Parachute Hopper, Madam X #8–14; Foam Beetle, Disc O'Beetle #14–16; Ants #16–18

M=morning; LM=late morning; A=afternoon; E=evening; D=dark; SF=spinner fall; /=continuation through periods

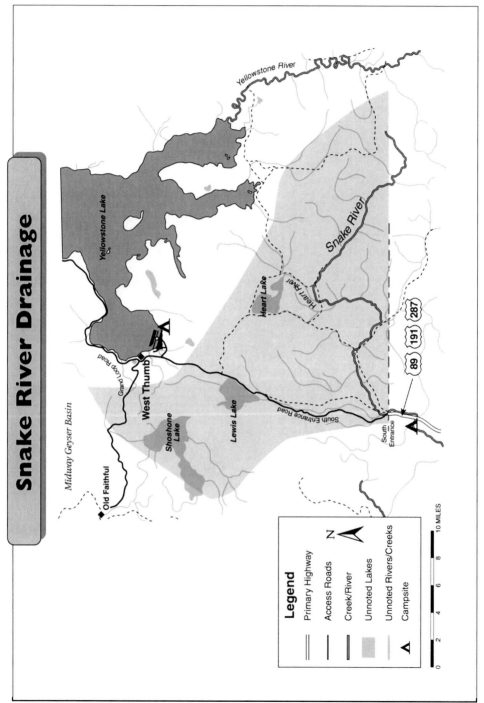

Snake River Drainage

Yellowstone River

Snake River

Yellowstone Lake

Heart Lake

Heart River

West Thumb

Grand Loop Road

Midway Geyser Basin

Old Faithful

Shoshone Lake

Lewis Lake

South Entrance Road

89 191 287

South Entrance

Legend

N

Primary Highway

Access Roads

Creek/River

Unnoted Lakes

Unnoted Rivers/Creeks

Campsite

0   2   4   6   8   10 MILES

Snake River Drainage

Some of the park's most remote fishing waters are located in the Snake River Basin southwest of the Continental Divide bisecting the southern third of Yellowstone.

The Snake River briefly skirts the South Entrance–West Thumb Road before it exits the park en route to Jackson Lake and its run through Grand Teton National Park. The south road also offers access to the Lewis River and Lewis Lake. Shoshone and Heart Lakes are at the end of relatively short hikes from the loop road.

But other routes into the eastern regions of this broad basin are strictly by foot or astride a horse. Extensive trip planning is required to reach the upper Snake River. It is a turbulent and often unpredictable river that offers better fishing to the south in Jackson Hole. The Snake also offers an alternate route to Heart Lake via its outlet, but both the lake and better fishing in Heart River are more easily reached by the Heart Lake Trail, northeast of Lewis Lake on the loop road.

Flyfishers looking for more rewarding streams off the beaten path in this basin find the best options in the Fall and Bechler Rivers. To reach them, you have to start from another state, Idaho. Located in the park's little explored southwest corner, hiking trails to the lower Fall River and Bechler Meadows are at the end of a short drive east from Ashton to the Cave Falls Road.

Another route to the upper and lower Fall River, along with Beula Lake, the Fall's source, is a very primitive road that parallels the park's southern boundary from Flagg Ranch to Ashton.

THE UPPER SNAKE RIVER

The Snake River rises at about 9,000 feet on the shoulders of the high, rumpled Two Ocean Plateau, which defines Yellowstone's southeast corner and the Teton Wilderness Area north of Jackson Hole.

Beginning as a humble trickle south of Mariposa Lake, the Snake makes a brief loop south into the Teton Wilderness and turns north to return to the park. It collects small tributaries as it cuts a steep northwesterly course along the face of Big Game Ridge in a rapid descent of nearly 1,000 feet in 10 miles to pick up the Heart River in a short valley. It then turns abruptly south through a narrow 10-mile canyon that loops north again until the Red Mountains bounce its course to the southwest. The river's final 5-mile run in the park is through a broad valley above the South Entrance, where it turns almost due south and exits the park.

Few anglers venture very far upstream on foot from the park boundary to fish the Snake's banks during the early season. Spring runoff is often high and turbulent, and very murky. Later hikes upstream are along trails that dip and climb along the river and circle its canyon. Several stream crossings can be treacherous well into July in high water years. A few Jackson outfitters offer horseback trips into the upper Snake and to Heart Lake and other sites on the plateau.

Most years, the lower Snake fishes best after late July but it still must be approached with caution in swift runs or deep channels. Unstable gravel bars and

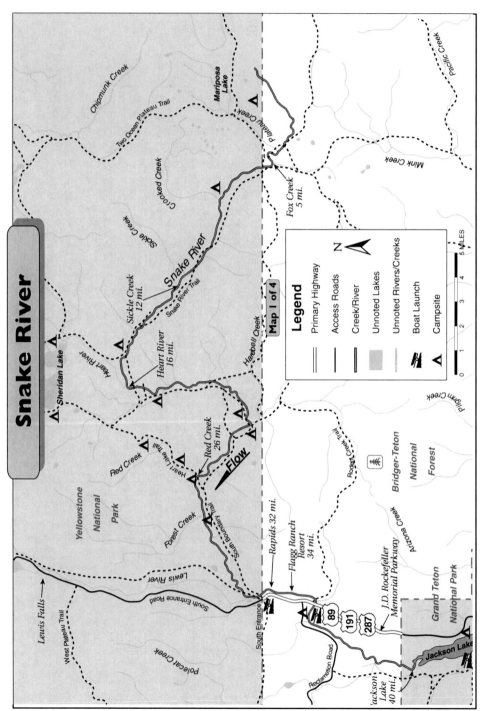

Snake River

Map 1 of 4

Legend

N

	Primary Highway
	Access Roads
	Creek/River
	Unnoted Lakes
	Unnoted Rivers/Creeks
	Boat Launch
	Campsite

0 1 2 3 4 5 MILES

undercut banks along the main channel of the braided river should be avoided. River crossings should be made only at the tops of shallow riffles. Care also must be taken when exploring deep pools, swift runs, and pocket waters in the canyon between Red Creek and Heart River.

Yellowstone cutthroat are the dominant species, ranging from 8 to 16 inches. A few Snake River finespotted cutthroat are still present in the upper river. Whitefish are numerous and, occasionally, quite large. Brown trout increase in number and size in fall as spawners run upstream from Jackson Lake. A few brook trout and lake trout, washed out of Lewis Lake, also are hooked by anglers.

Fishing is fairly straightforward with basic mayfly, caddis, and attractor patterns, as well as terrestrials in late summer. Moderate-sized stonefly nymphs and leeches are good prospecting options. Beadhead nymphs, emergers, and soft hackles tied as dropper flies beneath larger dry flies increase chances for hits. Streamers and large nymphs are the flies of choice when hunting brown trout spawners in late fall.

A mystical river of the West, the mighty Snake unfortunately demands more effort at its headwaters than most anglers are willing to expend, knowing that they'll find better fishing up the road in the park. Still, the lower river and its canyon present quiet backwater options to explore for those who time it right. But don't venture into this region alone; grizzly bears may be present. Keep a clean camp when staying overnight.

Heart River

The Heart River descends a steep, 4-mile course to its merger with the Snake about 15 miles east of the park's South Entrance.

Although it is the Snake's largest tributary in the park, the river's only good fishing access is along its half mile outlet from Heart Lake. A boggy marsh at the confluence and a deep canyon in between the outlet and the Snake make fishing the lower river difficult.

The most direct route to the outlet is a 12-mile hike via the Heart Lake Trail, northwest of Lewis Lake on the loop road. The lake and its outlet don't open to fishing until July 1 due to restrictions against entering prime grizzly bear country in early season.

The outlet meadow is a popular side trip for those who camp at the lake, especially during cool, late spring seasons. The river's canyon hosts a prolific stonefly hatch in late June that wafts upstream on the winds and draws robust, savvy cutthroat from the lake to the feast.

Callibaetis and smaller mayflies offer topwater action in summer, along with small terrestrials, for 8- to 14-inch cutthroat.

Stream Facts: Upper Snake River

Season

- Memorial Day weekend through first Sunday in November.

Possession and length limits:

- Catch and release all native species, including Yellowstone and Snake River finespotted cutthroat trout.
- Catch and release all rainbow trout and brown trout.
- Possession limit: 5 combined brook trout or lake trout, any size.
- Heart Lake opens to fishing July 1 due to bear activity.
- No size or possession limit on lake trout caught in Heart Lake.

Trout

- Mostly moderate-sized cutthroat and smaller numbers of brown trout in the 8- to 16-inch range. Brown trout increase in numbers and size with their fall spawning run out of Jackson Lake. Numerous whitefish are present, along with a few brook and lake trout.

Miles

- Mile 0: Source on Two Ocean Plateau south of Mariposa Lake
- Mile 5: Park boundary
- Mile 12: Confluence of Sickle Creek
- Mile 16: Confluence of Heart River
- Mile 26: Mouth of canyon
- Mile 32: Park boundary at South Entrance

Character

- The river descends a steep narrow course from its source down a high valley for about 15 miles to its confluence with the Heart River, where it almost doubles in size and enters a high-walled canyon. Its canyon stretch is a series of swift runs, rapids, and deep pools. The river braids into channels, riffles and runs, and undercut banks on its final run through a broad valley to the South Entrance.

Flows

- Spring runoff is high and off-color from late May into July. Most years the river isn't fishable until mid-July or later. In dry years, flows can be quite low in autumn.

Access

- South Boundary Trail and Snake River Trail, starting from the South Entrance.

Camping

- Lewis Lake Campground
- Flagg Ranch
- Snake River Campground in Bridger-Teton National Forest

THE LEWIS RIVER

Divided into four distinct sections, almost like a jigsaw puzzle, the Lewis River is the most quixotic stream in Yellowstone.

It rises at the mouth of Shoshone Lake and meanders 4 miles through a picturesque meadow to Lewis Lake. Exiting the lake, it rambles for 2 miles down a low-walled canyon to cascade over one of the park's most scenic waterfalls and spills out onto a broad marshy valley. At the lip of the 4-mile meadow the river plunges into a deep narrow canyon and gallops 10 miles to its confluence with the Snake.

Closely linked to its two lakes, the Lewis River's mixed bag of fishing options draws the most attention from flyfishers during the fall spawning runs by brown trout. In late September and October, browns in the 14- to 26-inch range migrating from both lakes into the channel are followed by large lake trout. A similar migration occurs at the outlet from Lewis Lake into the upper canyon.

Fishing for fall spawners and lake trout with large streamers and nymphs is intense, but smaller beadhead nymphs also can be effective. This is about the only time the river is crowded, although the window of opportunity is short. Fishing ends after the first weekend of November.

The river's other seasons are equally rewarding for anglers with different agendas. After ice-out on Lewis Lake in late May or early June, look for brown and lake trout

The Lewis River Falls.

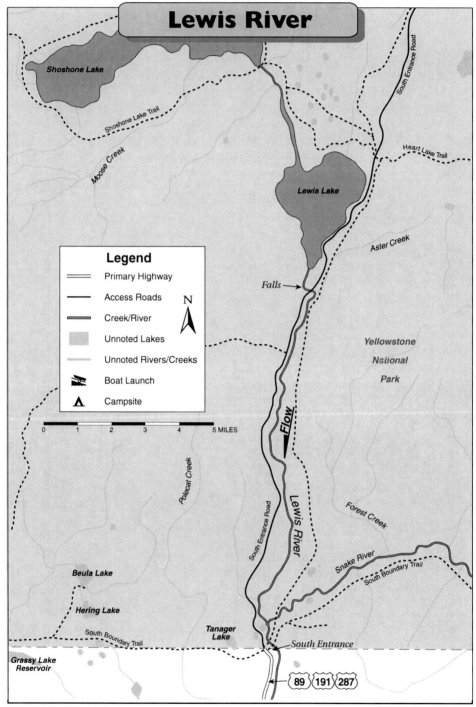

Lewis River

Shoshone Lake

Shoshone Lake Trail

Moose Creek

Lewis Lake

Heart Lake Trail

Aster Creek

South Entrance Road

Legend

Primary Highway

Access Roads

Creek/River

Unnoted Lakes

Unnoted Rivers/Creeks

Boat Launch

Campsite

N

0 1 2 3 4 5 MILES

Falls →

Flow

Yellowstone
National
Park

Polecat Creek

Lewis River

South Entrance Road

Forest Creek

Snake River

South Boundary Trail

Beula Lake

Hering Lake

South Boundary Trail

Tanager
Lake

South Entrance

Grassy Lake
Reservoir

89 191 287

© 2009 Wilderness Adventures Press, Inc.

congregating at the mouth of the Lewis River Channel or explore the lower meadow run of the channel as it warms and hatches erupt.

Mayflies in the channel include Green Drakes in late June and Pale Morning Duns and Baetis in July and August. Caddis and attractor patterns also are effective through the season, along with small terrestrials in late summer. Midges and tiny Baetis provide some topwater action in late fall.

In early summer, good-sized brown trout take up feeding lies at the outlet of Lewis Lake and in downstream shelter areas for about a half mile of the river's upper run. The trout lie in wait for caddis, midges, and Callibaetis and other mayfly spinners flushed out of the lake. The short canyon above the waterfall also produces a prolific overlapping hatch of Small Dark Stoneflies, Golden Stones, and Little Yellow Stones around the Fourth of July.

The browns attack the smorgasbord with abandon, although they can be as selective in their feeding habits as rainbows. The bonus is that they offer a tussle just as acrobatic as a rainbow's.

The riffles and runs of the canyon immediately above the waterfall offer a pleasant diversion for smaller browns and an occasional large trout that may have over-wintered in a deep pool or under a logjam. The plunge pool below the waterfall also gives up occasional surprises and in high water years is sometimes full of lake trout flushed out of Lewis Lake.

The Lewis River's most challenging fishing is in the long deep channels of the meadow above its second canyon. It is full of 8- to 12-inch browns but also harbors a good population of wily adults in the 16- to 20-inch range.

A spring creek in nature, this stretch requires long, delicate leaders and precise presentations to score on its larger browns. Wading can be a bit difficult in silt-laden areas, and in high water years marshes and flooded flats hinder hiking into some parts of the meadow. But anglers who make the effort to get away from easy access sites along the road generally find better fishing.

A mid-June Green Drake hatch offers early season topwater action, along with stoneflies blown out of the canyons in early July. Tiny Baetis and Pale Morning Duns and small caddis patterns are the most common options through most of the summer when casting to rising trout. In late season, terrestrials sometimes pound up large fish. And prospecting undercut banks and pools with moderate-sized Woolly Buggers or leeches may be effective during quiet periods.

Attempting to fish the upper Lewis Canyon is dangerous and not worth the effort for the small trout it holds. But the flatter riffles and runs in its mouth above the Snake offer another interesting diversion for still another trout in this complex stream. Cutthroats join the browns in the lower river, and even here an occasional lake trout may be encountered in cool waters of tributaries like Moose Creek.

The Lewis River's name derives from Lewis Lake. It was named for Meriwether Lewis, of Lewis & Clark fame. Ironically, the closest the Corps of Discovery got to the park was when William Clark and a small party of men descended the Yellowstone River from present-day Livingston, Montana, well above its northern border.

The South Entrance–West Thumb Road parallels the river's lower meadow for about 2 miles. Other access routes to the river are by trails above and below Lewis Lake or by boat or canoe from the boat ramp at the Lewis Lake Campground.

A 1.5-mile footpath near the campground leads to the outlet and the upper canyon. Trying to take a shortcut through the forest is virtually impossible because of numerous barriers created by downed timber. The lower end of the canyon can be reached from a footpath that loops south around the waterfall from a parking lot on the loop road.

Two trails into the Lewis River Channel start from a trailhead at the north end of Lewis Lake. The Doghead Trail, which goes directly to the top of the channel, is 4 miles long. The Lewis Channel Trail is 3 miles along the top of the lake to the inlet and then 4 miles to the top of the channel.

A short trail from the South Entrance leads to the river's confluence with the Snake and provides access to the mouth of the Lewis Canyon.

The Lewis River Channel is the only stream in the park that can be floated in hand-propelled watercraft. The top .75 mile of the channel is a shallow rapid and must be portaged. Boats and canoes are not permitted below a posted line on the outlet bay of Lewis Lake.

The Lewis Lake Campground is an excellent base for exploring the river. It is one of the few in the park that doesn't require reservations. Camping also is available at Flagg Ranch and the Snake River Campground, just below the park's South Entrance.

Boat permits are available at ranger stations at the campground and South Entrance.

Stream Facts: Lewis River

Season

- Memorial Day weekend through the first Sunday in November.

Possession and length limits:

- Catch and release all native species, including Yellowstone and Snake River finespotted cutthroat.
- Catch and release brown trout below Lewis River Falls.
- Possession limit: 5 combined brook trout or lake trout. Above Lewis River Falls, this combination may include two brown trout.
- Above Lewis River Falls, only one fish more than 20 inches.
- All fish in possession must remain whole.

Trout

- Good populations of brown trout in the 10- to 18-inch range. Brown trout increase in number and size with fall spawning runs into the Lewis River Channel and the Lewis Lake outlet. Large lake trout follow the migrations and also occur in the lower river when flushed out of Lewis Lake. Yellowstone cutthroat join the browns in the mouth of the Lewis Canyon. The Lewis River Channel's 91-percent satisfaction rating is the highest reported by park anglers. Its catch rate is .91 fish per hour for trout averaging 14.5 inches.

Miles

- Mile 0: Outlet of Shoshone Lake
- Mile 4: Inlet of Lewis Lake
- Mile 6: Lewis Falls below Lewis Lake outlet
- Mile 10: Top of Lewis Canyon
- Mile 20: Mouth of canyon and confluence with Snake River

Character

- The river is divided into four distinct sections: A meadow run through the Lewis River Channel between Shoshone and Lewis Lakes; a short canyon and waterfall below Lewis Lake; a marshy meadow run below the waterfall; and a long steep canyon above its confluence with the Snake River.

Flows

- Spring runoff is somewhat moderated by outflows from Shoshone and Lewis Lakes, although runoff from tributaries can muddy the lower river. Most years the river fishes well in late June and through the remainder of the season.

Access

- South Entrance–West Thumb Road.
- Trailheads above and below Lewis Lake, and the Lewis Lake Campground boat ramp.

Camping

- Lewis Lake Campground
- Flagg Ranch
- Snake River Campground in Bridger-Teton National Forest

LEWIS RIVER MAJOR HATCHES

Insect	A	M	J	J	A	S	O	N	Time	Flies
Stonefly			■						A	Dry: Bird's Stone, Orange Stimulator, Salmonfly #4–8; Wet: Black Rubberleg, Girdlebug, Woolly Bugger #2–6
Golden Stone			■						A	Dry: Golden Stone, Yellow Stimulator #6–10; Wet: Bitch Creek Nymph, Montana Stone #4–10
Little Yellow Stone			■						A/E	Yellow Sally, Blonde Humpy, Yellow Stimulator #10–14
Green Drake			■						A/E	Green Drake, Olive Wulff, Flav, Para-BWO #10–12
Pale Morning Dun			■						M/E	Dry: PMD, Light Cahill, Rusty Spinner, Yellow Sparkle Dun #14–18; Wet: Hare's Ear Nymph, Pheasant Tail #14–20
Baetis			■	■	■	■			A/E	Dry: Blue-Winged Olive, Blue Dun, Olive Sparkle Dun, Para-Adams #16–22; Wet: Pheasant Tail, Baetis Nymph #16–18
Caddis			■	■	■				A/E	Dry: Elk Hair Caddis, Renegade, Yellow or Royal Humpy #12–16; Wet: Soft Hackles, Squirrel Tail #14–16
Terrestrials				■	■				M/A/E	Joe's Hopper, Jacklin's Hopper, Para-Hopper #12–14; Dave's Cricket #14–16; Ants #16–18
Callibaetis					■				A	Thorax Callibaetis, Crystal Spinner, Para-Adams, Rusty Spinner #12–14
Flav		■	■						M/E	Dry: Para-Olive Hare's Ear, CDC Olive Quill, Green Wulff, CDC Spinner #14–16; Wet: Quigley Cripple, CDC Cripple, Olive Sparkle Emerger #12–16

M=morning; LM=late morning; A=afternoon; E=evening; D=dark; SF=spinner fall; /=continuation through periods

An angler fishes the meadow section of the Lewis River.

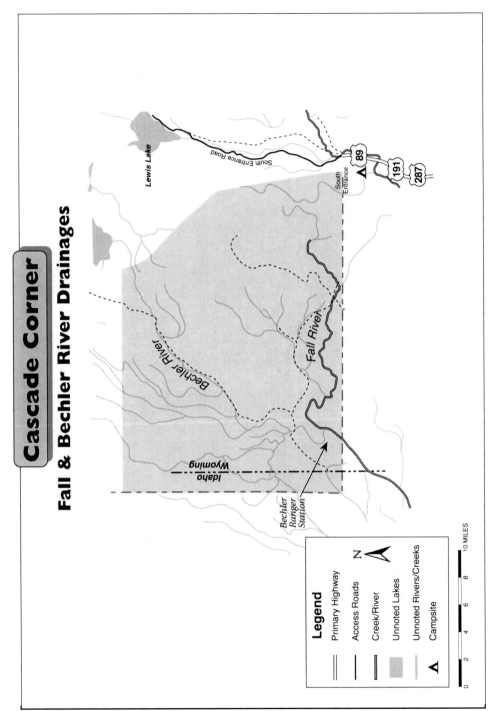

Cascade Corner

Fall & Bechler River Drainages

Lewis Lake

South Entrance Road

Bechler River

Fall River

Idaho
Wyoming

Bechler Ranger Station

South Entrance

Legend

Primary Highway

Access Roads

Creek/River

Unnoted Lakes

Unnoted Rivers/Creeks

Campsite

N

0   2   4   6   8   10 MILES

Cascade Corner:
Idaho's Entrance to Yellowstone

The little explored southwest corner of Yellowstone is Idaho's only entry into the park. Called Cascade Corner, the Fall and Bechler Rivers and their tributaries flowing off the slopes of the Pitchstone Plateau are adorned with 21 of the park's 40 waterfalls.

Scholarly rainbows in the Bechler River's meadows are among the most challenging in Greater Yellowstone's golden circle of trout. The Bechler Canyon, the upper Fall River, and Beula Lake harbor healthy populations of Yellowstone cutthroat.

Rainbows in the Bechler and its tributaries are protected by a special catch-andrelease regulation, as are all cutthroat in this corner of the park. However, several lakes south of Yellowstone's boundary permit a chance to broil a brace of trout over a campfire in the John D. Rockefeller Memorial Parkway and Wyoming's section of the Targhee National Forest. The "parkway" is a wilderness area linking Grand Teton and Yellowstone National Parks. The Targhee's tiny Winegar Wilderness Area is southwest of the park on the Idaho border.

To get to the Bechler and lower Fall Rivers from Idaho, turn east off US 20 at Ashton, 60 miles north of Idaho Falls and 65 mile south of West Yellowstone. At Ashton, drive east about 6 miles on ID 47 to the Cave Falls Road. A 10-mile gravel road ends at the scenic falls and the Bechler Ranger Station. There also is a small campground at Cave Falls.

From the east, Cascade Corner is reached via the primitive Reclamation Road that runs from Flagg Ranch (south of the park's South Entrance and 60 miles north of Jackson) to Ashton. The western end of its 35-mile course parallels the south rim of the Fall River. Turn north at the first bridge in Idaho to reach the Cave Falls Road and Bechler Ranger Station. Four-wheel-drive vehicles with good clearance are strongly advised for travel over the Reclamation Road. Trailers are prohibited on the unmaintained, deeply rutted, one-way stretch between Calf Creek and Gibson Meadows.

Good references for trip planning are the Targhee National Forest Island Park–Ashton Ranger Districts map and the Bridger-Teton National Forest Buffalo-Jackson Ranger Districts map. Topographic trail maps include Trails Illustrated's SW Yellowstone map and American Adventures Association's South Yellowstone Park map.

Snow or flooded meadows may make two-track sections of the Reclamation Road impassible in late spring. Late-fall visitors to this remote region should check weather forecasts before setting out. Snow storms can occur as early as mid-October.

A park fishing permit can be purchased at Flagg Ranch or at the Bechler Ranger Station. Reservations are required to camp overnight at designated backcountry campsites in the park. A Forest Service campground is located at Cave Falls. It fills fast in midsummer, so get there early. In fall, it is largely deserted. Also, numerous undeveloped campgrounds are available in the surrounding national forests.

One of Yellowstone's wettest regions, Cascade Corner fishes best in late summer and early fall. Mosquitoes are thick in spring and early summer until marshes start to dry. This is also grizzly bear country. It is best to hike in parties of three or more and to keep a clean camp.

Some of the more interesting fishing requires longer hikes or rock scrambling into canyons. Carry topographic maps and a compass, and know how to use them. At the end of the rainbow are wild trout in spectacular mountain forest country. Views of the Teton Range pop up to the south as you come out of a canyon or crest a rise in the trail.

Fishing these waters is a fairly straightforward proposition. Backcountry trout are less wary than those pounded unmercifully on better known streams.

For topwater action, Elk Hair Caddis, Stimulators, Humpies, and other highriding attractor patterns like Renegades, Trudes, and Wulffs work through the season, along with generic mayfly patterns like the Adams and Light Cahill. Don't forget grasshoppers, ants, and beetles.

The best wet fly choices are general stonefly and Golden Stone nymphs, Woolly Buggers, and smaller nymph and larva patterns like Hare's Ears, Pheasant Tails, soft-hackle nymphs, and caddis emergers. Beadhead patterns also are best since Yellowstone bans the use of lead jigs, split-shot, wires, or ribbon twist-ons. Nontoxic options are available for the last of the above weights.

The Fall River Flasher, in green or brown, is a popular variation on the Woolly Bugger theme. It has a chenille body and rainbow crystal strands tied along the sides of its marabou tail. The matching-color saddle hackle is wrapped only on the head of the fly. It's also a good pattern on other fast-water streams.

Some mayfly hatches may arrive latter than expected in high water years, but this quiet backwater has them all.

The most nitty-gritty, match-the-hatch situations are likely to occur in Bechler Meadows. Choices may include midges, Tricos, *Callibaetis,* or Green Drakes in summer and, in fall, the Gray Drake and Mahogany Dun. Always hope for overcast days and carry a selection of Pale Morning Duns and Blue-Winged Olives.

BECHLER RIVER

The Bechler rises at 8,000 feet at the confluence of the Phillips, Gregg, and Ferris Forks and flows about 20 miles to its merger with the Fall River at Cave Falls.

Waterfalls on each of the headwater tributaries set the pace for the Bechler's dash down its narrow canyon in a series of waterfalls, cascades, and roaring pocket waters. Mostly pan-sized cutthroat reside in its canyon waters.

At the canyon mouth, the Bechler plunges over two-tiered, 100-foot Colonnade Falls to enter its 4-mile meadow run. The crystal-clear waters of the meadow meander through a broad, marshy flat. The final couple miles of river gallop down a lava-rock cascade to the Fall River.

Bechler Meadow holds good numbers of 9- to 14-inch rainbows, with a fair amount in the 16- to 20-inch range. Tributaries of the Bechler hold mostly 9- to 12inch rainbows and cutthroat, with chances for occasional larger fish. Rainbows in the tributaries are protected by the catch-and-release rule since they are wild trout and contribute to the Bechler's pristine fishery.

Channels in Bechler Meadow are usually too deep to wade, and the trout are extremely skittish. If you can see them, they can see you.

Fish cautiously from the banks as you would on a spring creek, with delicate leader tippets and refined presentations. Surface swirls frustrate attempts at drag-free floats. It's best to work to rising fish early and late in the day, or hope for heavy cloud cover. Grassy overhangs along banks and deep pools may harbor large trout and offer nymphing opportunities. Prospecting in late summer with grasshoppers can be fruitful.

The relatively flat 5-mile trail to the meadows starts from the Bechler Ranger Station. A suspension bridge crosses the river at the top end of the meadow near Ouzel Creek. Rocky Ford, on the Union Falls Trail at the bottom end of the meadow, has to be waded.

For day hikes into the meadows, set up a base camp at the Targhee National Forest campground below Cave Falls.

Stream Facts: Bechler River

Season

- Memorial Day weekend through the first Sunday in November.

Regulations

- Cutthroat, rainbows, and cutthroat-rainbow hybrids are catch and release only, including in tributaries like Boundary and Ouzel Creeks. Brook trout limit is 5, any size.

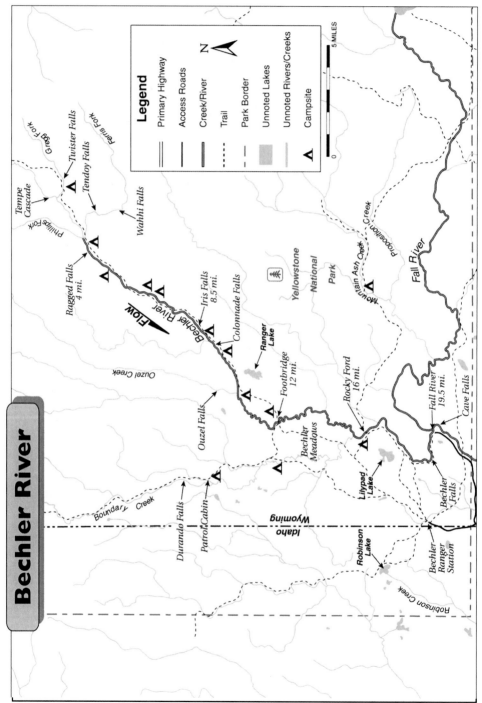

Bechler River

Legend

	Primary Highway
	Access Roads
	Creek/River
	Trail
	Park Border
	Unnoted Lakes
	Unnoted Rivers/Creeks
	Campsite

N

0   5 MILES

Gregg Fork

Twister Falls

Ferris Fork

Tendoy Falls

Tempe Cascade

Phillips Fork

Wahhi Falls

Ragged Falls 4 mi.

Bechler River

Flow

Iris Falls 8.5 mi.

Colonnade Falls

Ouzel Creek

Ranger Lake

Footbridge 12 mi.

Yellowstone National Park

Mountain Ash Creek

Proposition Creek

Fall River

Ouzel Falls

Bechler Meadows

Rocky Ford 16 mi.

Fall River 19.5 mi.

Cave Falls

Boundary Creek

Durando Falls

Patrol Cabin

Lilypad Lake

Bechler Falls

Idaho
Wyoming

Robinson Lake

Bechler Ranger Station

Robinson Creek

Trout

- Bechler Meadow holds a strong population of 10- to 14-inch rainbows, with a fair number in the 16- to 18-inch range and a few larger fish. Numerous pan-sized cutthroat are found above Colonnade Falls in the canyon run. Anglers report a 61percent satisfaction rate with a .63-fish-per-hour catch rate for fish averaging 10.7 inches.

Miles

- Mile 0: Confluence of Phillips, Gregg, and Ferris Forks
- Mile 4: Ragged Falls
- Mile 8.5: Iris Falls
- Mile 10.5: Colonnade Falls
- Mile 12: Footbridge at the top of Bechler Meadows
- Mile 16: Rocky Ford trail crossing
- Mile 19.5: Confluence with Fall River

Character

- The upper Bechler cascades down a narrow canyon and plunges over a series of waterfalls to the 100-foot Colonnade Falls at its mouth. The crystal-clear waters of its 4-mile meadow run below the falls meander through a marshy flat. The final couple miles of river are a shallow gallop down a lava-rock cascade to the Fall River. Channels in the meadow are usually too deep to wade. Fish cautiously, as you would on a spring creek. There are grassy overhangs along the banks, and the deep pools of cutbanks harbor larger trout. A suspension bridge crosses the river at the top end of the meadow. Marshes in this corner of park are often mosquito-infested into August. It is also grizzly bear country. Hike in groups of three or more and keep clean camps.

Flows

- Spring runoff on Bechler usually peaks in late June, but may extend into July. It fishes best in late summer and early fall.

Access

- Cave Falls Road east of Ashton, Idaho
- Reclamation Road, which connects Ashton with Flagg Ranch, at Yellowstone's South Entrance north of Jackson

Camping

- Targhee National Forest
- Bridger-Teton National Forest
- Flagg Ranch Resort

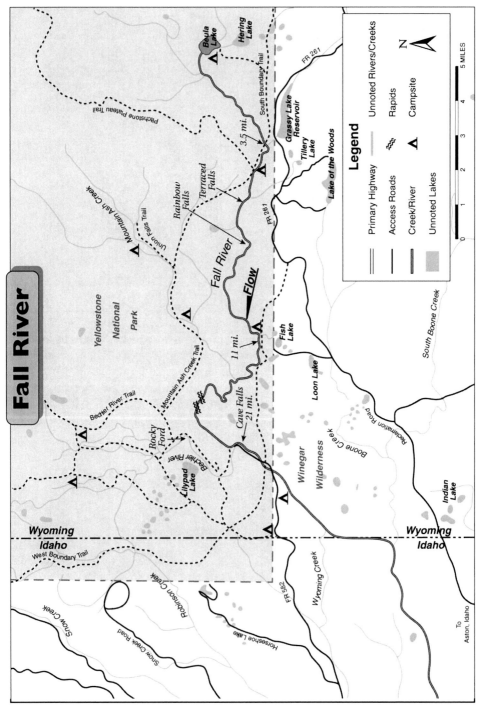

Fall River

© 2009 Wilderness Adventures Press, Inc.

THE FALL RIVER

The Cave Falls Campground offers an excellent opportunity to tackle the lower Fall River at the plunge pool below Cave Falls and in the rocky pocket waters of its lower canyon. The two best options for hiking into the upper river and its tributaries are at trailheads on the Reclamation Road: at Grassy Lake Reservoir on the east side of the road and at Fish Lake on the west side.

Headwaters of the Fall rise at 8,500 feet on the south slopes of the Pitchstone Plateau. It meanders across meadow and forest below Beula Lake, the Fall's official source, and then drops dramatically down a string of swift cascades and over a series of waterfalls to scenic Cave Falls. Interspersed along its swift course are a series of long meandering forested runs. Its 50-mile southwesterly course ends at the Henry's Fork of the Snake in eastern Idaho. The average rate of descent is more than 50 feet per mile. Its canyons are often deep and picturesque.

While it is listed on many maps as the Falls River, its name was officially changed to Fall River by the U.S. Geological Service. The alteration in the mid-1980s was made to agree with the name local residents use for the river.

The many waterfalls along its course are the source of its original name. For the flyfisher, the name reflects the chance that one might take a tumble in its refreshing waters. It is tough wading, more difficult than Box Canyon on the Henry's Fork. Feltbottomed boots are needed to negotiate its slick basalt lava streambed carpeted with slippery cobblestones.

The upper river holds mostly cutthroat and its lower reaches hold rainbows and a few cutthroat-rainbow hybrids. Most are in the 9- to 15-inch range, with a few exceeding 20 inches. Its tributaries are loaded with cutthroat in similar sizes.

The two most popular hikes into the Fall River Basin are to Beula Lake and its outlet and to 260-foot Union Falls on Ash Mountain Creek. Both can be reached from trails starting from the eastern tip of Grassy Lake, 10 miles west of Flagg Ranch. Another Union Falls trail starts from Fish Lake, about midway along Reclamation Road.

The 2.5-mile jaunt into 107-acre Beula Lake is most productive for float-tubers. Hering Lake (60 acres) lies just upstream. There's a minor climb at the start, but the rest of the route is flat.

The 7-mile hike to Union Falls is more of a workout, with more ups and downs, but you get a chance to fish three of the Fall's better cutthroat tributaries—Cascade, Proposition, and Ash Mountain Creeks. The hike from Fish Lake is slightly longer. Pools below waterfalls and at stream confluences often harbor larger fish.

The general rule of thumb on cutthroat waters is that if the fish aren't hitting, move on. If it still isn't happening, move on again. Remember, this is get-away-fromit-all country. Keep exploring. Have fun. Take a photograph or two. And watch out for grizzlies.

Stream Facts: Fall River

Season

- Memorial Day weekend through the first Sunday in November.

Regulations

- Cutthroat and cutthroat-rainbow hybrids are catch and release.
- Limit on rainbow and brook trout combined is 5, any size.

Trout

- Moderate-sized rainbows outnumber cutthroat in the lower section of river. Mostly moderate-sized Yellowstone cutthroat in upstream pocket waters of the Fall and in Beula Lake, its source. Fish average in the 9- to 15-inch range, with a few exceeding 20 inches. Its tributaries are loaded with cutthroat in similar sizes. Anglers report 86-percent satisfaction with a 1.38-fish-per-hour catch rate for fish averaging 8.3 inches.

Miles

- Mile 0: Beula Lake
- Mile 3.5: Cascades trail crossing, west of Grassy Lake
- Mile 6: Rainbow Falls
- Mile 12: Fish Lake trail crossing
- Mile 21: Cave Falls
- Mile 24: Idaho border
- Mile 50: Confluence with Henry's Fork River

Character

- The river meanders a few miles through meadows and forests below Beula Lake to its canyon runs over the Cascades, Terrace Falls, and Rainbow Falls. It continues to drop dramatically down a string of swift cascading runs to scenic Cave Falls, interspersed with long riffles and runs and pocket waters. Flows increase significantly with the mergers of Mountain Ash Creek and the Bechler River. Meadow marshes in this corner of park are often mosquito-infested into August. It is also grizzly bear country. Hike in groups of three or more and keep clean camps.

Flows

- Spring runoff on the Fall usually peaks in late June, but may extend into July. It fishes best in late summer and early fall.

Access

- Cave Falls Road east of Ashton, Idaho
- Reclamation Road, which connects Ashton with Flagg Ranch at Yellowstone's South Entrance, north of Jackson

Camping

- Targhee National Forest
- Bridger-Teton National Forest
- Flagg Ranch Resort

BECHLER AND FALL RIVERS MAJOR HATCHES

Insect	A	M	J	J	A	S	O	N	Time	Flies
Stonefly			█						A	Dry: Sofa Pillow, Salmonfly, Orange Stimulator #2–8; Wet: Brook's Stone Nymph, Black Rubberlegs, Woolly Bugger, Fall River Flasher #2–8
Golden Stone				█					A	Dry: Golden Stone, Yellow or Orange Stimulator, Yellow Sally #6–10; Wet: Bitch Creek Nymph, Montana Stone, Girdlebug, Woolly Bugger #6–10
Caddis						█	█		A/E	Dry: Olive or Tan Elk Hair Caddis, Goddard Caddis, Yellow, Royal, or Blonde Humpy, Renegade #12–16; Wet: Prince Nymph, Bead-head Emerger, Caddis Pupa, Soft Hackles #14–16
Fall Caddis						█	█		A	Orange Stimulator, Orange Bucktail #10–12
Baetis					█	█			A/E	Blue-Winged Olive, Para-BWO, Para-Adams, Blue Dun #14–18; Tiny BWO #18–22
Pale Morning Dun				█	█				M/E	Dry: PMD, Thorax PMD, PMD Cripple, Sparkle Dun, Rusty Spinner #14–18; Wet: Hare's Ear Nymph, Pheasant Tail, Beadheads #14–16
Green Drake					█				A/E	Dry: Green Drake, Olive Wulff, Quigley Cripple #10–12; Wet: Ida Mae, Prince Nymph, Zug Bug #10–12
Gray Drake						█	█		A/E	Gray Sparkle Dun, CDC Spinner, Para-Adams #10–12
Mahogany Dun						█	█		A	Dry: Mahogany Dun, Sparkle Dun, Mahogany Thorax, #14–18; Wet: Mahogany Emerger
Trico					█	█	█		A	Dry: Black and White, Trico Spinner, Para-Adams #18–22; Wet: Pheasant Tail #18–22
Callibaetis						█	█		A	Thorax Callibaetis, Crystal Spinner, Para-Adams #14–16
Terrestrials				█	█	█	█		M/A	Joe's Hopper, Dave's Hopper, Henry's Fork Hopper, Parachute Hopper #8–14; Foam Beetle, Disc O'Beetle, Dave's Cricket #14–16; Black Ant, Rusty Ant #14–18

M=morning; LM=late morning; A=afternoon; E=evening; D=dark; SF=spinner fall; /=continuation through periods

WYOMING WILDERNESS LAKES

Float-tubers or canoers who want to buy only a Wyoming fishing license can stick to the Reclamation Road west of Flagg Ranch. It's possible to tackle Grassy Lake, Tillery Lake, Lake in the Woods, Fish Lake, and Indian Lake just beyond the Yellowstone Park border. Lake trout and brook trout are added to the mix of opportunities.

Grassy Lake—346 acres; 9- to 20-inch cutthroat and lake trout, a few cutthroatrainbow hybrids. Rated by Wyoming Game and Fish as good fishing.

Tillery Lake—15 acres; 6- to 18-inch rainbows; rated as fair.

Lake in the Woods—245 acres; 8- to 16-inch rainbows; rated as good.

Fish Lake—20 acres; 8- to 16-inch brook trout; rated as good.

Indian Lake—40 acres; moderate-sized cutthroat; not rated.

Several other lakes in the region—South Boundary, Tanager, Loon, and Winegar— are fishless. Be sure to check current state or park regulations wherever you plan to fish.

Yellowstone's Lake Country

The breathtaking scenery of Yellowstone Lake and its grand expanses, tinctured by its brooding power, have fascinated visitors through the years.

In 1869, Charles Cook, David Folsom, and William Peterson of Helena, Montana Territory, were the first to visit the wilderness with the express purpose of confirming Yellowstone's wonders, although a variety of trappers and explorers had already wandered through the area. The vast lake was at the top of their agenda. They were not disappointed. Reports of their ebullient Yellowstone observations in the press spurred further exploration parties and eventually led to the creation of the first national park.

"As we were about departing on our homeward trip we ascended the summit of a neighboring hill and took a final look at Yellowstone Lake," Folsom wrote. "Nestled among the forest crowned hills which bounded our vision, lay this inland sea, its crystal waves dancing and sparkling in the sunlight as if laughing with joy for their wild freedom. It is a scene of transcendent beauty which has been viewed by few white men, and we felt glad to have looked upon it before its primeval solitude should be broken by the crowds of pleasure seekers which at no distant day will throng its shores."

A year later Nathaniel Langford of the Washburn Expedition offered an equally enthusiastic picture of the lake's awesome strength.

"How can I sum up its wonderful attractions! It is dotted with islands of great beauty.... The winds from the mountain gorges roll its placid waters into a furious sea, and crest its billows with foam."

The throngs eventually came to the lake, but more often for its spectacular fishing than for the scenery. Yellowstone Lake is home to the largest inland cutthroat trout population in the world. Its Yellowstone cutthroat survived decades of exploitation and rebounded to historic proportions under strict regulations to limit harvest. Now, unfortunately, it faces its greatest challenge in the illegal presence of lake trout, a voracious predator.

Yellowstone Lake is the largest natural freshwater lake above 7,000 feet of elevation in the United States. Shaped like a giant hand with two fingers pointed south and a thumb extended to the west, it is 20 miles long and 14 miles wide. Its 110-mile shoreline encircles a surface area of 196 square miles. The lake's average depth is 140 feet and its maximum depth is at least 320 feet.

Following its creation 600,000 years ago, when a cataclysmic volcanic explosion carved out the Yellowstone caldera, the lake was 300 feet higher and covered an area twice its present size. West Thumb was formed about 150,000 years ago in the region's last major volcanic eruption.

The Yellowstone River originally flowed south to the Snake and the Pacific. Floods from melting glaciers carved the Grand Canyon of the Yellowstone during the last Ice Age, and the river was ultimately directed by resurgent ice caps into the Missouri and the Atlantic. At 671 total miles, it is the longest undammed river in the Lower 48 States.

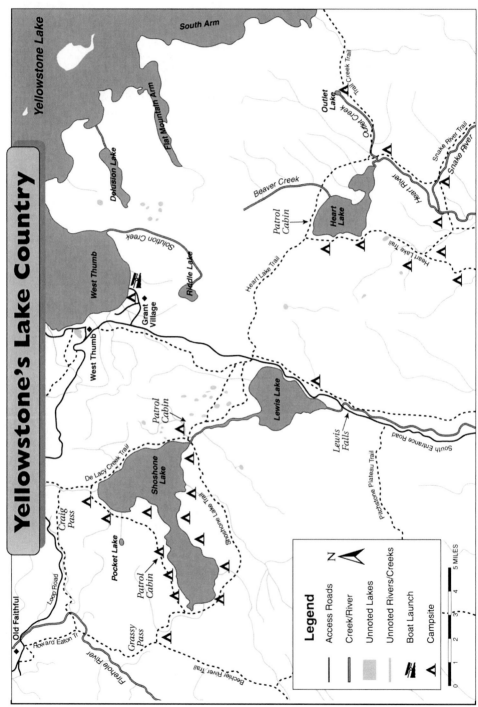

Yellowstone's Lake Country

Legend

N

Access Roads

Creek/River

Unnoted Lakes

Unnoted Rivers/Creeks

Boat Launch

Campsite

0 1 2 3 4 5 MILES

© 2009 Wilderness Adventures Press, Inc.

The park's other three big lakes, located across the Continental Divide in the Snake River drainage, are significantly smaller. Lewis Lake is easily reached from the loop road, and relatively short hikes take you to Shoshone and Heart Lakes, two of Yellowstone's best wilderness fishing destinations.

Shoshone Lake, at 8,050 acres, is the largest backcountry lake in the Lower 48 States. It is connected to the 2,716-acre Lewis Lake by the Lewis River Channel, and both lakes offer excellent fishing for brown and lake trout. The two non-native trout species were established in the previously fishless lakes in 1890.

Heart Lake is the most fertile body of water in the park and holds more species, including forage fish, than any other. This remote 2,150-acre gem established unofficial park records for lake trout and Yellowstone cutthroat.

Boating and Canoeing Dangers

An abiding feature of the four big lakes is that they can be fished well from shore, by wading their shallows, or by float-tubing. Boats really aren't necessary to fish them. But those who venture away from shore need to be aware of almost daily high winds and the threat of sudden storms. The chilly waters can become death traps for capsized boaters.

Yellowstone Lake harbors a malevolent beauty, notes park historian Lee Whittlesey. "All things considered, no body of water in Yellowstone Park and probably in all of the United States is more potentially dangerous," he writes in Death in Yellowstone: Accidents and Foolhardiness in the First National Park.

Despite its macabre topic, the book is a fascinating read. Among other points, it refutes an often held misconception that geysers have killed the most Yellowstone visitors. Cold water has slain six times more people than hot water. Of the approximately 300 deaths caused by natural phenomena, 115 people have died from drowning compared to 19 falling into hot springs. Yellowstone Lake is the biggest killer, with 41 deaths, followed by the Yellowstone River's 29 fatalities.

Fed by melting snows, Yellowstone Lake barely gets to 60 degrees in summer. Its average year-round temperature is just 45 degrees. Prevailing winds from the southwest routinely kick up 4- to 5-foot waves, and storms push crests to 6 feet or more. The winds begin to stir around 11 a.m. almost daily. Storms are most likely to occur between 1 and 6 p.m. Squalls may occur at any time.

The same combinations of cold temperatures, prevailing winds, and sudden storms occur on Lewis and Shoshone Lakes. Anglers in small boats and canoes are cautioned to hug the shorelines on all three. Lewis Lake has recorded seven deaths and Shoshone Lake has tallied four.

The majority of accidents on the lakes occur when small boats capsize or canoes tip over in sudden squalls or when larger boat are caught in the open by storms, according to Whittlesey. The water is so cold people can't hold onto capsized vessels as hypothermia takes its toll in as little as 20 minutes.

Russ Pollard of the Wyoming Game and Fish Department encourages anglers and floaters to keep the 50-50-50 rule in mind on coldwater lakes. "If you fall in 50-degree water, and stay in the water for 50 minutes, your chances of survival are about 50 percent."

Boating Regulations and Fees

A permit is required for all motorized and non-motorized vessels, including float tubes. Permits can be purchased at the South Entrance Ranger Station, Lewis Lake Campground, Grant Village Visitor Center, Bridge Bay Ranger Station, or Lake Ranger Station. At Canyon and Mammoth Visitor Centers, only non-motorized boating permits are available. The fee is $20 for an annual permit or $10 for a week for motorized vessels and $10 annual or $5 for a week for non-motorized vessels. A Coast Guard–approved, wearable personal flotation device is required for each person boating, including float-tubers.

Grand Teton National Park's boat permits are honored as a one-time, 7-day permit, or can be applied toward a Yellowstone annual permit. However, Grand Teton boat permits must be verified at a park entrance ranger station or visitor center before the boat can be used in Yellowstone.

All vessels are prohibited on park rivers and streams except the channel between Lewis and Shoshone Lakes, where only hand-propelled vessels are permitted. Only hand-propelled vessels are permitted at the tips of Yellowstone Lake's South and Southeast Arms and the Flat Mountain Arm.

Outboards and rowboats may be rented at Bridge Bay Marina on Yellowstone Lake. The marina also provides guided fishing boats, which may be reserved in advance by calling 307-344-7311. Numerous other commercial businesses have permits to offer guided services for canoeing, kayaking, and motorized boating.

YELLOWSTONE LAKE

Yellowstone Lake is the most heavily fished water in the Greater Yellowstone region. Even after a 100-year history of overfishing and commercial exploitation and a half-century of hatchery meddling, the lake has endured as the finest citadel of inland cutthroat in North America. Its fishing has been legendary, but the lake once again is facing troubling times forced upon it by outside intervention.

An estimated 6,873 anglers fished the lake in 2008, down from a high of more than 30,000 anglers in the late 1990s.

"The angler reported catch of cutthroat trout was 0.73 fish per hour in 2008 (in Yellowstone Lake), a higher catch rate than the previous three years," according to the park's 2008 annual fisheries report. "The average size of cutthroat trout reported by anglers decreased slightly in 2008 to 437mm (17.2 inches) due to an increase of cutthroat trout in the 12- to 16-inch size classes rather than a decrease of larger fish."

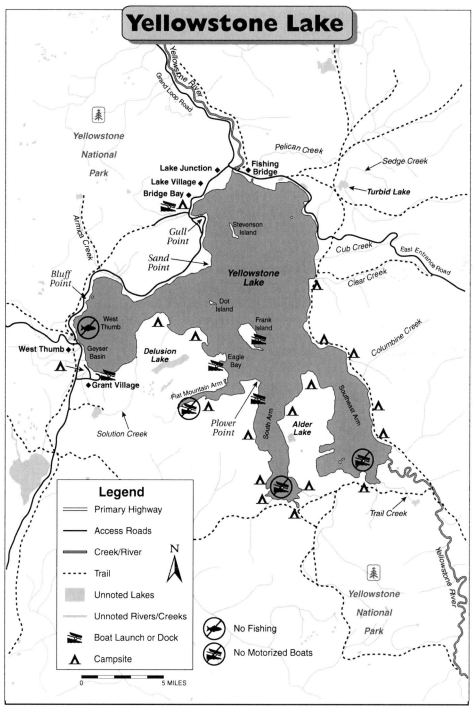

Yellowstone Lake

Yellowstone National Park

Pelican Creek

Sedge Creek

Lake Junction ◆
Fishing Bridge ◆

Lake Village ◆

Turbid Lake

Bridge Bay ◆

Armica Creek

Gull Point

Stevenson Island

Sand Point

Cub Creek

East Entrance Road

Bluff Point

Yellowstone Lake

Clear Creek

Dot Island

West Thumb

Frank Island

Columbine Creek

West Thumb ◆

Geyser Basin

Delusion Lake

Eagle Bay

Southeast Arm

◆ Grant Village

Flat Mountain Arm

South Arm

Solution Creek

Plover Point

Alder Lake

Trail Creek

Legend

Primary Highway
Access Roads
Creek/River
Trail
Unnoted Lakes
Unnoted Rivers/Creeks
Boat Launch or Dock
Campsite

N

No Fishing

No Motorized Boats

Yellowstone National Park

Yellowstone River

0   5 MILES

Yet, in 2002 the Federation of Fly Fishers declared Yellowstone Lake's cutthroat trout population to be the most threatened trout population in the United States. Serious concerns about the declining number of cutthroat in the lake, including an apparent complete loss of some age classes in the early 2000s, precipitated the declaration.

The lake's native Yellowstone cutthroat trout are engaged in mortal combat with their deadliest nemesis, illegally introduced lake trout, as well as the pernicious presence of whirling disease in key spawning tributaries. However, park biologists leading the fight against these foes are hopeful that over time the intricate mix of subpopulations in the enormous lake and varied spawning and rearing strategies will enable the cutthroat to survive the alien invasions.

As part of an ongoing survey, data collected in 2003 from 11 collection sites around the lake "... provided some of the first evidence in several years that the Yellowstone cutthroat trout population may be responding positively to efforts to remove nonnative lake trout from Yellowstone Lake," states the Yellowstone Fisheries & Aquatic Sciences 2003 annual report.

"An average of 7.4 cutthroat were collected per net in 2003, up from 6.1 fish per net in 2002 (which was the lowest point recorded since the lake netting program began in 1969). Prior to 2003, the reduction in catch had been 0–21% each year (averaging 11% per year) since 1994, the year lake trout were first discovered in Yellowstone Lake.

"Examination of length-frequency data from the fall netting survey has indicated an annual, continuous loss of adult cutthroat trout numbers in Yellowstone Lake. Entire age classes are virtually missing from the lake population. In 2003, few fish between the lengths of 300 mm (12 inches) and 430 mm (17 inches) were caught. Historically, most cutthroat trout noted in spawning tributaries such as Clear Creek and at LeHardy Rapids of the Yellowstone River have fallen into this size range.

"Despite this, we see an apparent increase in juvenile cutthroat trout in recent years (2001–2003) as encouraging, and an additional signal that the lake trout removal program's effects may be significant, making a major contribution to the preservation of Yellowstone cutthroat trout. The South Arms of Yellowstone Lake may continue to act as refuges for cutthroat trout due to the low numbers of lake trout found there.'"

A century-old tradition of keeping a limit of cutthroat for a campfire meal ended at Yellowstone Lake in 2001 when catch-and-release rules were imposed on the lake, too. Nowadays, biologists prefer that the meal be lake trout, which must always be kept by anglers.

Unfortunately, the dramatic turnaround in the lake's cutthroat population dampened one of the park's greatest success stories. A series of increasingly stricter fishing regulations—imposed in the 1970s and 1990s on Yellowstone Lake, the Yellowstone River, and their tributaries—had brought the Yellowstone cutthroat back from a disconcerting downward spiral that had begun in the 1950s.

A 14-inch minimum catch size imposed in 1970 helped curb the intense overfishing of the 1950s and 1960s, but still allowed too many adult cutthroat to be taken from the lake. The two-fish-under-13-inches limit imposed in 1973 was designed to improve the population's age structure and gain an increased number of older, larger trout. It was hoped this would provide additional stability and productivity that would more closely resemble historic cutthroat populations. The under-13-inch limit worked, along with the closure of Fishing Bridge and delayed openings of the upper river and spawning tributaries until July 15.

Before the lake trout invasion, biologists were highly encouraged by the lake's comeback, said Lynn Kaeding, former Yellowstone research director for U.S. Fish and Wildlife Service. "We were very close, if not there, to correcting the adverse human activity."

Population estimates in the late 1990s for the sport fishery of catchable-sized fish—8 to 10 inches and larger—was 2.5 million cutthroat. The total population, including immature cutthroat, was 4 million or more.

Gillnet surveys by the Fish and Wildlife Service showed that the cutthroat population's size structure was approaching equilibrium, with an average size of 15 inches. The capture of a 10-year-old cutthroat in 1994 indicated the population was approaching its historical age structure.

First officially recorded in 1994, illegal transplant of the predatory non-native lake trout was described as an "appalling act of environmental vandalism" by former Superintendent Bob Barbee. "The potential consequences of this thoughtless act are enormous," he said. "It could mean the destruction of the last major stronghold of inland cutthroat. Yellowstone Lake has been an almost museum-pure home of these fish for thousands of years, and it would be a tragic loss to Yellowstone's wilderness quality, to anglers and to science."

Barbee said other wildlife could be seriously harmed if lake trout succeed in taking over the lake. "If lake trout make serious inroads on the cutthroat trout population, many animals will suffer, including eagles, osprey, otters, and bears." Unlike cutthroat, which spawn in streams, lake trout spend almost all their time in deep waters, out of reach of other predators. "Many grizzly bears feed heavily on stream-spawning cutthroat trout and could simply lose that important food source," Barbee said.

Meanwhile, park biologists have taken great strides to perfect gillnetting techniques to capture large lake trout, which are the prime spawners. Most of their efforts have been focused on West Thumb where adult lake trout congregate, and between 1995 and 2003 more than 75,000 lake trout were removed from the lake through gillnetting. Anglers also have taken lake trout from numerous places around the lake, and they are asked to continue to assist in the battle as much as possible.

Fishing Yellowstone Lake

Nearly 35 miles of the park's loop roads offer easy access to the lake's west and north shores. Anglers can fish virtually anywhere they want, but the most popular areas are the banks north of Bridge Bay and to the south at Gull Point, Sand Point, and Rock Point. West Thumb is a favorite with float-tubers because the warm waters around its thermal features are prime feeding grounds for cruising trout.

Boat ramps are located at Bridge Bay and Grant Village, although the latter may be closed in early season during high water years.

The best hiking route is the Thorofare Trail, which starts from Lake Butte Drive on the northeast corner of the lake. It follows the east shore for about 20 miles to the Yellowstone River delta. The Trail Creek Trail, from the delta to Heart Lake, skirts the tips of the lake's two southern arms. Otherwise, the only access to the lake's south shore east of Grant Village is by boat or canoe.

Due to the devastating effects of whirling disease, Pelican Creek, on the north shore of the lake, was closed to fishing in 2004 until further notice. Cub Creek and Clear Creek, on the Thorofare Trail, are closed to fishing until August 11 because of grizzly bear activity. Areas near Lake Lodge, Grant Village, and Fishing Bridge often are closed for the same reason. Tributaries, including the upper Yellowstone River, don't open to fishing until July 15, and a 100-yard zone around their mouths also are closed. Fishing is not permitted in posted areas of the outlet above and below Fishing Bridge.

All cutthroat trout caught in the lake or its tributaries must be released. All lake trout caught in the lake, its tributaries, and the Yellowstone River must be killed. If you do not want to keep the fish, puncture the air bladder and drop it into water as deep as possible. Anglers that catch lake trout must report the number and catch location to the Park Service (verbally or by using the report card provided with each fishing permit).

Working along the shoreline of Yellowstone Lake.

Yellowstone Lake's 7,728-foot elevation means ice-out occurs in late May or early June.

Adult cutthroat cruise the shorelines to feed in 4 to 10 feet of water in shallow bays, along sandbars, and near points and inlets. Spring spawning migrations often keep the trout close enough to banks and points to be reached by fly casters without boats or float tubes. The lake fishes best in morning and evening because of its prevailing winds.

Anglers in float tubes cover more water, but need to hug the shore and dress warmly to avoid hypothermia. Boaters who embark for the shoals around the lake's few islands or its southern arms should be wary of high winds and sudden intense storms.

The most prudent option for canoers headed to the South or Southeast Arms is to arrange ferry shuttles to the Promontory. In addition to being safer, it saves a great deal of time and effort that could be better spent fishing. Advance reservations are required for backcountry campsites.

Early season float-tubers often do best slowly stripping small Woolly Buggers or leech patterns, size 4 to 6, or medium-sized nymphs, size 10 to 14, with a full-sink line or sink-tip and short leader. Hits are often subtle, so be prepared to set the hook at the first hint of a strike.

Wet fly choices include green or black Woolly Buggers, dark leeches, stonefly nymphs, damselfly nymphs, Zug Bugs, Marabou Muddlers, Spruce Flies, and beadhead nymphs (such as the Prince, Hare's Ear, and Pheasant Tail), soft hackles, and scuds. The same patterns also are most effective in autumn.

The best topwater action is usually sight casting to cruising cutthroat as the lake warms and clears. Shoreline casters find fishing improves by early July. Present dry flies on a long leader with a shooting -head floating line.

When prospecting, try Elk Hair Caddis, terrestrials, or attractor patterns, such as Adams or Royal Wulffs, size 10 to 14; also try giving them an occasional twitch. Callibaetis are the principal mayfly hatch on late July and August mornings. Try Callibaetis cripples, Parachute Adams, and gray Sparkle Duns, size 12 to 16. Sporadic mayfly hatches and spinner falls include Gray Drakes, Baetis, and Tricos, and usually occur near inlets. Midges often are a good option in quiet bays and near inlets.

Lake trout hunters lobbing large colorful streamers, size 2 to 6, are most likely to find them close to shore from ice-out until early July and again in late autumn as they migrate and congregate near spawning reefs. Tiny Carrington Island in West Thumb was the first documented spawning site. Others have been found along the southeast shore of the bay and near Breeze Channel.

Some anglers complain that Yellowstone Lake's cutthroat are cookie-cutter fish (all about the same size). The trout average 15 to 18 inches, and maximum size rarely exceeds 20 inches. However, it is reasonable to expect the lake's most exceptional trout to be in spawning tributaries at the height of the fishing season.

Small cutthroat are uncommon near shorelines because of their different feeding requirements. Young cutthroat in the lake ply its deeper reaches, feeding almost exclusively on zooplankton like water fleas and copepods. The tiny crustaceans are filtered from the water with specially developed gill rackers. Studies by biologists also indicate that significant subpopulations remain in perennial tributaries like Arnica Creek and Beaverdam Creek until they approach adult age. This means that the loss of the Pelican Creek fishery to whirling disease in the early 2000s was an extraordinary blow to the lake's cutthroat population.

But perhaps the lake's most unique feature is its dramatic spawning runs out of the outlet. It is a mirror image of other lake tributaries, notes Robert Gresswell, a U.S. Forest Service biologist. The adults go downstream to spawn and their fry swim upstream to the lake. Moreover, there are populations of robust resident cutthroat in the upper and lower river often overlooked in the dynamics of the basin.

When the lake's cutthroat reach 13 to 14 inches in size, they move to its warmer and shallower littoral zones, where they switch to eating invertebrates like leeches, larvae, and nymphs and larger crustaceans like scuds and snails. But unlike other Yellowstone cutthroat races, the lake's large trout do not switch to being predators as is common in Heart Lake and eastern Idaho waters.

Lake Trout War Terrifies Cutthroat Guardians

Once the presence of lake trout was officially recorded in Yellowstone Lake in 1994, a war of attrition was declared against the deadly predator despoiling the largest bastion of genetically pure Yellowstone cutthroat trout.

The first two years of the war were largely exploratory, devising ways and means to launch the attack. But by 1996 the escalating numbers and increased sizes of lake trout captured in gillnets terrified the U.S. Fish and Wildlife Service fisheries biologists in the vanguard of the battle against the predator. Even then they suspected lake trout were well established in the lake and had been there much longer than first believed.

"It's a beautiful fish, but it doesn't belong here," said Glenn Boltz, a USFWS biologist. "The numbers showing up this year are scary." Also, a 10-inch jump in size in a single year for the largest lake trout netted meant older than expected fish were in the lake. "Even with the [exceptionally prolific] feed base, the growth can't be expected from that alone."

In the first two weeks of the 1996 gillnetting season, his crew captured a 13-pound lake trout and a 12.5-pounder, both more than 30 inches in length. By year's end, a total catch of 580 in nets and 206 by anglers included other lake trout ranging from 17 to 21 pounds. The larger fish were estimated to be 20 to 25 years old. By comparison, the 204 fish captured in 1994 and 1995 had been in the 8- to 22-inch range.

The pattern was repeated in 1997, when 1,056 lake trout were taken from the lake, including 240 by anglers. The largest was 16 pounds, said Dan Mahony, a fisheries biologist for the park's aquatic resource center, which later assumed Yellowstone's fisheries management after the U.S. Fish and Wildlife Service ended its management program in the park.

The age of the lake trout debunked an "urban myth" that they got into the lake when helicopters were used to dip huge buckets of water from Lewis Lake to fight forest fires in 1988, Mahony said. One of the hardest fought battles against the fires saved Grant Village on Yellowstone Lake's West Thumb, where most of the lake trout have been netted.

Nevertheless, the seriousness of the unauthorized introduction of lake trout was immediately apparent and sent shock waves throughout the West upon "official" discovery of the fish in the lake.

The consensus of a coalition of experts brought to the park to assess the lake trout threat was that if no action was taken to fight the invasion, Yellowstone Lake would lose 80 percent of the 2.5 million cutthroat in its sport fishery in 20 years. And in a century all the cutthroat would be gone. Drastic measures to reduce lake trout populations, they said, would reduce losses to 30 percent in 20 years and to 60 percent in 100 years.

The experts agreed it would be virtually impossible to eradicate lake trout from the vast lake. But upper Midwest scientists offered some hope that expansion of the population might be contained through an aggressive gillnetting program such as the one used by commercial fishing operations in the Great Lakes.

The dire warnings were based on assumptions that lake trout had been present for only about eight to 10 years when first discovered in 1994. But even if their tenure has been longer and the impact much less, there was no cause for jubilation. It just meant a lot more information was needed.

Nor could there be any doubt the lake trout were making a dent in the cutthroat population. Annual consumption estimates range from 40 to 90 cutthroat per lake trout, depending on the size of an adult predator.

Weeding out sexually mature adults with gillnets has been the focus of suppression efforts from the outset, Mahony said. Discovery in 1996 of a key spawning area near Carrington Island in West Thumb enabled biologists to key on one of the largest concentrations of large lake trout in the lake. Early netting efforts also concentrated on Breeze Channel between West Thumb and the main lake, and along the southeast shore of West Thumb. Additional spawning sites have since been found near the West Thumb Geyser Basin and Solution Creek.

Radio-tagged "Judas fish" led the gillnetters to concentrations of adults in the late 1990s.

"That was our biggest contribution" in the war against the lake trout, said Jim Risch, a University of Utah graduate student. "We found spawners as soon as the surface temperature of the water dropped below 50 degrees. It was classic."

But, while they can take adults anytime they want in West Thumb, the juveniles are dispersed throughout the lake where they compete with young cutthroat for zooplankton, their principal food source. Biologists also are concerned about the large numbers of 12-inch lake trout in the lake, notes Risch. But using small-mesh nets to take them results in unacceptable losses of cutthroat—an almost 1-to-1 ratio.

Lake trout switch to a fish diet at about 12 inches and rapidly grow in size. Males become sexually mature at about 16 inches and females at 17 or 18 inches. When they surpass 20 inches, their appetite skyrockets.

Biological analysis shows lake trout are doing better in Yellowstone Lake than in Lewis Lake, said Boltz.

"The head size to body size ratio shows fast growth. They all have really good body fat. Scale studies show they have the fastest growth after they reach 20 inches," he said. "They surpass the cutthroat in reaching that size by as much as two years earlier."

Lake trout have an amazingly large mouth for a salmonid species.

"A large lake trout can easily take a fish one-half its own body weight," Boltz said. "Smaller ones can easily take fish one-third their body weight. The 12.5-pound lake trout we caught had the remains of a 20-inch cutthroat in its stomach."

It's particularly disconcerting the lake trout are hitting cutthroat rather than other prey species in the lake, including longnose dace, longnose sucker, redside shiner, and lake chub.

"What we have learned is that fish predation is keyed on cutthroat," Boltz said. "The longnosed sucker is abundant but is found only in shallow, warm water. Predation on cutthroat is occurring because their habitat overlaps."

While adult lake trout can consume large numbers of cutthroat, there are other scary aspects of this unequal competition. A cutthroat's life expectancy is about 10 years. A lake trout's is 25 to 40 years. That means a lake trout's lifespan equals two or more cutthroat generations. Cutthroats spawn once or twice in a lifetime. Lake trout may spawn eight to 10 years in a row. On average, a lake trout has 1,000 eggs per kilogram of body weight. That means a 20-pound fish could produce 10,000 eggs. If just 1 percent of those eggs survive, that's 100 new lake trout born to a single fish.

Also, in addition to being preyed on by lake trout, the cutthroat must compete for similar food resources, especially since both species feed on zooplankton when young.

Growth potential for lake trout in Yellowstone Lake is phenomenal, considering the histories of the park's other lakes. Unofficial trophy fish records from the three lakes range from 50 pounds in Heart Lake to 40 pounds in Shoshone Lake and 30 pounds in Lewis Lake.

The record angler catch was a 63-pound, 51.5-inch lake trout from Lake Superior in 1952. The largest one ever netted was a 121-pound gargantuan from a Canadian lake.

Some lake trout hunters may chomp at the bit to pursue trophies in the lake, but it isn't going to happen if park officials can prevent it. A lake trout sport fishery in no way would equal Yellowstone Lake's cutthroat fishery—ecologically, economically, or morally.

The group of experts collected back in 1994 to assess the lake trout threat to the park's cutthroat fishery offered a dramatic "bottom line" forecast:

"While the potential ecological losses are staggering, the potential economic losses can be summarized as equally immense. The 1994 value of the Yellowstone fisheries above the great falls (of the Yellowstone River), including the lake and its tributaries, is estimated at slightly more than $36 million. The cumulative 30-year value of the cutthroat trout sport fishery, assuming lake trout were absent, is estimated at more than a billion dollars ($1,080,000,000). Assuming lake trout are vigorously controlled, the consonant value declines to $685 million. If lake trout are not controlled, the value declines to $439,950,000. The last value represents a three-decade economic loss of $640 million, which can be considered the net economic effect of the illegal lake trout introduction if no actions are taken to control the species."

Mahony and others look upon their battles against the illegally introduced lake trout as an endless war.

"You just have to stay on top of it," he said. "If we can get this population to the point where it kind of collapses down there and if we can kill over half of the adults a year, then over a period of time that population will start to take a tumble and be at a real low level. The reason this project is so important is because of the native wild cutthroat, and we're doing everything we can to save those guys."

And after a decade of fighting the battle, park biologist were beginning to see encouraging results that their strategies might be working.

"The 2003 field season came to a close in early November, marking the end of the first decade of fieldwork since lake trout were discovered in Yellowstone Lake. This was a record year, as more than 18,000 of the non-native predators were killed

High water rising up to Gull Point.

to preserve our remaining native Yellowstone cutthroat trout of this system," states the Yellowstone Fisheries & Aquatic Sciences 2003 annual report. "Because each of the non-native lake trout would have consumed many cutthroat trout each year, the gillnetting effort has saved a tremendous number of cutthroat trout; 75,000 lake trout have been killed by gillnetting since they were first discovered in 1994. The angling community has also joined forces and has been contributing to a significant removal of lake trout from Yellowstone Lake each year.

"The result is a lake trout population that is suppressed and showing some signs of it. Catch per unit of effort for lake trout remains very low, and the average length of spawning adult lake trout continues to decline each year."

Lake Trout Mysteries

The lake trout bombshell ticking ominously in Yellowstone Lake was almost inevitable considering previous attempts—both official and unofficial—to fill supposed voids in its basin. Previous fish transplants in the upper Yellowstone drainage fizzled, but it will take a Herculean effort to defuse today's lake trout fiasco.

"Landlocked salmon planted in Yellowstone and Duck Lakes in 1908 have not been recorded since," F. Phillip Sharpe stated in a Yellowstone Library and Museum Association pamphlet from the 1960s. "Mountain whitefish were introduced above Yellowstone Falls in 1889, but none survived. Rainbow trout first planted above the falls in 1908 probably survived but were subsequently hybridized into the dominant cutthroat trout population."

By then a philosophical trend toward natural management was evolving. The U.S. Fish Commission employee who made an unauthorized transplant of rainbows into Yellowstone Lake in 1907 was reprimanded. A proposed transplant of smelt into Lewis Lake was rejected.

Still, at least one more attempt was made to establish rainbows in the upper river in 1929, according to records uncovered by Steve Pierce, author of The Lakes of Yellowstone.

Also, redside shiner, lake chub, and longnose sucker found their way into Yellowstone Lake, probably from the dumping of baitfish buckets.

"The only other exotic species in the (Yellowstone) lake drainage were brown trout in Duck Lake, and those were eradicated in 1967," stated Sharpe.

But two decades later brook trout showed up in Arnica Creek, a tributary of Yellowstone Lake's West Thumb. The U.S. Fish and Wildlife Service, the modern successor of the U.S. Fish Commission, struck hard and fast. Arnica was poisoned in 1985 and 1986 to eliminate the non-native species, which could have flourished in the lake.

Ironically, West Thumb is the star player in the riddle of how lake trout illegally got into Yellowstone Lake, apparently in the late 1980s.

Science Panel Reviews Lake Trout Suppression Program

In late August (2008), Yellowstone National Park invited 15 fisheries scientists from around the country to attend a conference at Chico Hot Springs designed to critically review the park's lake trout suppression program.

The conference was also attended by 35 - 40 interested participants from state agencies, non-profit groups, universities and several federal agencies, including the National Park Service, U.S. Geological Survey, and U.S. Fish and Wildlife Service.

The park tasked the science panel to (1) evaluate the effectiveness of the current program, (2) review emerging technologies that could possibly be employed for lake trout suppression, and (3) make recommendations for the future direction of the program.

The science panel overwhelming agreed that the Yellowstone Lake Yellowstone cutthroat trout population is in serious trouble, but that suppression efforts could restore this population to healthy levels. They stated that efforts to date, while certainly slowing the lake trout population growth rate, have not been substantial enough to collapse that population. Consequently, the cutthroat trout population remains in peril.

They strongly stated that very little time remains to turn the situation around and immediate action to increase suppression efforts should be taken. Increased monitoring and evaluation of the population status of both the cutthroat trout and lake trout should also be undertaken. Finally, although several emerging technologies show promise for future use in reducing lake trout populations, none currently exist that could replace direct removal efforts.

Long-range plans, however, should include further research in these areas. A report with complete findings of the science panel, including strengths and weaknesses of the current program and specific recommendations to the park, is expected in 2009.

Yellowstone Science
Volume 17 • number 1 • 2009

"Fish Story," published in 1991 by Gray's Sporting Journal, might be the title of just another tall tale or a clue to solving the mystery. An intriguing piece of fiction, it revolves around the search for a park ranger who drowned in West Thumb. According to the story, he was fishing for lake trout planted in the lake in the 1960s to produce trophy-sized fish. A sonar search for his body reveals monster fish in the lake, but the story ends with a plot to keep the presence of the "trophy" fish in the lake secret.

Law enforcement authorities talked extensively with the author, Gary Parks, a former Yellowstone Lake fishing guide. They concluded there is no basis to the story, said Cheryl Mathews, a Yellowstone spokeswoman. "It was just pure fiction, there was nothing to it."

Investigation of the illegal transplant of lake trout continued. A $10,000 reward for information leading to the arrest and conviction of those involved was offered in 1996.

"We have had no solid leads, which leads us to conclude that lake trout have been in the lake longer than we previously anticipated," Mathews said.

Still, the magazine story was intriguing to Lynn Kaeding, former research director of Yellowstone fisheries for the Fish and Wildlife Service. "I don't know if we will ever get to the bottom of it. There are some elements of fact in it, and there are some elements of barroom talk.

"I would say that whoever did it was a misdirected lake trout enthusiast."

There's strong evidence that more than one unwarranted transplant of lake trout has occurred in Yellowstone Lake, according to Kaeding.

Glenn Boltz, a colleague, agreed.

"If I were to guess, the West Thumb area was planted years ago," he said. The large number of lake trout captured there at the outset of the park's gillnetting efforts would seem to be more than coincidence. Boltz suspected many small lake trout were slipped into the lake several times. "It's not human nature to give up a trophy fish" to produce a brood stock.

The assumption of Boltz and other fisheries experts that the lake trout transplants most likely came from Lewis Lake, a short drive across the Continental Divide from Yellowstone Lake, gained credence through continued scientific analysis of the fish in the lake.

According to the park's 2002 fisheries and aquatic science report, lake trout otolith "fingerprints" helped unravel questions of both stocking origin and timing of the lake trout. "Otoliths are calcium carbonate structures located in the inner ears of fish that grow by continually adding new layers, and they are used to age fish. Trace elements from the water, such as strontium, are incorporated into the new layers of otolith, imparting a unique elemental signature, or fingerprint, that can then be used to help identify where a fish lived at different times of its life...

"During lake trout removals in 1996–'97, some comparatively large fish were captured in Yellowstone Lake. Aquatics biologists suspected that these larger fish could be original transplants.... [Otolith] studies suggest that lake trout have been naturally reproducing in Yellowstone Lake since 1986 or 1987. Many lake trout were transplanted into Yellowstone Lake from Lewis Lake, or from a lake with a similar Sr:

Ca fingerprint, and the introductions began as early as the mid-1980s and possibly continued as late as 1996. Our initial detective work will guide management strategies to prevent future illegal introductions."

Lake trout planted in Lewis Lake and Shoshone Lake in 1890 are the Bear Island strain from the northwest shore of Lake Michigan. The fish eventually migrated to Heart Lake and Jackson Lake in the Snake River drainage. Heart Lake's apparently special breed of Yellowstone cutthroat have been holding their own, but Jackson Lake's cutthroat population—identified today by most biologists as another subspecies called the Snake River finespotted cutthroat—were virtually eliminated by the lake trout and exist today, perhaps, only through massive early-day stocking of hatchery fish.

Lewis and Shoshone Lakes, which also hold brown trout from the 1890 transplants, were previously barren of fish. They were stocked with non-native species because they are across the Continental Divide from Yellowstone Lake. The danger of infiltration was considered impossible.

Famous last thoughts.

YELLOWSTONE LAKE MAJOR HATCHES

Insect	A	M	J	J	A	S	O	N	Time	Flies
Callibaetis			X	X	X	X			A/E	Dry: Thorax Dun, Crystal Spinner, CDC Quill Spinner, Para-Adams #10–14; Wet: Hare's Ear Nymph #10–12
Pale Morning Dun			X	X	X				A/E	Dry: PMD, Sparkle Dun, PMD Cripple, Para-Adams #14–18; Wet: Hare's Ear Nymph, Pheasant Tail, Beadheads #14–18
Gray Drake			X	X					A/E	Dry: Para-Drake, Gray Wulff, Sparkle Dun, Para-Adams, CDC Spinner #10–12; Wet: Hare's Ear Nymph #10
Caddis			X	X					A/E	Elk Hair Caddis (tan), X-Caddis #14–16
Baetis			X	X	X	X			A/E	Dry: Blue-winged Olive, Blue Dun, Olive Sparkle Dun #14–18; Adams, Para-Adams #16–18; Wet: Pheasant Tail #16–18
Terrestrials					X	X	X		A	Dave's Hopper, Tan Para-Hopper #10–14; ants #16–18; beetles #12–16
Scuds/Leeches	X	X	X	X	X	X	X	X		Olive Scud #14–16; Leech (black, brown, green) #2–10; Woolly Bugger (crystal, brown, olive, black) #6–8

M=morning; LM=late morning; A=afternoon; E=evening; D=dark; SF=spinner fall; /=continuation through periods

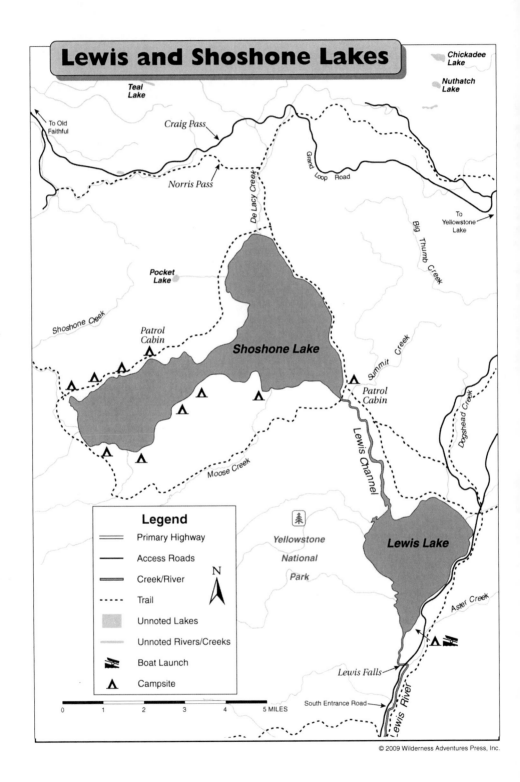

Lewis and Shoshone Lakes

Chickadee Lake

Nuthatch Lake

Teal Lake

To Old Faithful

Craig Pass

Grand Loop Road

Norris Pass

De Lacy Creek

To Yellowstone Lake

Big Thumb Creek

Pocket Lake

Shoshone Creek

Patrol Cabin

Shoshone Lake

Summit Creek

Patrol Cabin

Dogshead Creek

Moose Creek

Lewis Channel

Lewis Lake

Legend

- Primary Highway
- Access Roads
- Creek/River
- · · · · Trail
- Unnoted Lakes
- Unnoted Rivers/Creeks
- Boat Launch
- Campsite

Yellowstone National Park

N

Aster Creek

Lewis Falls

South Entrance Road

Lewis River

0   1   2   3   4   5 MILES

© 2009 Wilderness Adventures Press, Inc.

Lewis Lake

Lewis Lake offers a mixed-bag of fishing opportunities that deserve more attention than they receive. Despite its easy access from the South Entrance–West Thumb Road, this lake is rarely crowded.

The lake's reputation for big trout is often associated with the channel linking it to its larger sister, Shoshone Lake. Anglers who only visit Lewis Lake during brown trout spawning runs into the Lewis River Channel in late fall are missing the boat. The lake fishes well with streamers and nymphs throughout the seasons and offers good topwater action in midsummer. But it is difficult to separate the lake from the river running through it, and the outlet is another positive link to its dynamic fishery.

The bottom line is that each of the lake's many options needs to be explored to fully appreciate its rewards. It has one of the prettiest campgrounds in the park, and it is one of the few that doesn't fill early.

Lewis Lake is loaded with smaller-than-average lake trout in the 14- to 18-inch range because of its limited prey base. However, those that succeed in making the conversion to full-sized predators may exceed 36 inches in length and 25 pounds in weight. The unofficial record for the lake was a 30-pound lake trout.

Brown trout fare better in Lewis Lake, and plump, acrobatic fish in the 12- to 20inch range are common, with a fair number exceeding 26 inches.

Anglers also take an occasional brook trout, and a few report cutthroat in the lake. The latter apparently have worked their way down from Pocket Lake, a small pond above Shoshone Lake. Heart Lake cutthroat were planted there in the 1970s as a safeguard against losing the unique race of Yellowstone cutthroat.

Angler reports give Lewis Lake a 74-percent satisfaction rating for its .49-fish-perhour catch rate and fish averaging 14.5 inches.

More than a century ago, Lewis Lake and Shoshone Lake had no fish in their pristine waters. The Lewis River waterfall blocked upstream migration of Yellowstone cutthroat. In 1890, lake trout from the Bear Island area of Lake Michigan and Loch Leven brown trout from Scotland were planted in the lakes, where they quickly took hold and were reproducing within a decade. Lewis Lake also received a transplant of lake trout in 1941.

In a unique switch in roles in the 1980s, lake trout from Lewis Lake returned to their natal waters. Brood stocks created from eggs collected from the lake helped reestablish Lake Michigan's lake trout fishery, which had been decimated by sea lampreys in the 1960s. However, pollution in the second largest of the Great Lakes has thwarted attempts to accomplish natural reproduction by Lewis Lake progeny.

Efforts to establish cutthroat and grayling in Lewis Lake in the 1930s failed, as did rainbow transplants in tributary streams. The few brook trout in tributaries are holdovers from fish stocked in 1893.

Shaped like a crudely drawn valentine, Lewis Lake is about 5 miles long and 3.5 miles wide at the top. The third largest of the park's lakes, it rests at 7,779 feet in a pine-rimmed bowl on the Pacific side of the Continental Divide. Puffs of steam rising from small thermal features at its outlet remind visitors it also is on the southern rim of the Yellowstone caldera.

The lake opens to fishing Memorial Day weekend, but it often isn't completely free of ice until mid-June.

Motorized boats are permitted, although small boats and canoes should hug its shores and avoid the center of the lake. Prevailing winds kick up a heavy chop or white-capped waves almost daily by midafternoon. Sudden storms can capsize small craft without warning, and the lake has claimed seven lives over the years.

Its high elevation means the water never has time to warm much above 50 degrees and hypothermia is an acute danger. Float-tubers should dress warmly to avoid becoming too chilled.

Early summer and autumn anglers do best searching the lake's in-shore ledges, shallows, points, and coves with moderate-sized streamers and black or olive Woolly Buggers and dark leech patterns. A floating line with a long stout leader can be used in shallow waters and around weed beds, but a sink-tip or full-sink line is needed for deeper waters off ledges and points.

Actually, two reels are better than one in midsummer. A second reel loaded with a floating line comes in handy as the waters warm and cruising trout sipping Callibaetis or caddis draw attention away from the lake's depths.

After ice-out, also look for brown and lake trout congregating at the mouth of the Lewis River Channel, or explore the lower meadow run of the inlet as it warms and hatches start to erupt. The channel between Lewis and Shoshone Lakes is the only stream in the park that can be floated in hand-propelled watercraft.

Hatches in the channel, which are often flushed into the inlet bay, include Green Drakes in late June and PMDs and BWOs in July. Small terrestrial patterns are effective in late summer. Midges and tiny BWOs also provide some topwater action in late fall.

In late June and July, good-sized brown trout also take up feeding lies at the outlet of the lake and in downstream shelter areas for about a half mile of the river's upper run to its scenic waterfall. The trout lie in wait for caddis, midges, Callibaetis, and other mayfly spinners being flushed out of the lake. And in the afternoon this is the one place on the lake where the winds work to an angler's advantage. The short canyon between the waterfall and the lake produces a prolific overlapping hatch of Small Dark Stoneflies, Golden Stones, and Little Yellow Stones in early July.

Unlike the inlet channel, boats or canoes are not permitted past a posted line on the outlet bay. Boaters can either anchor near the top of the outlet or land their craft and work the outlet bay and upper river from the banks.

In late September, lake trout start to follow brown trout into both the Lewis-Shoshone channel and the outlet on their fall spawning runs. Fishing with large streamers can be intense, but beadhead nymphs also may be effective. This is about the only time the lake is crowded, but the window of opportunity is short. Fishing ends the first weekend of November.

There is an excellent boat ramp at the campground on the south end of the lake. Canoes and float tubes also can be bank launched at several coves along the South Entrance–West Thumb Road, which parallels the lake for about 2.5 miles.

It is shallow enough in a few places near the campground for wading anglers, although float-tubers cover more water. Shore anglers also can find a few places along coves and points, as well as shallows and bays near the outlet and inlet, to cast to cruising or rising fish. Fishing is best in early morning and on warm summer evenings since afternoon winds blow from the southwest.

Footpaths skirt much of the east shore near the campground and the loop road. Stick to the path on the 1.5-mile hike to the outlet. Trying to take a shortcut through the forest is virtually impossible because of numerous barriers created by downed timber.

Two trails into the Lewis River Channel start from a trailhead at the north end of the lake. The Doghead Trail, which goes directly to the top of the channel, is 4 miles long. The Lewis Channel Trail is 3 miles along the top of the lake to the inlet and then 4 miles to the top of the channel.

The Lewis Lake Campground is one of the few in the park that doesn't require reservations. Camping also is available at Flagg Ranch and the Snake River Campground, just south of the park's South Entrance.

Boat permits are available at the ranger stations at the campground and South Entrance.

Boats are allowed on Lewis Lake, but not on the river.

Shoshone Lake:
YELLOWSTONE'S HIDDEN GEM

By Bruce Staples

Open any angling magazine and you can expect an article on a famous stream or lake. The Henry's Fork, Henry's Lake, the Madison River, and the South Fork are common subjects. It's nice to see these fisheries gain the attention they deserve, but the fanfare can crowd rivers and, for some people, diminish the experiences touted in the articles.

On the other end of the spectrum, there are waters that deserve attention and can absorb a few more anglers without destroying the experience. One such place is Yellowstone's Shoshone Lake.

If the huge lake were located next to a highway, it would receive the same fanfare. But even though it is hidden in the shadows of the region's other angling heavyweights, Shoshone still shines. Fish it and you'll experience a true wilderness adventure. At 12 square miles, it is the largest lake in the Lower 48 without a road to its doorstep.

A little more than 100 years ago, Shoshone Lake didn't have trout. The same was true for its sister, Lewis Lake, and all the waters above Lewis Falls in the river's drainage. In 1890, brown trout and lake trout were released into Shoshone Lake. A bit later, brook trout were released into its tributaries.

Shoshone Lake is so fertile that in the 1920s it sustained a commercial fishery. Anglers got the idea to fish the lake after being served some of its trout at eateries in the park. The result was four decades of degradation. Powerboats roared up and down the lake, and anglers camped indiscriminately on its shores. Garbage and human waste littered the shores and polluted its waters. Bag limits were not enforced and often scoffed at by many anglers. Complaints finally brought the Park Service to the rescue.

In the early 1960s, bag limits were enforced, and powerboats were removed despite howls of protest. Later, bag limits were rolled back to compensate for the increasing number of visitors. At the same time, backcountry camping permits were required and the number of visitors per campsite was limited.

Shoshone Lake has a surprising mix of trout.

The result of the new regulations is Yellowstone Park's greatest population of brown trout. That may come as a surprise to many anglers, particularly those who frequent the Madison River. But it is certain that Shoshone Lake hosts more brown trout than the entire Madison River drainage within the park.

Shoshone Lake's other major salmonid resident is lake trout. The lake trout, which received a black eye because of its illegal introduction into Yellowstone Lake, are doing well in Shoshone Lake. In fact, the park's largest population of lake trout is in Shoshone Lake.

The lake's brown trout can range up to 8 pounds, while its lake trout tip the scales at 30 pounds. Brook trout make up a minor part of the fish population and can run up to 3 pounds. Brook trout-lake trout hybrids, known as splake, are also present and achieve the same size as the brookies.

Another resident is the Heart Lake strain of Yellowstone cutthroat trout. In the 1970s, these were planted in nearby Pocket Lake after its brook trout population was eradicated. Some Pocket Lake cutthroat descended to Shoshone Lake and grew large. I can verify this. In 1985, I caught and released a 20-inch cutthroat in Moose Creek Bay on the other side of Shoshone Lake from Pocket Lake's outlet.

Shoshone Lake's climate is as harsh as you would expect to find in northern Alberta or the Northwest Territories. Because it sits at nearly 8,000 feet, winter stays late and comes early. As a result, lake waters are cold.

The elevation also means the angling season is short, beginning with a late May to early June ice-out. Wintry weather usually closes the lake to angling in mid-October.

Storms can lash the lake's surface without warning, turning it from glass smooth to 4-foot whitecaps in minutes. Over the years, a number of people have drowned or died of hypothermia after being pitched into the lake.

The fishing experience reveals that Shoshone Lake is best early in the season. As if celebrating spring, the fish feed to the point of gorging right after ice-out.

Any streamer, nymph, or attractor pattern allowed to sink near bottom around dropoffs, shoals, inlets, submerged hot springs, or weed beds will bring action from juvenile browns and lake trout that range in size from 15 to 23 inches. Find one of these natural features and enjoy the action. Use a full-sink or sink-tip line depending on depth. A long, tapered leader is a must in Shoshone Lake's ultra-clear waters.

As the surface water warms in June, midge and Speckled Dun mayfly emergences grab the attention of cruising browns. If you rise early, you can experience the lake's best dry fly fishing during these emergences. Again, it is important to use a long, tapered leader.

The results can be acrobatic and beautiful browns that take several minutes to subdue. Once in a while, a brookie or juvenile lake trout will respond to these tactics. Midmorning winds usually end this action, but when winds die down in the evening, it repeats.

By early July, waters in the shallows warm to the point where the trout move to deeper water. So the tactics mentioned above become increasingly less effective. In a sense, fishing on Shoshone Lake "takes a nap" during midsummer, and I recommend that you seek better action elsewhere.

Fishing improves again after Labor Day. The cool weather makes the fish more active and signals the upcoming spawning season. Throughout September and early October, both browns and lake trout move to shallower waters. The lake trout head toward rocky shoals and the browns move toward the lake's outlet.

During the fall, use large, colorful streamers to explore waters around the shoals and outlet. The fish that respond will be the largest the lake has to offer. Fall is the best time of year for flyfishers to encounter the huge lake trout in Shoshone Lake. The rest of the year they reside in the lake's depths, which range to 300 feet.

There are two basic approaches to Shoshone Lake: by water and by land. For the more adventurous, a float trip starting from the boat ramp at Lewis Lake Campground is the choice. By this route, visitors travel across Lewis Lake to the outlet of the Lewis River Channel. From there, motors are not allowed. Visitors must paddle up the river, which runs through a beautiful meadow. Above the meadow, the river changes to a riffle-and-run stream. This demands a .75-mile portage to the outlet bay of Shoshone Lake.

If you prefer to backpack, here are the three routes to consider:

The shortest starts from a trailhead near DeLacey Creek on the Old Faithful-West Thumb Road. The trail follows the creek for about 3 miles to the lake. It is a flat walk, and is the best choice for carrying a float tube.

The next most convenient route starts at the trailhead just north of Lewis Lake and off the South Entrance-West Thumb Road. It's a 5-mile walk over easy terrain to the outlet bay of the lake. This is a good choice in the autumn when the brown trout are migrating to spawning redds in the channel.

If you wish to see the west end of Shoshone Lake, which hosts a large and beautiful geyser basin and very few anglers, then take the Lone Star Geyser Trail, which begins just a few miles east of Old Faithful. This choice is an 8-mile walk, but it lets you explore very lightly fished Shoshone Creek and its brook and brown trout.

No matter how you reach it, Shoshone Lake offers a wilderness angling experience of high quality—more difficult to achieve as time goes by.

(*Bruce Staples is the author of* Trout Country Flies: From Greater Yellowstone Masters, Yellowstone Park: A River Journal, *and* Snake River Country: Flies and Waters.)

Heart Lake:
A CUTTHROAT BONANZA
By Bruce Staples

Where would you fish if you could only fish one place? My choice is Yellowstone's Heart Lake Basin, without hesitation.

Its primary quarry—Yellowstone cutthroat—are found elsewhere in the region, but nowhere else will you find a stronger and more beautiful race of this native trout. Hefty lake trout are prime drawing cards, too, and whitefish complete the basin's fishing options.

Many anglers are not familiar with Heart Lake Basin for a good reason: It's 8 miles from the nearest highway. But its remoteness assures exceptional water quality and all other requirements for excellent trout populations. The long hike guarantees a wilderness angling experience because it keeps all but the most hardy away.

The most direct route is the Heart Lake Trailhead a few hundred yards north of Lewis Lake, on the east side of the South Entrance–West Thumb Road. A longer trail from the South Entrance along the Snake River requires stream crossings not always safe in wet years.

The Heart Lake Trail winds through a monotonous pine forest for the first 5 miles, but then the sulfide aroma of hot springs wafts through the trees and a sight of rare beauty meets the eyes. At the top of Heart Lake Geyser Basin, known as Paycheck Pass, the trees part to reveal Heart Lake 3 miles in the distance and 500 feet below. At the east end of the lake, the outlet to the Snake River can be seen. Traces of Outlet and Surprise Creeks are visible. On the horizon is the Absaroka Mountain Range, the park's east boundary.

As you get closer, you can guess the course of Beaver Creek through its picturesque meadow. Right at your feet, Witch Creek gurgles. It traverses the geyser basin and ends in the lake below. At certain times of the year, all these streams host cutthroat trout.

The entire vista is dominated by Mount Sheridan, which towers over the basin at 10,308 feet. Its impressive figure is graced by snow throughout the year. Its numerous springs feed the lake. Mount Sheridan resembles an enormous ice-cream sundae slipping into Heart Lake, an illusion brought about by the faults that ripped at its eastern flank.

The basin is hugely impressive in stature, especially since you know that you are already 5 miles from the closest road.

But it hasn't always been that way. Until 1960, a primitive road coursed the easy grade from the trailhead to the top of Paycheck Pass. Anglers would park at the top of the pass and portage boats down the 3-mile trail through

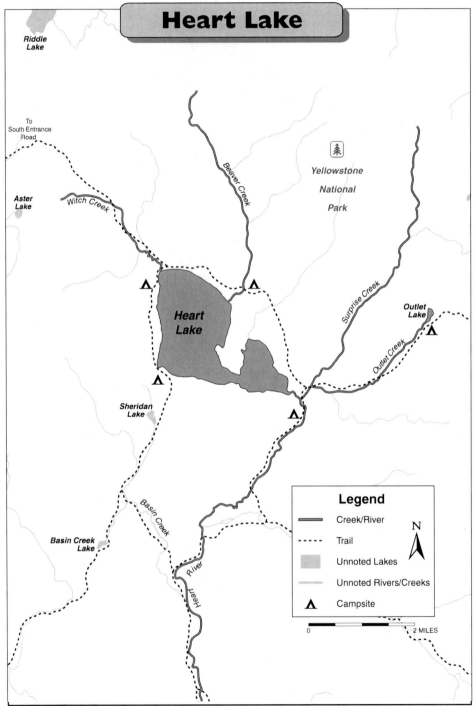

Heart Lake

Riddle
Lake

To
South Entrance
Road

Aster
Lake

Witch Creek

Beaver Creek

Yellowstone

National

Park

Heart
Lake

Surprise Creek

Outlet
Lake

Outlet Creek

Sheridan
Lake

Basin Creek

Basin Creek
Lake

Heart   River

River

Legend

— Creek/River

- - - Trail

Unnoted Lakes

Unnoted Rivers/Creeks

Λ Campsite

N

0   2 MILES

the geyser basin to the lake. Damage to the habitat—garbage—was collecting in alarming amounts, so the Park Service closed the road. Lazy anglers complained, but the rewards were quickly apparent to those who hiked to the improved fishery.

My first visits to the Heart Lake Basin were in the early 1970s, not long after my love of fly fishing began. In those days, my fishing efforts were focused on the park's fourth largest lake. Elegant cutthroat could be caught on dry or wet flies from shore right under Sheridan's heights or at the mouth of Witch Creek. Occasionally a lake trout could be lured from the depths, especially early in the season. In time I began to explore the basin's other waters.

I first discovered Heart River during a Fourth of July weekend. Its first half mile is as beautiful as a trout stream can be. It meanders through a beautiful meadow, and its crystal-clear water allows visitors to watch schools of cutthroat search for food. After the first half mile, the river drops down into a brawling canyon.

A thick, giant stonefly emergence was in full stride, and windborne adults were wafting up the river to the lake. The catching was fabulously easy. In addition to the river's residents, trout from the lake were feasting on the giant bugs. It was an unforgettable experience. I exhausted my supply of floating imitations and was left to encourage my companions as they spotted, fooled, and released all the largest trout in sight.

On another trip, I fished the river in June, only to discover that its trout ravenously accepted anything offered, from PMDs to caddis patterns to Woolly Worms. It was on that trip that I noticed the giant grizzly bear tracks that had obliterated the tracks I made that morning. It is something I will never forget.

In the early 1980s, I discovered cutthroat and occasional lake trout would be in Witch and Beaver Creeks in June. They were feasting on roe from spawning suckers. They would fatten to the point of being grotesque, yet still remained wary. The slightest hint of danger triggered a dash to the lake below. They were great sport and remain the prettiest and strongest cutthroats I have ever encountered. Fish up to 8 pounds could be fooled with almost any large, brightly colored wet fly and, occasionally, with a dry fly.

The only problem was they were not the only ones who fed off the suckers. For grizzlies, both the suckers and the trout were the main course. As a result, fishing required vigilance. Bears and man in such close proximity worried the Park Service, especially since bear habitat was diminishing while the basin was becoming more popular.

Over time, I discovered the remainder of the basin. During one trip, I ventured up Outlet and Surprise Creeks, where I was greeted by small, but eager, cutthroat. I received the same greeting in Outlet Lake. Torrential rains drove me back to camp before I could really enjoy this remote gem, so it remains a personal goal to return to it and systematically test its waters.

It was during a four-day stay in June 1985 that we learned our Heart Lake fishing patterns were going to be interrupted. The ranger at the Heart Lake Patrol Cabin told us the Park Service had determined the basin was critical grizzly bear habitat in June when they were still in the lower country. She told us the basin would no longer be open in June in order to lessen conflicts and to help the grizzlies survive.

The rule eliminated a month of great fishing, a pain I have found hard to endure. I still go to the basin today, but I've had to learn the nuances of its other seasons.

The forest fires of 1988 scarred the face of Heart Lake Basin, but they didn't impact the fishing. In the years after the fires, I learned the basin was not just a springtime fishery.

An angler gets a strike on Beaver Creek, a half mile north of Heart Lake. (Bruce Staples photo)

One of my angling friends from Jackson Hole invited me on a float-tubing trip during the second week of September to look for spawning lake trout. It taught me the best tactic for lake trout is to pitch big streamers and let them sink close to the rocky bottom and then vary the retrieve until the right combination is found. The result is huge lake trout and superb cutthroats that follow the lake trout to snitch eggs as they do from the suckers in June in the basin's creeks.

Float-tubing provides the most mobility, but also the biggest chance of a back ache after a 16-mile round trip. Chest waders also can get you out deep enough to take part in the action.

Since June is closed, pick early July for a trip. Float-tube or wade around the creek confluences using leeches and streamers. There are some caddis and Speckled Dun hatches, so be prepared for everything. There is also the stonefly hatch on the river just below the lake. To enjoy it, a 24-mile round trip is required, and camping is a must. It is important to make campsite reservations in advance and to know and follow all the park rules in bear country.

One of the newest rules is the Park Service's requirement that anglers keep all lake trout they catch to help protect the lake's unique race of cutthroat. And since you can't effectively carry them out, be prepared for a lake trout dinner. Again, beware of the bears. That may sound like a lot to consider, but the extra planning is worth the effort.

If you go, remember Heart Lake Basin is a rare resource. It offers a total wilderness with scenic surroundings and waters inhabited by perhaps the world's best cutthroat trout. Take care of it.

(Bruce Staples is the author of Trout Country Flies: From Greater Yellowstone Masters, Yellowstone Park: A River Journal, *and* Snake River Country: Flies and Waters.)

SMALL LAKES IN YELLOWSTONE

Less than 35 of Yellowstone's 140 small lakes and ponds contain trout today. However, only 17 lakes harbored fish in 1872 when the park was founded.

Stocking and hatchery programs that began in the late 1880s attempted to establish native or non-native fish in all the big lakes and the majority of the smaller ones. Yellowstone's put-and-take philosophy ended in the mid-1950s, but many of the transplants never took hold or were only briefly sustained through supplemental stockings. Others dwindled into oblivion due to inadequate spawning habitat, a fate still facing several small lakes.

Small backcountry lakes in the Yellowstone drainage contain cutthroat, except for a few isolated waters with brook trout. Some lakes in the Snake, Madison, and Gallatin drainages hold cutthroat, but most are rainbow or brook trout fisheries. Only three backcountry lakes—Grebe, Wolf, and Cascade—hold grayling.

A few ponds with trout are located near the park's loop roads, and several of the most popular fisheries are reached by hikes of 5 miles or less. Fishing in some remote lakes is not worth the hike if that is your only purpose for venturing off the beaten path. Still, they are in scenic locations and many have backcountry campsites.

Topographic hiking maps are recommended for trips into the backcountry, including day hikes. An excellent hiking guide, with notes on fish transplant attempts, is Steve Pierce's The Lakes of Yellowstone. Hikers may cross paths with grizzly bears anywhere in the park, and it's safer to hike in groups of three or more. Campers, who must make reservations in advance, need to follow rules for keeping a clean camp and campfire restrictions. Float-tubers must purchase boating permits and wear a life vest when on the water.

Park biologists rarely get enough time to sample remote lakes. Completing angler report cards greatly assists data collection on the health of Yellowstone's fisheries.

The following list details locations of small lakes and ponds by principal drainages in the park. Lakes without fish are named to help avoid confusion in making trip plans.

Upper Yellowstone River Drainage

Fishless lakes in the upper Yellowstone drainage include Glade, Aster, and Forest Lakes.

Indian Pond

- Location: 3 miles east of Fishing Bridge on East Entrance Road; Indian Pond is named Squaw Lake on older maps.
- Access: Just south of loop road.
- Topography: 24 acres; maximum depth 72 feet; elevation 7,780 feet.
- Trout: Marginal fishery for small cutthroat.
- Comments: Most people just give it a glance when walking along a scenic nature trail to a point on Yellowstone Lake.

Eleanor Lake

- Location: 7 miles west of East Entrance; 17 miles west of Fishing Bridge.
- Access: Just south of loop road.
- Topography: 2.5 acres; maximum depth 13 feet; elevation 8,450 feet.
- Trout: Cutthroat average 10 inches.
- Comments: It gets a lot of pressure after it opens to fishing on July 15; float tubes are prohibited. Also, there is better fishing down the road.

Sylvan Lake

- Location: 10 miles west of East Entrance; 16 miles east of Fishing Bridge.
- Access: Just south of loop road.
- Topography: 28 acres; very shallow, with maximum depth of 21 feet; elevation 8,410 feet.
- Trout: Cutthroat in 10- to 14-inch range.
- Comments: It gets a lot of pressure after it opens to fishing on July 15; float tubes are prohibited. Lake's outlet flows into Clear Creek, a principal spawning stream on Yellowstone Lake.

Riddle Lake

- Location: Southeast of Yellowstone Lake.
- Access: Trailhead is 2.5 miles south of Grant Village Junction on South Entrance Road; 2.5-mile hike over flat terrain.
- Topography: 274 acres; maximum depth 27 feet; elevation 7,913 feet.
- Trout: Cutthroat mostly in 14-inch range, possibilities for a larger fish.
- Comments: This lake is often closed in the early season due to grizzly bear activity in the area. Check at Grant Village or Lewis Lake Ranger Stations before setting out.
- Solution Creek, which flows out of the lake, is closed to fishing until July 15.

Trail Lake

- Location: South of South Arm of Yellowstone Lake.
- Access: 2 miles south of Trail Creek Trail to Yellowstone River delta; Trail Creek Trail connects Heart Lake Trail and Thorofare Trail to delta; total length from either direction is 25 miles or more; terrain is more extreme along Heart Lake route.
- Another option is to canoe to the bottom of the South Arm of Yellowstone Lake.
- Topography: 55 acres; maximum depth 12 feet; elevation 7,748 feet.
- Trout: Cutthroat in 14- to 18-inch range.
- Comments: This lake could be the icing on the cake during a backcountry trip of a lifetime to the upper Yellowstone. To fish it requires adding an extra overnight camp to an itinerary that involves a minimum of four days just to hike into and out of the delta. Canoers might find it a more attractive option.

Alder Lake

- Location: West side of Promontory Point separating the South and Southeast Arms of Yellowstone Lake.
- Access: Boat or canoe to the South Arm, hike about a half mile to the lake; 4-mile cross-country bushwhack hike from Trail Creek Trail.
- Topography: 123 acres; maximum depth 20 feet; elevation 7,752 feet.
- Trout: Cutthroat in 10- to 14-inch range.
- Comments: Effort involved to reach this lake makes it a questionable fishing destination for most hikers.

Middle Yellowstone River Drainage

Fishless lakes in the middle Yellowstone drainage include Beach Springs, Turbid, Wrangler, Dewdrop, Wapiti, Mirror, Tern, and Clear.

Cascade Lake

- Location: Northwest of Canyon Village.
- Access: 2.5-mile hike up Cascade Creek from trailhead on Norris Canyon Road, just west of junction; 2.5-mile hike from first picnic area on Canyon–Tower Road, north of junction; 4.5 miles west of Grebe Lake on loop hike; moderate climbs on all trails.
- Topography: 36 acres; maximum depth 27 feet; elevation 7,980 feet.
- Fish: Grayling, mostly in the 10-inch range; cutthroat in the 12-inch range.
- Comments: Cascade Lake contains the only grayling in the Yellowstone drainage of the park. Cascade Creek also is a pleasant diversion for small cutthroat when the Yellowstone River is running high or before the upper river opens.

Ribbon Lake

- Location: Northeast of Yellowstone's waterfalls.
- Access: 2-mile hike from the trailhead near scenic Artist Point; flat terrain.
- Topography: 11 acres; maximum depth 19 feet; elevation 7,820 feet.
- Trout: Marginal fishery for small rainbow.
- Comments: Marsh and thick water lily growth around lake's edges make fishing very difficult. Basically, it's a nice hiking or camping destination.

Fern Lake

- Location: North of Pelican Valley.
- Access: 12-mile hike via Pacific Creek Trail to Broad Creek Trail; moderate terrain.
- Topography: 90 acres; maximum depth 25 feet; elevation 8,245 feet.
- Trout: Marginal fishery for a few small cutthroat.
- Comments: Not worth the hike.

White Lakes

- Location: North of Pelican Valley.
- Access: 9-mile hike via Tern Lake Trail; moderate terrain.
- Topography: 90 acres; maximum depth 25 feet; elevation 8,245 feet.
- Trout: Marginal fishery for few small cutthroat.
- Comments: Not worth the hike.

Lamar River Drainage

Fishless lakes in the Lamar drainage include Buck, Shrimp, Trumpeter, Foster, and Rainey Lakes.

Trout Lake

- Location: 1.5 miles west of Pebble Creek Campground.
- Access: Half-mile steep climb from unmarked parking lot on Tower–Cooke City Road.
- Topography: 12 acres; maximum depth 17 feet; elevation 6,900 feet.
- Trout: Rainbows in the 14- to 20-inch range; a few go to 30 inches.
- Comments: Trout Lake was once the park's hatchery site for rainbows. It gets hit hard the first weeks after its June 15 opening day, especially by park employees and the region's residents, and it rarely offers a solitary experience. If there are more than a half-dozen cars in the tiny parking lot, look for a better fishing experience elsewhere. Nearby Shrimp and Buck Lakes are fishless. Inlet to Trout Lake is closed to fishing until July 15.
- This is basically a nymph fishery with small leech and damselfly patterns, Woolly Buggers, scuds, soft hackles, and beadheads. Callibaetis is the principal hatch in July and August, but sporadic hatches of other mayflies, midges, and terrestrials draw topwater action. Fishing from float tubes is the best option, but many anglers patrol its banks to sight-cast to cruising trout. Trout Lake's 90-percent satisfaction rating is the second highest in the park reported by anglers, who record a 0.74-fish-per-hour catch rate for fish averaging 14.3 inches.

McBride Lake

- Location: Above First Meadow of Slough Creek.
- Access: 3-mile hike up Slough Creek Trail, and 2-mile cross-country bushwhack to lake; moderate climbs on both routes.
- Topography: 23 acres; maximum depth 22 feet; elevation 6,560 feet.
- Trout: Cutthroat in the 10- to 14-inch range; a few larger fish.
- Comments: Mosquitoes and deerflies are fierce in marshes above Slough Creek, and this is prime grizzly bear country. Carry spray repellents for both contingencies, and don't hike alone. A topo map is recommended whenever a hike departs from a groomed trail.
- McBride Lake was the source of Montana's brood stock for Yellowstone cutthroat. Wyoming developed one of its brood stocks from Montana's McBride cutthroat,

but currently is developing a new brood stock from eggs collected at the LeHardy Rapids of the Yellowstone River.

Lower Yellowstone and Gardner River Drainages

Fishless lakes in the lower Yellowstone and Gardner drainages include Mammoth Beaver Ponds, Rainbow, Cache, Twin, Swan, Crevice, Geode, Nymph, Beaver, Phantom, Floating Island, Lake of the Woods, and Obsidian.

Blacktail Ponds

- Location: 7 miles east of Mammoth on Mammoth–Tower Road.
- Access: Near loop road.
- Topography: 11 acres; shallow with maximum depth of 26 feet; elevation 6,600 feet.
- Trout: Cutthroat and brook trout average 14 inches.
- Special regulations: Release all cutthroat. Limit on brook trout is five fish under 13 inches.
- Comments: In early season, the lakes are often closed to protect nesting trumpeter swans or sandhill cranes. A very popular fishery, it is called "Shaky Lake" by some because of marsh and spongy banks surrounding it, plus mud-sucking flats as levels diminish. It's basically a small nymph, leech, damselfly, and scud fishery. Callibaetis is the main mayfly hatch; small terrestrials may bring topwater action in late summer.

Fawn Lake

- Location: Southwest of Mammoth above Gardner Meadows.
- Access: 5-mile hike via Glenn Creek–Fawn Pass Trail; moderate terrain.
- Topography: 5 acres; shallow lake with maximum depth of 18 feet; elevation 7,800 feet.
- Trout: Brook trout in the 10- to 14-inch range.
- Special regulations: Brook trout limit on Fawn Lake is five fish under 13 inches. Children 11 or younger may fish with worms as bait.
- Comments: This is a possible side trip on a popular hiking and horseback riding trail in the scenic northwest corner of Yellowstone.

Joffe Lake

- Location: 1 mile southeast of Mammoth.
- Access: Just off the bottom of Bunsen Peak Road, which passes through the employee housing area east of the Mammoth–Norris Loop Road.
- Topography: 1.5 acres; maximum depth 9 feet; elevation 6,500 feet.
- Trout: Pan-sized brook trout.
- Comments: Great spot to teach a child to fly cast to eagerly rising trout. Children 11 or younger may fish with worms as bait.

Slide Lakes

- Location: 2 miles northwest of Mammoth.
- Access: Gravel road behind Mammoth Inn that goes to North Entrance; no trail to lower lake, which holds rainbow trout.
- Topography: 1 acre; maximum depth 43 feet; elevation 5,170 feet.
- Trout: Sparse population of rainbows.
- Comments: The chances of spotting antelope and other wildlife up close on this road outweigh fishing opportunities. The road is usually closed during wet weather.

Grizzly Lake

- Location: 6 miles northwest of Norris Campground on Norris–Mammoth Road.
- Access: Steep 2-mile climb from trailhead; easier route in is to follow Straight Creek upstream from Apollinaris Springs Trailhead, a mile or so north on the loop road.
- Topography: 136 acres; maximum depth 36 feet; elevation 7,508 feet.
- Trout: Pan-sized brook trout.
- Comments: Grizzly Lake is a popular day hike, although campsites on Straight Creek are available for a loop trip. Brookies are a little bigger in Straight Creek.

Madison River Drainage

Fishless lakes in the Madison drainage include Ice, Feather, Harlequin, Nymph, Lower Basin, Mary, Nuthatch, Isa, Scaup, and Mallard.

Grebe Lake

- Location: Northeast of Virginia Cascade on Gibbon River.
- Access: 3.5-mile hike from trailhead on Norris Canyon Road; relatively flat terrain.
- Topography: 156 acres; maximum depth of 32 feet; elevation 8,000 feet.
- Fish: Rainbows mostly in the 14-inch range; grayling around 11 inches.
- Comments: Grebe Lake is the source of the Gibbon River. By far the most popular small backcountry lake in the park, it sees relatively heavy pressure early in the season when grayling spawn at the outlet in mid-June. The hike along an old grayling hatchery road crosses marshy areas in wet years, and mosquitoes can be fierce. This region is prime grizzly bear country and should not be entered alone.
- The best option is to pack in a float tube. Small nymphs and emergers work very well for grayling, along with medium-sized black or purple Woolly Buggers, damsel nymphs, leeches, and Zug Bugs. Watch for sporadic caddis and mayfly hatches, primarily Callibaetis, and terrestrials as the summer progresses. Rainbows help keep the fishing hopping. Grebe Lake has the highest catch rate in the park—1.94 fish per hour—and anglers give it an 89-percent satisfaction rating for fish averaging 9.9 inches.
- In wet years, grayling spill out of the lake and into the Gibbon and down into the upper Madison River.

Wolf Lake

- Location: 2 miles southwest of Grebe Lake outlet.
- Access: 5-mile hike from Ice Lake Trailhead on Norris Canyon Road, or backtrack from Grebe Lake Trail.
- Topography: 5 acres; maximum depth of 32 feet; elevation 7,998 feet.
- Fish: Grayling and rainbows average 10 inches.
- Comments: Wolf Lake is a stopping point on the Gibbon River's course downstream. Spawning habitat is sparse and grayling and rainbows are smaller than in Grebe Lake. There are no fish in nearby Ice Lake.

Goose Lake

- Location: Fountain Flats south of Firehole River.
- Access: 2-mile hike from Fairy Falls Trailhead south of Nez Perce bridge on Madison–Old Faithful Road; 3-mile hike from Steel Bridge Trailhead west of Black Sand Basin; flat terrain.
- Topography: 34 acres; maximum depth of 31 feet; elevation 7,170 feet.
- Trout: Very marginal fishery for rainbows.
- Comments: Rarely fished, Goose Lake was poisoned in 1937 to eliminate the unauthorized transplant of yellow perch. Attempts to establish browns failed, and the rainbow population continues to dwindle.

Gallatin River Drainage

Fishless lakes in the Gallatin drainage include Gallatin, Divide, Shelf, Crescent, and Crag.

High Lake

- Location: On park's northwest boundary in the Gallatin Mountains.
- Access: 10-mile hike via north spur off Sportsman Lake Trail, which starts from mouth of Bacon Rind Creek on Gallatin River, on US 191; rugged terrain.
- Topography: 7 acres; maximum depth of 18 feet; elevation 8,774 feet.
- Trout: Cutthroat in the 8- to 11-inch range.
- Comments: Remote location of this lake makes it more a hiking destination or an overnight camping site.

Sportsman Lake

- Location: 5 miles west of Electric Peak in Gallatin Mountains.
- Access: 12-mile hike from trailhead at mouth of Specimen Creek on Gallatin River, on US 191, or 14-mile hike from south of Mammoth via the Glenn Creek Trail to Sportsman Lake Trail; eastern route much more extreme.
- Topography: 7 acres; shallow lake with maximum depth of 26 feet; elevation 7,730 feet.
- Trout: Cutthroat in the 8- to 11-inch range.

- Comments: Remote location of this lake makes it more a hiking destination or an overnight camping site. The Mammoth route crosses a high, steep pass south of 10,992-foot Electric Peak, the highest point in Yellowstone.

Snake River Drainage

Fishless lakes in the Snake drainage are mostly in the Fall River Basin. They include Lilypad, Winegar, Robinson, Wyodaho, Buffalo, South Boundary, and Summit.

Sheridan Lake

- Location: Southwest of Heart Lake.
- Access: 12-mile hike via Heart Lake Trailhead on South Entrance Road.
- Topography: 15 acres; very shallow lake; elevation 7,378 feet; rugged terrain.
- Trout: Small population of pan-sized cutthroat.
- Comments: There is much better fishing in nearby Heart Lake.

Basin Creek Lake

- Location: Southwest of Heart Lake.
- Access: 2.5 miles southwest of Heart Lake; or 11-mile hike via Southern Boundary Trail, starting at South Entrance, and Heart Lake Trail from Snake River; rugged terrain.
- Topography: 8 acres; maximum depth of 17 feet; elevation 7,390 feet.
- Trout: Pan-sized cutthroat.
- Comments: There is much better fishing in nearby Heart Lake.

Outlet Lake

- Location: East of Heart Lake below rim of Continental Divide.
- Access: 4-mile hike from Heart Lake on Trail Creek Trail; rugged terrain.
- Topography: 16 acres; very shallow lake; elevation 7,749 feet.
- Trout: Pan-sized cutthroat.
- Comments: Possible overnight campsite on hike into or out of upper Yellowstone delta.

Mariposa Lake

- Location: On Two Ocean Plateau northeast of headwaters of Snake River.
- Access: 30-mile hike from Southern Boundary Trailhead at South Entrance; very rugged terrain.
- Topography: 12 acres; very shallow; elevation 8,950 feet.
- Trout: Cutthroat and cutthroat-rainbow hybrids in the 8- to 12-inch range.
- Comments: This is the highest and most remote backcountry lake in Yellowstone. It is also in the heart of grizzly bear country. Campsites offer possible stopovers on the longest route to the upper Yellowstone River, across the Continental Divide.

Pocket Lake

- Location: Above Shoshone Lake.
- Access: Half-mile steep climb from northwest corner of Shoshone Lake; easiest route in is the 3-mile hike on DeLacy Creek Trail from Old Faithful–West Thumb Road, and 2-mile hike to mouth of lake's outlet.
- Topography: 14 acres; maximum depth of 24 feet; elevation 8,100 feet.
- Trout: Cutthroat average 14 inches, with a few in the 18- to 20-inch range.
- Comments: Heart Lake cutthroat were planted in Pocket Lake in the mid-1980s to establish a second population as a hedge against anything happening to the unique strain of Yellowstone cutthroat. Brook trout in the lake were poisoned but have returned. In 1998, the park issued a mandatory kill order for brook trout hooked by anglers in Pocket Lake. The cutthroat, which occasionally show up in Shoshone Lake, are protected by a catch-and-release rule.

Beula Lake

- Location: West of South Entrance and Flagg Ranch.
- Access: 2.5-mile hike from trailhead at Grassy Lake, 9 miles west of Flagg Ranch on rough gravel road that skirts southern boundary of the park; relatively flat terrain.
- Topography: 107 acres; maximum depth of 36 feet; elevation 7,377 feet.
- Trout: Cutthroat in the 10- to 14-inch range, with some larger fish.
- Comments: Beula Lake is the source of the Fall River. It fishes best in late summer and fall from a float tube. Sporadic caddis and mayfly hatches and small terrestrials offer topwater options. Moderate-sized leeches, Woolly Buggers, small nymphs, emergers and beadheads, and scuds are all effective for prospecting with wet flies. Hering Lake is just upstream. Grizzly bears are common, so don't enter this littleexplored corner of the park alone, and keep a clean camp on overnight stays.

Hering Lake

- Location: Half mile southeast of Beula Lake.
- Access: Backtrack from Beula Lake Trail by following inlet channel.
- Topography: 60 acres; maximum depth of 44 feet; elevation 7,381 feet.
- Trout: Cutthroat average about 12 inches.
- Comments: Good side trip from Beula Lake if trip allows enough time to explore.

Ranger Lake

- Location: East of Bechler River.
- Access: Half-mile hike from northeast side of Bechler Meadows; no trail, moderate climb.
- Topography: 58 acres; maximum depth of 38 feet; elevation 6,980 feet.
- Trout: Rainbows in the 8- to 10-inch range.
- Comments: This lake offers minor reward for a lot of extra effort.

Bozeman, Montana
Elevation – 4,950 • Population – 39,282

Known for its blue-ribbon trout fishing and great skiing, Bozeman is a rapidly growing resort and college town. There has been a recent population boom, resulting in crowded conditions and high prices. However, Bozeman has a lot to offer the flyfisher. There is still a small town atmosphere with big city amenities: good air service, shopping, fine restaurants, and outdoor activities. Bozeman's zip code is 59715.

Accommodations

Days Inn, 1321 North 7th Avenue / 406-587-5251 / 80 rooms / Cable, continental breakfast / Dogs allowed, $25 deposit / $$ / www.daysinn.com

Fairfield Inn, 828 Wheat Drive / 406-587-2222 / 57 rooms, 12 suites w/kitchenettes / Continental breakfast, pool, and jacuzzi / Dogs allowed, no restrictions / $$-$$$ / www.marriott.com

Holiday Inn, 5 Baxter Lane / 406-587-4561 / 178 units / Restaurant, bar, pool and jacuzzi, cable / Dogs allowed, but not unattended in rooms / $$$ / www.hibozeman.com

Holiday Inn Express, 6261 Jackrabbit Lane, Belgrade / 406-388-0800 or 800-542-6791 / 67 rooms / Dogs allowed / $$ / www.hiexpress.com

Super 8, 6450 Jackrabbit Lane, Belgrade / 72 rooms / 406-388-1493 800-800-8000 / dogs allowed / www.super8.com

The Bozeman Inn, 1235 North 7th Avenue / 406-587-3176 / 45 rooms / Outdoor pool, sauna, cable / Mexican restaurant and lounge / Dogs allowed for a $5 fee / $$ / www.bozemaninn.com

TroutChasers Lodge, 77017 Gallatin Rd / 406-763-9049 / www.montanatroutchasers.com

Gallatin River Lodge, 9105 Thorpe Road / 406-388-0148 / restaurant and guide service / www.grlodge.com

Campgrounds And Rv Parks

Bozeman KOA, 8 miles west on US 91 / 406-587-3030 / Open year–round / 50 tent and 100 RV spaces / Full services including laundry and store

Sunrise Campground, 31842 Frontage Road / 406-587-4797

Bear Canyon Campground, at I-90 Exit 313 / 800-438-1575 / www.bearcanyoncampground.com

Restaurants

John Bozeman's Bistro, 242 East Main / 406-587-4100 / International and regional specialties / www.johnbozemansbistro.com

Pickle Barrel, 809 W. College, 406-597-2411 / Sub Sandwiches / www.picklebarrelmt.com

Mackenzie River Pizza Co., 232 E. Main St., 406-587-0055 / North 19th St & Rawhide Ridge, 406-582-0099 / 409 W. Main St., Belgrade, 406-388-0016 / Fancy pizzas, pasta, salad / www.mackenzieriverpizza.com

Montana Ale Works, 611 East Main St. / 406-587-7700 / Sunday-Wednesday 4 p.m.-12 a.m., Thursday-Saturday 4 p.m. – 1 a.m. / Regional American cuisine and microbrewed ales / www.montanaaleworks.com

Ferraro's Fine Italian Restaurant, 726 N. 7th Ave. / 587-2555 / fine Italian cuisine cocktails / open for dinner / www.ferrarosfineitalian.com

Mama Mac's, SW Corner of Four Corners / 522-8690 / open from 6a.m. to 3p.m. for breakfast and lunch, will pack lunches

Ted's Montana Grill, 105 West Main Street (in the Baxter Hotel) / 406-587-6000 / Ted Turner's hamburger joint / www.tedsmontanagrill.com

Mint Bar and Grill, 27 East Main Street, Belgrade / 406-388-1100 / Great steaks and seafood / Good selection of single malt Scotches / www.themintmt.com

VETERINARIANS

All West Veterinary Hospital, 105 All West Trail / 406-586-4919 / Gary Cook, Honor Nesbet, David E. Catlin, DVMs / 24-hour emergency service

Animal Medical Center, 216 North 8th Avenue / 406-587-2946 / Sue Barrows, DVM / Emergency service / www.amcbozeman.com

Faithful Friends Animal Clinic, 205 Edelweiss Drive (behind Perkins) / 406-585-7387

FLY SHOPS AND SPORTING GOODS

Bob Ward and Sons, 3011 Max Ave. / 406-586-4381 / www.bobwards.com

Greater Yellowstone Flyfishers, 29 Pioneer Way / 406-585-5321 / www.gyflyfishers.com

The River's Edge, 2012 North 7th Avenue / 406-586-5373 / www.theriversedge.com

Yellowstone Gateway Sports, 21 Fork Horn Trail / 406-586-2076 / www.yellowstonegateway.com

Montana Troutfitters, 1716 West Main / 406-587-4707 / www.troutfitters.com

Bozeman Angler, 23 East Main / 406-587-9111 or 800-886-9111 / www.bozemanangler.com

Fins 'n' Feathers, SW Corner of 4 Corners, 81801 Gallatin Rd / 406-585-2917 / www.finsandfeathersonline.com

Wholesale Sports, 2214 Tschache Lane / 406-586-0100 / www.wholesalesports.com

OUTFITTERS

(all fly shops offer guide services)

C. Francis & Co., Chris Francis / guided flyfishing trips in Montana and Argentina / 877-898-4005 / www.c-francis.com

Dave McKee Fly Fishing, 431 N. Grand Ave / 406-582-0980 / www.davemckeeflyfishing.com

Grossenbacher Guides / 406-582-1760 / www.grossenbacherguides.com
Montana Angler, 76 Lucille Lane / 406-522-9854 / www.montanaangler.com

Auto Rental And Repair

Budget Rent-A-Car of Bozeman, Gallatin Field / 406-388-4091
Avis Rent-A-Car, Gallatin Field / 406-388-6414
Hertz Rent-A-Car, Gallatin Field / 406-388-6939
Enterprise Rent-A-Car, 1238 West Main Street / 406-586-8010

Air Service

Gallatin Field Airport, 8 miles west of Bozeman in Belgrade on Frontage Road
/ 406-388-6632 / Served by Delta, United, Northwest, Horizon and Frontier /
Charter service available / www.bozemanairport.com

Medical

Bozeman Deaconess Hospital, 915 Highland Boulevard / 406-585-5000.

For More Information

Bozeman Chamber of Commerce
2000 Commerce Way
Bozeman, MT 59715
406-586-5421
www.bozemanchamber.com

Big Sky, Montana
Elevation – 6,200 • Population – 1,559

Accommodations

Best Western Buck's T-4 Lodge, US Hwy. 191 / 406-995-4111 or 800-822-4484 / 74
rooms / pets allowed / Dining room serves dinner / www.buckst4.com
River Rock Lodge, 3080 Pine Drive / 866-995-4455 / www.riverrocklodging.com
Lone Mountain Ranch, Big Sky Spur Road / 406-995-2782 / www.lmranch.com
320 Guest Ranch, Hwy. 191, Mile Marker 36 / 800.243.0320 or 406.995.4283 /
www.320ranch.com

Restaurants

Buck's T-4 Lodge, Hwy 191 / dinner nighty from 6–9:30pm / 406-995-4111
Lone Mountain Ranch, Big Sky Spur Road / fine dining / 406-995-2782
Lone Peak Brewery, 48 Market Place / 406-995-3939 / www.lonepeakbrewery.com

Fly Shops

East Slope Outdoors, Hwy. 191 / 406-995-4369 / www.eastslopeoutdoors.com
Gallatin River Guides, Hwy. 191 / 406-995-2290 / www.montanaflyfishing.com
Wild Trout Outfitters, Hwy 191 / 800-423-4742 / www.wildtroutoutfitters.com

Cody, Wyoming
Elevation—5,016 • Population—9,317

Founded by William F. "Buffalo Bill" Cody in 1896, Cody is the quintessential Old West tourist town. The Cody Nite Rodeo has been a summer feature since 1938. The Buffalo Bill Historical Center has a vast collection of western exhibits in its four museums—the Buffalo Bill Museum, the Plains Indian Museum, the Cody Firearms Museum, and the Whitney Gallery of Western Art.

Only an hour's drive to the west is Yellowstone National Park via the Wapiti Valley of the North Fork of the Shoshone River. President Teddy Roosevelt called it the most scenic 50 miles in North America. Just two miles from the park is Buffalo Bill's original hunting lodge, Pahaska Teepee. And The Irma, the hotel named for his daughter, is still the town's favorite watering hole. An hour northwest of town is Sunlight Basin and Wyoming's only Wild and Scenic River, the Clark's Fork of the Yellowstone. The Clark's Fork and North Fork Shoshone are rated as two of the best dry fly streams in the West. Their feeder streams flowing down the Absaroka Mountains in the Shoshone National Forest further entice flyfishers to the highlands. Cody's zip code is 82414.

ACCOMMODATIONS

AmericInn, 508 Yellowstone Ave. / 800-634-3444 / www.americinn.com / 46 rooms
Best Western Sunset Motor Inn, 1601 8th St. / 307-587-4265 / 120 rooms, pets allowed with fee
Big Bear Motel, 139 West Yellowstone Avenue / 307-587-3117 / www.bigbearmotel.com / 42 rooms / Pets allowed / $
Buffalo Bill Village, 1701 Sheridan Avenue / 800-527-5544 / www.blairhotels.com / 83 rooms / $$
The Irma Hotel, 1192 Sheridan Avenue / 307-587-4221 / www.irmahotel.com / Historic hotel, 40 rooms / $$
Buffalo Bill Cody House (B&B), 101 Robertson Street / 307-587-2528 / www.buffalobillcodybb.com / Hosts: Mr. & Mrs. Philip W. Robertson
The Cody Hotel, 232 West Yellowstone Avenue, Cody, Wyoming 82414 / 307-587-5915 / thecody.com
The Lambright Place, 1501 Beck Ave / 307-527-5310 / www.lambrightplace.com
Pahaska Teepee, 183 Yellowstone Hwy. / 307-527-7701 or 800-628-7791 / www.pahaska.com / Cabins, restaurant and lounge, and grocery/gas station
Crossed Sabres Ranch, 829 North Fork Highway / 307-587-3750 / Guest ranch
Rimrock Ranch, 2728 North Fork Route / 307-587-3970 / www.rimrockranch.com / Guest ranch
Shoshone Lodge, 349 Yellowstone Hwy., 3 miles east of the park / Resort & Guest Ranch / 307-587-4044 / www.yellowstone-lodging.com/shoshone.html

CAMPGROUNDS AND RV PARKS

Cody KOA Kampground, 5561 Greybull Highway / 307-587-2369 / Open May 1 to October 1 / 100 RV and 90 tent sites / Full services / www.codykoa.com

Gateway Motel & Campground, 203 Yellowstone Avenue / 307-587-2561 / Open April 1 to October 1 / 74 RV and tent sites / Full services

Ponderosa Campground, 1815 8th Street / 307-587-9203 / www.codyponderosa.com

Parkway Trailer & RV Park, 132 Yellowstone Avenue / 307-527-5927

Absaroka Bay RV, 2002 Mountain View Drive / 307-527-7440 / www.cody-wy.com

RESTAURANTS

Adriano's Italian Restaurant, 1244 Sheridan Ave. / lunch & dinner / 307-527-7320

Granny's Restaurant, 1550 Sheridan Avenue / 307-587-4829

The Irma Hotel, 1192 Sheridan Avenue / 307-587-4221 / www.irmahotel.com

La Comida, 1385 Sheridan Ave. / Lunch & dinner / 307-587-9556

The Proud Cut Saloon, 1227 Sheridan Avenue / 307-527-6905

Zapatas, 1362 Sheridan Avenue / 307-527-7181

VETERINARIANS

Chadwick Veterinary Hospital, 3008 Big Horn Avenue / 307-527-7213

Cody Animal Health, 2320 Sheridan Avenue / 307-587-2631

OUTFITTERS

North Fork Anglers, 1438 Sheridan Avenue / 307-527-727 / www.northforkanglers.com

Monster Lake, Desert Ranch 10 miles south of Cody on WYO 120 / 800-840-5137 / www.monsterlake.com

Eastgate Anglers, 548 County Rd. 2AB / 307-587-3059 / www.eastgateanglers.com

FLY SHOPS

North Fork Anglers, 1438 Sheridan Avenue / 307-527-7274 / www.northforkanglers.com

The Humble Fly Shop, 1183 Sheridan Ave / 307-587-2757 / www.thehumblefly.com

Rocky Mountain Discount Sports, 1526 Rumsey Ave / 307-527-6071

AUTO RENTAL AND REPAIR

Hertz Rent-A-Car, Box 847, Cody, WY 82414 / 307-587-2914 / www.hertz.com

Thrifty Cody Car Rental, 3001 Duggleby Dr, Cody -307-587-8855 / www.thrifty.com

Avis Rent-A-Car: Cody - Yellowstone Regional Airport, 3001 Duggleby Drive / 307-587-4082 / www.avis.com

Dollar Rent-A-Car, 3001 Duggleby Drive / 307-587-4082 / www.dollar.com

AIR SERVICE

Yellowstone Regional Airport, 1 mile south of Cody / Served by Skywest–Delta
Connection via Salt Lake and United Express via Denver / Charter services
available / 307-587-5096 / www.flyyra.com

MEDICAL

West Park Hospital, 707 Sheridan Avenue / 307-527-7501 or 800-654-9447 /
www.westparkhospital.org

FOR MORE INFORMATION

Cody Chamber of Commerce
836 Sheridan Avenue
Cody, WY 82414
307-587-2777
www.codychamber.org

Cooke City, Montana

Elevation—7,500 • Population—142

Cooke City and its sister community, Silver Gate, are rustic mountain hamlets
retaining elements of their gold mining history that preceded the founding of
Yellowstone National Park. Yellowstone's Northeast Entrance is 4 miles west of Cooke
City at the end of the two most picturesque drives to the park: The Beartooth
Scenic Highway via U.S. 212 from Red Lodge, Montana, and the Chief Joseph Scenic
Highway via WYO 296 from Cody. Soda Butte Creek flows through the two hamlets
and leads anglers to the Lamar River and Yellowstone's superb fishing. Just over
Colter Pass and east of Cooke City, you will find the headwaters of the Clark's Fork of
the Yellowstone, an unforgettable invitation to Wyoming's blue ribbon trout streams.
Beartooth Pass (11,000 feet) and Colter Pass (8,000 feet) on U.S. 212 are blocked by
snow until late May. The road from Gardiner, Montana, via Mammoth and the Park's
Lamar Valley is open year-round. Cooke City's zip code is 59020.

ACCOMMODATIONS

Alpine Motel, 105 Main Street, Box 1030, Cooke City, MT 59020 / 406-838-2262 or
888-838-1190 / www.ccalpinemotel.com / 88 rooms / $$
Antlers Lodge, 311 Main Street East / 406-838-2432 / 18 rooms / $ /
www.cookecityantlerslodge.com
Elkhorn Lodge, 103 Main Street / 406-838-2332 / www.elkhornlodgemt.com / 6
rooms / Pets allowed / $$$
Grizzly Lodge, U.S. 212, Box 9, Silver Gate / 406-838-2219 /
www.yellowstonelodges.com / 17 rooms / $$
Silver Gate Cabins, 107 US Hwy 212 / Silver Gate MT 59081 / 406-838-2371 /
www.silver-gate-cabins.com

Whispering Pines Cabins, HC 84 Box 48 Silver Gate MT 59081 / 406-838-2371 / www.yellowstone-park-lodging.com

CAMPGROUNDS AND RV PARKS

Big Moose Resort, 3 miles east of Cooke City on U.S. 212 / 406-838-2393 / www.bigmooseresort.com / Open June 1 to September 30 / 10 tent and 6 RV sites / 7 cabins / Store / Pets allowed
(Many other campgrounds in Yellowstone)

RESTAURANTS

Beartooth Cafe, Highway 212 / 406-838-2475 / www.beartoothcafe.com
Buns N Beds, 201 E Main St / 406-838-2030

OUTFITTERS

Beartooth Plateau Outfitters, Main Street (P.O. Box 1127) / 406-838-2328 or 800-253-8545 / www.beartoothoutfitters.com
Greater Yellowstone Outfitters, 211 W. Main (P.O. Box 1150) / 406-838-2468
Skyline Guide Service, Box 507, Cooke City, MT 59020 / 406-838-2380 / www.flyfishyellowstone.com

FLY SHOPS AND SPORTING GOODS

Beartooth Plateau Outfitters, Main Street (P.O. Box 1127) / 406-838-2328 or 800-253-8545 / www.beartoothoutfitters.com
Parks' Fly Shop, 202 South 2nd Street, Gardiner / 406-848-7314 / www.parksflyshop.com

AUTO RENTAL AND REPAIR

No auto rental. Nearest repair shop and wrecker service is Yellowstone National Park at Canyon Village.

MEDICAL

Call 911 in case of an emergency. Emergency medical services are provided by rangers on duty.
Yellowstone National Park's Lake Hospital, 307-242-7241 / Lake Hospital is open from mid-May to mid-September
Mammoth Clinic, 307-344-7965 / Mammoth Clinic is open year-round
Old Faithful Clinic, Old Faithful Clinic is open from early May to mid-October

FOR MORE INFORMATION

Cooke City Chamber of Commerce
109 W. Main St.
Cooke City, Montana
406-838-2495
www.cookecitychamber.org

Gardiner and the Northeast Entrance to Yellowstone.

Gardiner, Montana
Elevation—5,286 • Population—867

Gardiner is located at the confluence of the Gardner and Yellowstone rivers at Yellowstone's north entrance. Named for a fur trapper, Gardiner was founded in 1880 and was originally a mining boomtown. It is the only year-round entrance to the park, and the only year-round road through the park runs through the Lamar Valley from Gardiner to Cooke City, Montana. There is incredible scenery in the area, as well as access to excellent fishing. Gardiner's zip code is 59030.

ACCOMMODATIONS

Absaroka Lodge, Hwy. 89 / 406-874-7414, 800-755-7414 / On the Yellowstone River / 41 rooms / $$$ / www.yellowstonemotel.com

Comfort Inn, 107 Hellroaring Street / 406-848-7536 / www.comfortinn.com

Yellowstone River Motel, 14 East Park Street / 406-848-7303 / www.yellowstonerivermotel.com

Super 8 Motel, 702 Scott Street West / 406-878-7401 / $ / www.yellowstonesuper8.com

Camping

Rocky Mountain Campground, Hwy. 89 / 406-848-7251 /
www.rockymountaincampground.com
Yellowstone RV Park and Campground, 117 Highway 89 S (west of Gardiner) /
406-848-7496 / www.ventureswestinc.com
(Many other campgrounds in Yellowstone)

Restaurants

Town Café, Motel, Lounge & Gift Shop, 120 East Park Street / 406-848-7322
Sawtooth Deli, 220 W. Park Street / 406-848-7600
Outlaw's Pizza, 906 Scott Street / 406-848-7733
Pedalino's, 204 Park St / 406-848-9950 / Italian food

Fly Shop

Park's Fly Shop, 202 Second Street South (US-89) / 406-848-7314 / Licenses /
Flyfishing guides and instructors / Full service fly shop / www.parksflyshop.com
Knoll's Fly Shop, 104 Chicory Road, Pray / 406-333-4848 / www.knolls.us / Hackle
specialists

For More Information

Gardiner Chamber of Commerce
233 Main Street
Gardiner, MT 59030
406-848-7971
www.gardinerchamber.com

Island Park, Idaho

Elevation—6,380 • Population—winter, 229; summer, 20,000

Island Park, located near Island Park Reservoir on the Henry's Fork of the Snake, is
an easy drive from West Yellowstone and the West Entrance of the park. From here,
you can also drive south to Ashton and the park's Cascade Corner to fish the Fall and
Bechler rivers. Also nearby are the famed waters of the Henry's Fork, Henry's Lake,
and Island Park Reservoir. Island Park and its surrounding areas share the zip code
83429.

Accommodations

Henry's Fork Lodge, 2794 S Pinehaven Dr / 208-558-7953 /
www.henrysforklodge.com
Mack's Inn Resort, 4292 U.S. 20 / 208-558-7272 / www.macksinn.com
Phillips Lodge, 3907 Phillips Loop Rd / 208-558-9939 / www.pinesislandpark.com
Lazy Trout Lodge, 4771 North Hwy 20 / 208-558-7407
Pond's Lodge, 3757 N. Hwy 20 / 208-558-7221 / www.pondslodge.com

Wild Rose Ranch, 3778 Highway 87, on Henry's Lake / 208-558-7201 /
www.wildroseranch.com

Island Park Lodge, 4149 N Big Springs Loop Rd / 208-558-7281 /
www.islandparklodge.org

CAMPGROUNDS

Redrock RV & Camping Park, 3707 Red Rock Rd / 208 558-7442 /
www.8004redrock.com / Open May through September

Sawtelle Mountain Resort, 4133 Lodge Pole Dr / 800-574-0404 /
www.sawtellemountainresort.com

Henry's Lake State Park, 3917 E. 5100 N. / 208-558-7532

Buffalo Run RV Park, 3402 N Highway 20 / 208-558-7112 /
www.buffaloruncampground.com

RESTAURANTS

Henry's Fork Lodge, 2794 S Pinehaven Dr / 208-558-7953 /
www.henrysforklodge.com

Ponds Lodge, 3757 N. Hwy 20 / 208-558-7221 / www.pondslodge.com

Angler's Lodge, 3363 Old Hwy 191 / 208-558-9555 / www.anglerslodge.net

Henry's Fork Landing, 4298 Highway 20, Macks Inn / 208-558-7672

FLY SHOPS AND SPORTING GOODS

Henry's Fork Anglers, 3340 Highway 20 / 208-558-7525 / Mike Lawson /
www.henrysforkanglers.com

Trout Hunter, 3327 N. Highway 20 / 208-558-9900 / www.trouthunt.com

Three Rivers Ranch, 3386 N Hwy 20 / 208-558-7501 / www.threeriversranch.com

BS Flies Shop, 3757 N. Hwy 20 (in Pond's Lodge) / 208-390-2177 / www.bsflies.com

Hyde Outfitters & Last Chance Lodge, 1520 Pancheri Drive, Idaho Falls /
800-428-8338 / www.hydeoutdoors.com

AIRPORT

Idaho Falls Regional Airport, 2140 N. Skyline Drive, Idaho Falls, 75 miles south

AUTO RENTAL

Closest is in Idaho Falls, or West Yellowstone, Montana

AUTO SERVICE

Hungry Bear Auto Repair and Towing, 4562 Highway 20 / 208-558-0100

FOR MORE INFORMATION

Island Park Chamber
4149 S Big Springs Rd
Macks Inn, ID 83433
208-558-7755
www.islandparkchamber.org

Livingston, Montana
Elevation – 4,503 • Population – 7,380

Livingston is located in south-central Montana, on a big bend of the Yellowstone River 53 miles north of Yellowstone National Park and 25 miles east of Bozeman. It sits in the lovely Paradise Valley, surrounded by the Absaroka-Beartooth Wilderness and the Gallatin, Bridger, and Crazy Mountain Ranges. Livingston is a hospitable western town, with over six hundred rooms in its hotels, motels, and bed and breakfasts. It offers excellent eateries and is considered by many seasoned flyfishers the king of western trout fishing towns. Campgrounds, scenic areas, and fishing access sites are readily available. Livingston's zip code is 59047.

ACCOMMODATIONS

The Murray Hotel, 201 West Park / 406-222-1350 / Located downtown, next to Dan Bailey's Fly Shop / Newly renovated, deluxe, turn-of-the century hotel / 40 charming guest rooms with or without adjoining baths / The Winchester Cafe and Murray Bar are adjoining / Dogs allowed / $$ / www.murrayhotel.com

Comfort Inn, 114 Loves Lane, right off free way exit / 49 rooms / 406-222-4400 / www.comfortinn.com

Chico Hot Springs, Pray / 406-333-4933 / Located 23 miles south of Livingston on route 89 / Inn has 50 Rooms / Motel has 24 rooms, 4 cabins, 3 cottages with kitchens, log house with kitchen, 2 condos with kitchens / Mineral hot springs pool / Chico Inn gourmet dining room / Poolside Grill, Saloon / Dogs allowed, $2 charge / $$ / www.chicohotsprings.com

Best Western Inn, 1515 W.Park St. / 98 rooms / 406-222-6110 / pets allowed / www.bestwesternmontana.com

Country Motor Inn, 814 E. Park St / 406-222-1923

Livingston Inn, 5 Rogers Ln, / 406-222-3600

RESTAURANTS

Montana Rib and Chop House, 119 West Park / 406-222-9200 / Spirits, beer, wine, steaks, and ribs / www.ribandchophouse.com

Chico Hot Springs, Pray / 406-333-4933 / 23 miles south of Livingston on Route 89 / Fine dining, reservations recommended / Great wine list / Poolside Grill has great homemade food, bar / www.chicohotsprings.com

Neptune's Brewery, 119 N. L Street / 406-222-7837 / Good beer, thai and seafood / www.neptunesdock.com

Adagio, 101 N. Main Street / 406-222-9400 / www.livingstonpizza.com

Second Street Bistro, located in the Murry Hotel W. Park / open for lunch and dinner / 406-222-9463 / www.secondstreetbistro.com

Pickle Barrel, 131 S Main St / Hearty sandwiches / 406-222-5469 / www.pickelbarrelmt.com

Fiesta En Jalisco Mexican Restaurant, 119 W Park St / 406-222-5444 / www.fiestaenjalisco.net

VETERINARIANS

Colmey Veterinary Hospital, 5288 US Highway 89 S / 406-222-1700 / Duane Colmey, DVM / Pet food, supplies, grooming, kennel

Livingston Veterinary Hospital, 1104 East Park Street / 406-222-3011

FLY SHOPS AND SPORTING GOODS

Dan Bailey Fly Shop, 209 West Park Street / 800-356-4052 / Flies, tying material, fishing equipment, clothing, and accessories / www.dan-bailey.com

George Anderson's Yellowstone Angler, 5256 Highway 89 South / 406-222-7130 / Flyfishing specialties, outdoor clothing / www.yellowstoneangler.com

Hatch Finders Fly Shop, 113 West Park #3 / 406-222-0989 / www.hatchfinders.com

Sweetwater Fly Shop, 5082 US Highway 89 S / 406-222-9393 / www.sweetwaterflyshop.com

Angler's West Flyfishing Outfitters, 206 Railroad Lane, Emigrant / 406-333-4401 / www.montanaflyfishers.com

Knoll's Fly Shop, 104 Chicory Road, Pray / 406-333-4848 / www.knolls.us / Hackle specialists

AIR SERVICE

Gallatin Field Airport, 8 miles west of Bozeman in Belgrade on Frontage Road / 406-388-6632 / Served by Delta, United, Horizon and Frontier / Charter service available / www.bozemanairport.com

AUTO RENTAL AND REPAIR

Yellowstone Country Motors, 1415 West Park Street / 406-222-7200 / All models, 4wd and vans

A-1 Muffler and Auto Repair, 1226 West Front Street / 406-222-3039

MEDICAL

Livingston Memorial Hospital, 504 South 13th Street / 406-222-3541 / www.livingstonhealthcare.org

FOR MORE INFORMATION

Livingston Area Chamber of Commerce
303 East Park Street
Livingston, MT 59047
406-222-0850
www.livingston-chamber.com

West Yellowstone, Montana

Elevation – 6,666 • Population – 1,502

West Yellowstone sits on the western edge of Yellowstone National Park, and it is an ideal location for flyfishers to call home for as long as they want. You should not have any trouble finding a nice spot to stay, whether in a plush hotel or an improved campground. West also hosts excellent eateries, lively bars and some nice bookstores. There are also many well-stocked fly shops. West Yellowstone's zip code is 59758.

ACCOMMODATIONS

Alpine Motel, 120 Madison Avenue / 406-646-7544 / $ /
www.alpinemotelwestyellowstone.com

Best Western, 201 Firehole Lane / 406-646-9557 Hwy 2 West / 406-293-8831 / $$

Firehole Ranch, Denny Creek Road (northwest shore of Hebgen Lake) /
406-646-7294 / www.fireholeranch.com

Campfire Lodge, 155 Campfire Lane / 406-646-7258 / $$ / In between Hebgen and Quake lakes / www.campfirelodgewestyellowstone.com

RESTAURANTS

Gusher Pizza and Sandwich Shoppe, 40 Dunraven Street / 406-646-9050

Bullwinkles Saloon & Restaurant, 19 Madison Avenue / 406-646-7974

Three Bear Restuarant, 217 Yellowstone Avenue / 800-646-7353 /
www.threebearlodge.com

Eino's, 155 Einos Loop (Just north of Hwy 287 off of Hwy 191) / 406-646-9344 /
choose your meat and cook it yourself on Eino's grills

FLY SHOPS AND SPORTING GOODS

Arrick's Fly Shop, 37 North Canyon Street / 406-646-7290 / www.arricks.com

Bud Lilly's Trout Shop, 39 Madison Avenue / 406-646-7801 / www.budlillys.com

Madison River Outfitters, 117 Canyon Street / 406-646-9644 /
www.madisonriveroutfitters.com

Blue Ribbon Flies, 305 Canyon Street / 406-646-7642 / www.blue-ribbon-flies.com

Jacklin's Fly Shop, 105 Yellowstone Avenue / 406-646-7336 /
www.jacklinsflyshop.com

West Yellowstone Fly Shop, 140 Madison Ave / 406-646-1181 / www.wyflyshop.com

AUTO REPAIR

Randy's Auto Repair, 415 Yellowstone Avenue / 406-646-9353

FOR MORE INFORMATION

West Yellowstone Chamber of Commerce
30 Yellowstone Avenue
West Yellowstone, MT 59758
406-646-7701
www.westyellowstonechamber.com

Bald eagle.

Close Encounters:
WILDLIFE OBSERVATIONS ACCENTUATE FISHING

An enthralling aspect of fishing in Yellowstone and its wild environs is the privilege of sharing each river's moods and whims with an abundant array of wildlife. Even if the trout don't cooperate, I'm satisfied it's been a good day when an antelope comes to a stream bank to drink or a great blue heron remains fixated on spearing dinner as I quietly wade upstream.

Wildlife observations are recorded as faithfully in my journals as the trout and mayfly hatches. Large fish brought to the net are measured and released. Ones that get away are listed as "LDRs" for Long Distance Releases. Wildlife captured on film rate "stars" in my notes. And, most years, autumn "stars" outnumber those of other seasons.

Fall is the favorite time of many western anglers. Tourist crowds depart for home; hunters abandon the streams for the woods. A renewed sense of quiet and solitude prevails. Rivers and lakes reflect the shimmering gold of frost-nipped cottonwoods and the salmon-orange blush of lingering sunsets. Yearlings entering these beguiling times embark on their first adventures a tad too inquisitive. Their peregrinations almost guarantee an unplanned rendezvous.

Juvenile predators often ignore, or at least don't worry about, solitary anglers because finding dinner is a major preoccupation. Such was the case with a coyote on the Yellowstone River.

Coyotes spotted in farm and ranch country rarely pause for a second glance back. But in a sanctuary like Yellowstone National Park they are less skittish. Juveniles often prowl throughout the day. Grassy meadows and knolls in the upper Lamar, Gibbon, and Yellowstone valleys are prime hunting grounds for coyotes stalking deer mice and meadow voles.

The tans and golden browns of a coyote's new winter coat blend perfectly into the autumn colors of sun-bleached grasses, wilted wildflowers, and dusty sagebrush along the Yellowstone. Fishing a sheltered alcove in the river, I almost missed seeing the small coyote exploring the bank a short distance downstream.

This time I was prepared, my camera set up nearby on a tripod. Wading back to shore, I slowly eased into position behind it. I was just in time as the coyote froze, cocked her head, and peered at a clump of grass. Her back curled catlike as she leaped into the air and dived headfirst into the bunchgrass. She came up empty-mouthed, probably with a bruised nose.

A classic moment in mouse hunting, it was over in seconds. But the cumbersome, sometimes frustrating, exertions involved in lugging a camera and tripod on fishing jaunts paid off again.

A telephoto lens—400mm at minimum—is best for bringing small animals and birds close enough to be more than just a dot on a slide or print. Long lenses also provide an element of security when photographing big game or large predators.

Coyote.

I have yet to confirm this axiom with a grizzly bear test, although I have spotted a few disturbingly fresh saber-clawed paw prints on gravel bars. A couple of twoyear-olds on Mount Washburn a few years ago were photographed in the safety of a crowd and two pistol-packing rangerettes. Still, the overgrown cubs provided a better appreciation of the great bear's formidable size. I no longer hike or fish alone in grizzly country.

It's also wise to stay back when moose and elk start polishing the velvet from their antlers. And bison are unpredictable and dangerous year-round.

Remember the song "You Can't Roller Skate in a Buffalo Herd"? Well, it's no picnic to fly fish in one, either. But the day the bison crashed the party at Buffalo Ford on the Yellowstone River was fairly comical.

The horde of flyfishers there for opening day was forced to retreat to the parking lot. About a dozen walked around the milling bison to get to the river, and four dumband-dumber types waltzed back through a split in the herd. Another guy declared with much bravado that he was going to eat his lunch at a picnic table.

The dude contentedly chomped on a sandwich until a buddy sneaked up and bumped the table. His sandwich flew in the air as the dude executed a long jump that probably set a world record from a sitting start.

Yellowstone's elk may seem docile, but they aren't shy about sticking to their appointed rounds, either.

One year I closed the park's season by searching for migrating brown trout in the Gardner River. A narrow, boulder-strewn stream, its swift current drowns out virtually all other sounds. So the herd of cow elk and fawns suddenly scrambling down a rocky cliff into my fishing hole took me by surprise. I backed up onto a gravel bar to retrieve my camera and to give them room to drink.

The herd boss wasn't far behind his harem. He sauntered down the slope with the stately cadence of a monarch. But it was a hot, dusty day. Plunging into the water up to the dark brown bib on his neck, the bull greedily stuck his snout into the river.

My picture complete, I savored the moment until the inevitable gaggle of photographers showed up. They made the elk nervous, and I retreated to a footpath along the cliff.

Twice I have seen photographers charged by elk. Each occurred when a bull was approached too closely. Both men had small point-and-shoot cameras. Once, I myself beat a hasty retreat from the Gibbon River when a herd boss decided his cows had strayed too far and went on a rampaging roundup.

Moose are less common in Yellowstone, and sightings are guaranteed traffic stoppers. Western Wyoming, however, has one of the largest moose populations in the West. Encounters along the Snake River below Jackson Lake in Grand Teton National Park dramatically enhance a day's fishing.

A bull elk wading in the Madison River.

Incredible swimmers and waders, moose range back and forth across even the largest of rivers. I once watched a bull plunge into the Snake directly across from me, swim the river, and climb up the bank only 40 yards downstream. The flow was more than 15,000 cubic feet per second. Another time, a young bull labored up through the deep water of a cutbank and waded into my fishing hole within 20 feet of me. Up to my waist in a side channel, I couldn't believe he kept coming. I froze, and we warily eyed each other as he waded through the eddy to an island and disappeared into the willows.

Bulls still in velvet are relatively stoic about human interlopers. Cows with calves remain sanguine as long as they aren't separated. But when a bull starts making that loony gurgling sound and his antlers are polished tawny white, admire him from a distance. Love-struck bulls cut and wheel in any direction when escorting cows.

Late one evening at the tip of a gravel bar island I stood entranced on the far side of a log for a half-hour. Vying for the attention of a cow in the inside channel was an amorous but frustrated bull. Much of his worrying and fussing was directed at trying to drive off the cow's calf. But mother and son finally bolted up the far bank and clattered off through the cottonwoods. The grumbling bull trailed the pair into the darkness.

Bull Moose on the Snake River.

Great horned owl.

A grizzly at Dunraven Pass.

Bison are dangerous; keep your distance.

Pronghorns are common in the northern part of the park.

Such moments are intriguing, but legions of two-legged characters also are princely players in daily dramas on nature's stage. Birdwatchers and anglers can learn a lot from each other.

An incredible array of birding hotspots accentuates the interconnected waterways of the northern Rockies. Sometimes you can get quite close, especially when fishing from a boat. In autumn, young birds appear almost tame in how closely they can be approached.

On rare occasions, a fish struggling at the end of a line may be too much to resist. That was the case one day on the Yellowstone River in the park. A young pelican was eager to share the river's bonanza with numerous flyfishers. He followed splashing cutthroat trout almost to the nets of several successful anglers.

Monitoring the fledging of generations of cygnets by a pair of trumpeter swans is as compelling a reason for me to return annually to the Madison River as its wily rainbow and brown trout. An osprey hovering over a shallow run instantly causes my fly line to go slack. It drifts unattended until the fish hawk plummets into the stream. When it struggles aloft with a wriggling whitefish or trout in its talons, I salute the master angler.

To me, osprey, bald eagles, pelicans, cormorants, mergansers, egrets, and herons are signs of healthy fisheries. Their shares of the bounty are not begrudged.

Many outfitters are expanding their services to include birding and photography. Guides are spending a lot of extra time rowing against the current to give clients time to identify or photograph streamside birds. It makes for a more interesting day on the stream.

Rivers never rest; their residents are ever busy. Birds amplify a stream's idyllic moods as flows of avian chatter wash through reeds and brush. But, just as often, the whims of nature catapult their prosaic pastimes into dynamic melodramas.

A strident chattering announces the flight of a kingfisher from one snag overhanging a river to another. It's a brief and welcoming background noise on a stream as the tiny indigo dive-bomber flies to a perch over a new fishing site. But one day an incessant clamor echoing off the walls of a canyon caused me to take a longer look around.

I spotted the screeching kingfisher darting and wheeling along the far bank, barely skimming the surface of the river. Splashes marked its flight as it weaved and bobbed in frantic maneuvers to escape a goshawk. Silence descended on the canyon when the kingfisher darted into a tangle of willows. The tumult irrupted again when the patrolling raptor flushed his prey. Their whirling aerial combat coursed up and down the river for another five minutes until the ghostly gray marauder gave up the chase.

It was just another electrifying day in paradise.

The Grand Tetons.

Grand Teton National Park and Jackson Hole

Towering above Jackson Hole, the Grand Teton rises to 13,770 feet. It is the second highest peak in Wyoming. Twelve Teton peaks reach above 12,000 feet, high enough to support a dozen mountain glaciers. Many of the most dramatic views of the Teton's jagged peaks are mirrored in large glacial lakes and the Snake River. The Snake, flowing through the center of the vast wilderness, is the connecting link between Grand Teton and Yellowstone National Parks.

The park's varied terrain is carpeted by ribbons of cottonwoods and willows bordering rivers and streams; sagebrush flats, lodgepole pine and spruce forests, subalpine meadows, and alpine boulder fields checker the valleys and mountains. Wildflowers bloom everywhere throughout spring and summer. Wildlife viewing opportunities in the park, Jackson Hole, and the Teton Wilderness rival the numbers and variety more commonly associated with Yellowstone National Park. The most diverse animal and plant communities are along the Snake River. Visitors are advised to keep their distance from big game animals like elk, moose, and bison. Black or grizzly bears may be encountered on park trails or in the backcountry.

Humans have visited Jackson Hole and used its abundant resources for approximately 11,000 years. Early residents occupied the valley during the short spring, summer, and fall seasons. During the other eight months of the year, they moved to lower elevations and warmer winter climates.

It was the route followed by fur trappers and Indian tribes during the region's fur trade era in the 19th century. Jackson Lake's Colter Bay is named for John Colter, a member of the Lewis & Clark Expedition who stayed on in the West when the Corps returned from the Pacific. The first of the mountain men, he explored the Teton-Yellowstone country alone during the winter of 1807–1808. Jackson Hole is named for David Jackson, who pioneered many other routes through the northern Rockies. The Bridger-Teton National Forest surrounding Jackson Hole and the Bridger Wilderness in the Wind River Mountains are named for the legendary Jim Bridger.

Beginning in the late 1800s, homesteaders, ranchers, and, later, dude ranchers moved into the valley, bringing the technologies of irrigation and insulation to allow them to stay through the long, harsh winter. With the establishment of Grand Teton National Park in 1929 and later additions in 1950, culminating in today's park, a wide variety of resources are protected for future generations in an area covering 485 square miles.

This is where western Wyoming's waters separate on their journeys to the sea. The parting of the waters occurs at a spring-fed trickle that splits and spills off Two Ocean Pass on the Continental Divide above Jackson. Atlantic Creek flows northeast to join the Yellowstone River, the largest tributary of the Missouri. Pacific Creek flows southwest to join the Snake River, the largest tributary of the Columbia.

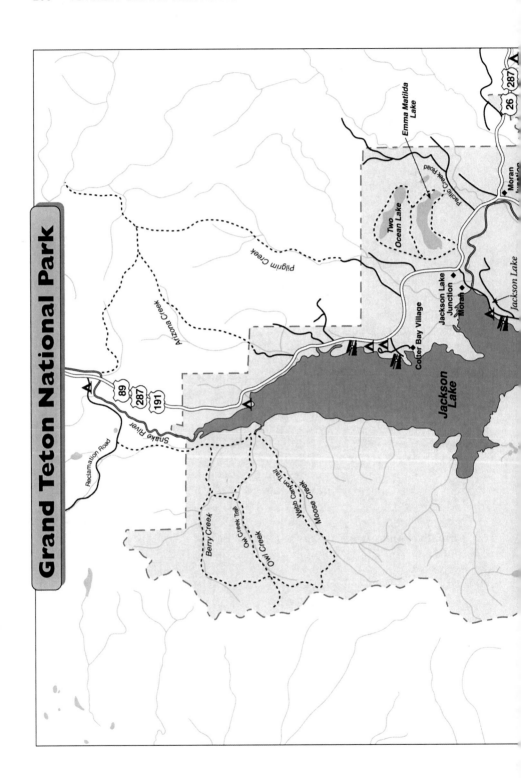

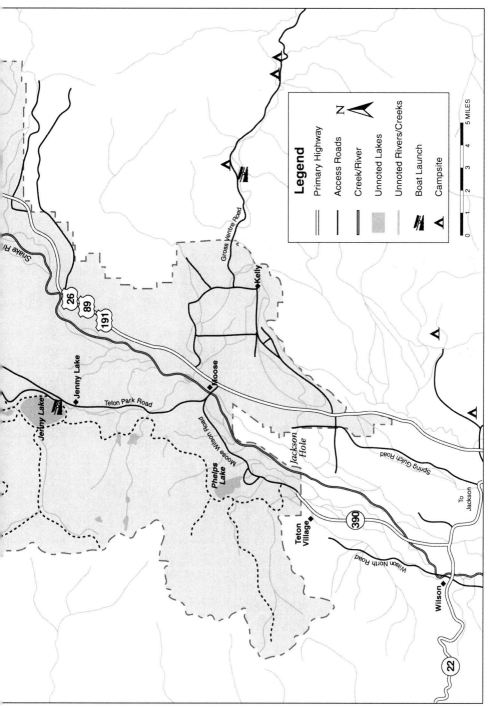

The Snake River finespotted cutthroat is the predominant trout on the Pacific side of the mountains. Its first cousin, the Yellowstone cutthroat, inhabits some of these waters, but its realm of dominance is in the park on the Atlantic side of the divide. Also present in the basin streams, in varying populations, are brown, rainbow, and brook trout, and lake trout inhabit Jackson Lake and a few other lakes. Whitefish are plentiful throughout the basin.

The Snake is a big, brawling river that demands respect. It fishes best from a boat, but newcomers or inexperienced boaters are advised to make their first floats with guides or friends who know the river. Fly casters who prefer to wade should stick to quiet, shallow sections of the river and side channels. Good access is found near boat ramps and bridges. Spring runoff is often late, so plan to fish the Snake in late summer or autumn.

More accommodating to wading and virtually undiscovered are the fine mountain streams flowing into the Snake. Although beyond the confines of Grand Teton Park, good prospects close to Jackson are the upper Gros Ventre River and Flat Creek, a challenging spring creek flowing through the National Elk Refuge. In between Jackson and Alpine, the Hoback River enters the Snake. Granite Creek, a tributary of the Hoback, is a classic small mountain stream.

North of Jackson and bordering Grand Teton Park is the Teton Wilderness. Its most tempting cutthroat fishing—a long hike over the divide—is the upper meadow section of the Yellowstone River and Thorofare Creek. On the west slopes of the divide, good streams to consider are Pacific Creek and the Buffalo Fork River.

Because more than 3.1 million tourists annually visit the park, primarily between Memorial Day and September 30, a visit requires some measure of planning and timing. During the summer season, all lodging and camping facilities throughout Yellowstone and Grand Teton National Parks fill by early afternoon, including overnight lodging in Jackson. Many dining establishments recommend or require reservations during summer. Waiting lists often exceed one hour.

Jackson Hole, the gateway to the park, is one of the West's most popular summer and ski resorts, and reservations are often needed in advance for accommodations or guided fishing trips in the area. Jackson has a host of well-stocked fly shops, outfitters, and guides available to fill equipment needs or help with fishing excursions.

Some basic services such as rental cars, rental equipment, and lodging are sold out every day. Reservations should be considered essential for peak-season visits. Campgrounds are frequently filled by noon, with the possible exception of Gros Ventre Campground near the park's south boundary, west of Kelly. Arrive early, plan carefully, and seek information at park visitor centers and ranger stations.

The Moose Visitor Center is 12 miles north of Jackson on US 89/191/287 and a half mile west of Moose Junction on the Teton Park Road. The Jenny Lake Visitor Center is 8 miles north of the Moose Visitor Center on the Teton Park Road. The Colter Bay Visitor Center is 30 miles north of Jackson on US 89/191/287 and a half mile west of Colter Bay Junction. The Flagg Ranch Information Station is 15 miles north of Colter Bay Junction on US 89/191/287.

The distance from Yellowstone's south boundary to Grand Teton's south boundary is 56 miles. The approximate driving time with no stops is 1.5 hours. Always consider driving time and distance to your next destination before setting out.

There are approximately 100 miles of roads and 200 miles of trails throughout the park. Most park trails are rough rock or dirt and are not accessible to visitors with disabilities. There are many asphalt trails in the Jenny Lake area, some of which are accessible. Some trails may begin as asphalt and deteriorate to dirt or gravel shortly thereafter. Hikes into the park's alpine backcountry range from moderate to strenuous.

Summer days are in the 70s and 80s, with cool nights in the 40s. Summer thunderstorms are common. Mild to cool temperatures linger through September and October. Rain gear is recommended during spring, summer, and fall. The first heavy snows fall by November 1 and continue through March, and snow and frost are possible during any month.

Grand Teton National Park is famous for its moose.

Grand Teton National Park and the John D. Rockefeller, Jr., Memorial Parkway offer a variety of activities from traditional mountain hiking, walking, wildlife viewing, photography, backpacking, camping, climbing, and fishing to swimming, boating, floating, canoeing, biking, and skiing, snowshoeing, and snowmobiling in the winter. Some activities, such as overnight backpacking, boating, floating, canoeing, fishing, and snowmobiling, require fee permits, licenses, or registration. Special regulations may also apply, so take the time to become informed at any visitor center or ranger station.

Permits Fees

A Wyoming fishing license is required to fish in Grand Teton National Park (along with a $12.50 Conservation Stamp for all but the one-day license). Seasons, regulations, and bag limits for the Snake River and the park's lakes are set by the Wyoming Game and Fish Department in cooperation with the National Park Service. With a few exceptions, Grand Teton is open to fishing year round. A park boating permit is required to float the Snake within its boundaries, both above and below Jackson Lake.

Permits are available at Grand Teton visitor centers. Fishing licenses may be purchased in fishing tackle stores in Jackson and Wilson, Dornan's at Moose Village, and at park marinas.

For more information, write Grand Teton National Park, P.O. Drawer 170, Moose, WY 83012; call 307-739-3300; or go online at www.nps.gov/grte/. Free printed publications are available for backcountry camping, hiking, mountaineering, fishing, boating, floating the Snake, bicycling, skiing, and snowmobiling.

License fees:

- Resident License: $24.00
- One-Day: $6.00
- Youth: (14–18) $3.00
- Under 14 (creel limit applies): no license needed
- Nonresident License: $92.00
- One-Day: $14.00
- Youth (14–17): $15.00
- Nonresidents under 14, accompanied by a person possessing a valid Wyoming fishing license, may fish free. Fish caught by persons under 14 are included in the licensed person's creel limit.
- Wyoming Conservation Stamp: $12.50

The Snake River

Tourists headed for Grand Teton National Park envision the Snake River as a silvery thread in the foreground of Ansel Adam's brooding portrait of the Tetons shrouded by storm clouds. Flyfishers are more intent on snapping their own pictures—ones with trout in them.

Both views are intertwined in the history and compellingly beautiful scenery of the region. The Teton Range sets the stage, but the Snake is the common link between the park and Jackson Hole.

The most heavily fished waters of the river's run through western Wyoming are the 35 miles in the park below Jackson Dam and the remaining 17 miles flowing through Jackson Hole. It ranks as one of the best dry fly streams in the West. The entire river is covered here, separately from the rest of Grand Teton National Park, because much of the river runs below the park.

The soaring cathedrals of the Tetons and Mount Moran are elegant distractions, but both the river and its trout demand attention from anglers. The Snake is a wild and woolly river. It punishes those who drop their guard but rewards prudent flyfishers with feisty native trout that inhale large easy-to-see dry flies like popcorn.

As remarkable as the scenery is the river's personal race of native trout. The home range of the Snake River finespotted cutthroat is Jackson Hole and its environs. A beautiful fish, it is unique in a breed that was once the only trout in the interior of the West, eventually evolving into 14 subspecies. Many feel the taxonomy list should be expanded to 15.

Cutthroat won the race up the Snake against rainbow trout, crossing the Continental Divide during the last Ice Age. The crossing was made at 8,200-foot Two Ocean Pass, north of Jackson. The rainbow were then confined to the lower Snake and Columbia drainages when a massive flood created southern Idaho's Shoshone Falls about 50,000 years ago.

The Yellowstone cutthroat, which still inhabits eastern Idaho waters, is the only native trout on the Atlantic side of the divide. It expanded throughout the headwaters of its drainage, including the Shoshone, Big Horn, and Tongue Rivers. Evolving separately, or staying behind, in the Jackson Hole area, was the Snake River finespotted cutthroat. Its native range is confined to the upper river from Heart Lake to Palisades Reservoir.

The Snake River cutthroat is unique in its ability to coexist with a species of its own genus. Its spotting pattern is heavier with many more small spots than the Yellowstone cutthroat, and it is considered less gullible and a stronger fighter. But while some argue otherwise, genetic studies indicate that it is not a separate subspecies.

The most vocal proponent for reclassifying the Snake River cutthroat is Colorado State University professor Robert Behnke. "They are visually different but genetically the same—but the trout know, they don't mix," he said. "They also are the least susceptible of the cutthroat to harvest."

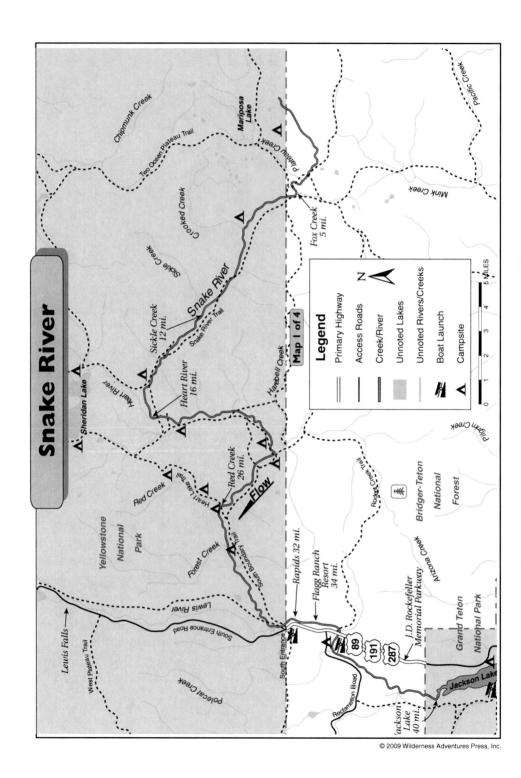

© 2009 Wilderness Adventures Press, Inc.

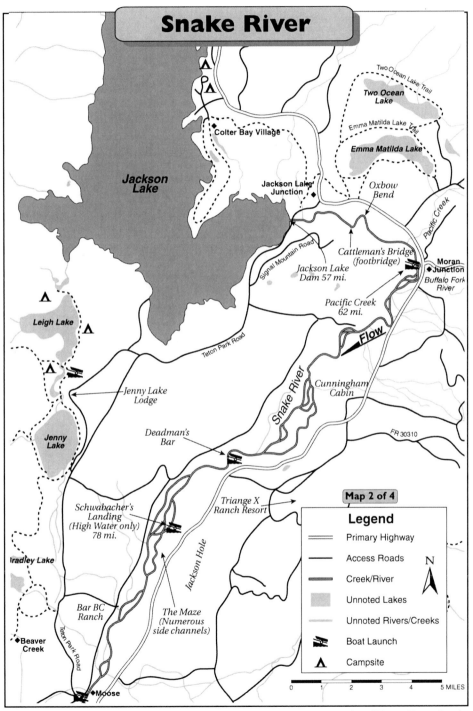

Snake River

Two Ocean Lake Trail

Two Ocean Lake

Emma Matilda Lake Trail

Emma Matilda Lake

Colter Bay Village

Jackson Lake

Jackson Lake Junction

Oxbow Bend

Pacific Creek

Cattleman's Bridge (footbridge)

Moran Junction

Jackson Lake Dam 57 mi.

Buffalo Fork River

Pacific Creek 62 mi.

Signal Mountain Road

Flow

Leigh Lake

Teton Park Road

Snake River

Cunningham Cabin

Jenny Lake Lodge

FR 30310

Deadman's Bar

Jenny Lake

Map 2 of 4

Triange X Ranch Resort

Schwabacher's Landing (High Water only) 78 mi.

Legend

Jackson Hole

Bradley Lake

Primary Highway

Access Roads

N

Creek/River

Unnoted Lakes

Bar BC Ranch

The Maze (Numerous side channels)

Unnoted Rivers/Creeks

Beaver Creek

Boat Launch

Teton Park Road

Campsite

Moose

0 1 2 3 4 5 MILES

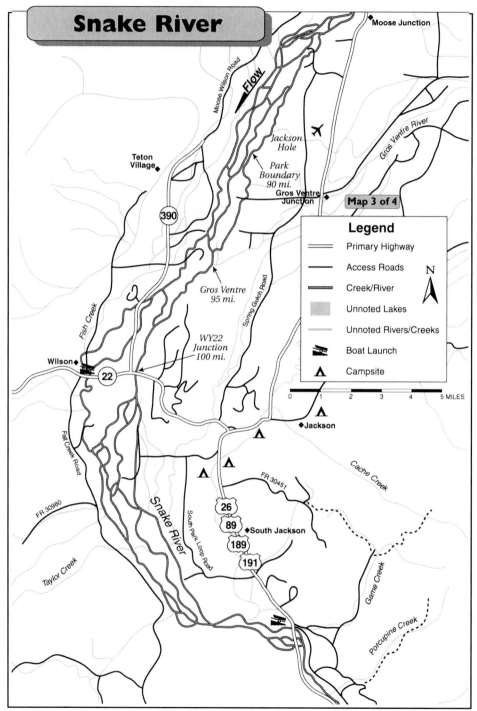

© 2009 Wilderness Adventures Press, Inc.

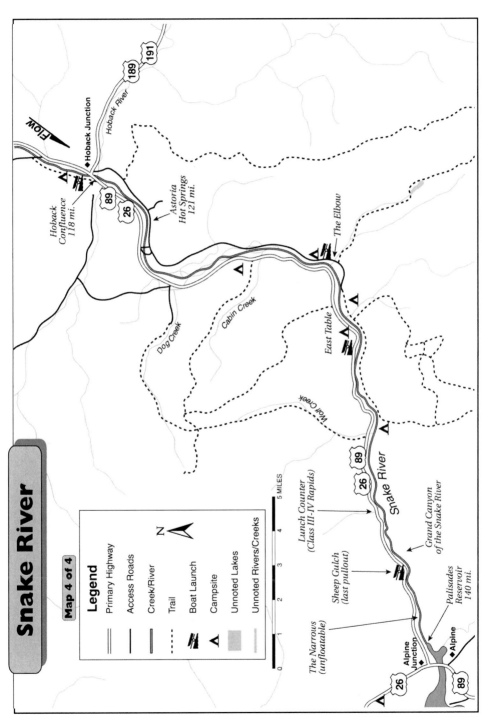

Snake River

Map 4 of 4

Legend

Primary Highway
Access Roads
Creek/River
Trail
Boat Launch
Campsite
Unnoted Lakes
Unnoted Rivers/Creeks

N

0 1 2 3 4 5 MILES

Flow

Hoback Junction

189
191

Hoback River

89
26

Astoria
Hot Springs
121 mi.

Hoback
Confluence
118 mi.

Dog Creek

Cabin Creek

The Elbow

East Table

Wolf Creek

89
26

Snake River

Lunch Counter
(Class III-IV Rapids)

Grand Canyon
of the Snake River

Sheep Gulch
(last pullout)

The Narrows
(unfloatable)

Palisades
Reservoir
140 mi.

Alpine
Junction

26

89

Alpine

© 2009 Wilderness Adventures Press, Inc.

Disputes over its genetics won't be settled soon, but Behnke maintains the Snake River cutthroat is hard to beat as a game fish. "It, to my mind, fights better than the Yellowstone cutthroat. It is the champion of cutthroat—but for the same reason: genetic quality. It can only be seen by the eye and at the end of your fly rod."

The trout's aggressive nature has evolved from its need to cope with a big, brawling river like the Snake. They eat just about anything: mostly aquatic insects and windblown terrestrials as juveniles, and forage fish and large aquatic invertebrates as adults.

The Snake River cutthroat has a well-deserved reputation as an excellent dry fly fish, but large streamers and nymphs are standard fare on the river, too. The cutthroat hits both hard. Large dry flies continue to be effective into late autumn on the Snake, unlike many other rivers.

Chris Tita fishes the Snake beneath the majestic Tetons.

Once spring runoff releases abate and topwater action kicks off in late July, fishing can be incredible with large attractors like Royal Trudes or Wulffs, Stimulators, Madam Xs, and terrestrial patterns. The average dry fly in summer is often size 12, and in early fall an effective strategy is to graduate to size 8 or larger patterns.

Two locally perfected patterns are Turk's Tarantula and the Chernobyl Ant. Both have wiggling, antennae-like rubber legs to help entice strikes. Another Jackson production, Joe Allen's Double Humpy, ups the ante for hits on one of the West's best gifts to pocket-water fly casters. All three incorporate provocative body colors like red, yellow, and green to further draw the attention of fish.

Snake River cutthroat are not total pushovers. While they often hit skating flies early in the season, as flows stabilize and the water clears the cutthroat start window shopping. Proper presentation to feeding lanes and lies and long dead drifts are critical in late summer and autumn.

One of the few places on the Snake where match-the-hatch challenges occur with standard flies is on the quieter waters of the Oxbow Bend stretch between Jackson Dam and Pacific Creek. There also are some quiet backwaters between Pacific Creek and Deadman's Bar accessible to boaters. And waders who make the effort to hike into braided channels in the floodplain find smaller waters with rising trout.

Hatches to watch for are stoneflies and Golden Stones soon after runoff wanes in July, along with caddis and Yellow Sallies. Pale Morning Duns appear in midsummer and Gray Drakes may be August options. September is the time to watch for Mahogany Duns. Still, grasshoppers are the prime candidates for good late summer fishing.

Small mayfly nymphs and caddis emergers are effective dropper flies in many sections of the river throughout the season. Beadhead patterns or small split shot on tag lines keep droppers down.

Good wet flies in the murky waters of early season are Woolly Buggers, leeches, Zonkers, black Rubber Legs, the JJ's Special, the Double Bunny, and other streamers.

A short-lived, fast-growing fish, the Snake River cutthroat reaches a maximum size of about 22 inches; a rare fish may go to 24 inches. Generally, trout in the upper river average 12 to 14 inches, but there are enough in the 16-inch range to keep things interesting. There are fewer cutthroat in the deeper channels below the Hoback River, but the fish are larger.

Brown trout also are found in the river above Jackson Dam, and whitefish are plentiful throughout the drainage.

The native trout has been hard-pressed to survive radical changes in its home range this century. It's taken a licking but keeps on ticking.

A 6.2-mile stretch of the Snake River above the Highway 22 bridge east of Wilson is routinely electrofished to obtain population estimates for Snake River finespotted cutthroat trout. The estimated number of Snake River finespotted cutthroat trout averaged 810 per mile during six sampling years, fisheries biologists reported in 2004.

Improved numbers and sizes of cutthroat in the Snake are largely the success of special regulations to restrict harvest, extraordinary efforts to rejuvenate spawning streams, and aggressive measures taken to maintain minimum winter flows.

A 1990 agreement with the Bureau of Reclamation guarantees a minimum winter flow of 280 cubic feet per second to provide cover for more age classes of trout.

Several regulations were refined to further protect the native trout:

- The Snake River is open year round for trout fishing. However, strict catch-and release regulations apply between November 1 and March 31. Artificial flies and lures only from 1,000 feet below Jackson Lake Dam to Wyoming Highway 22 bridge east of Wilson. It is closed to human access from the Buffalo Fork confluence at Moran to Menor's Ferry at Moose from December 15-April 1.
- Most of Area 1 of western Wyoming has new creel limits. The creel limit on trout is six per day or in possession. However, no more than three can be cutthroat trout and only one can exceed 12 inches. Also, only one trout can exceed 20 inches. There are exceptions, so check the regulations for full details. The restrictions on cutthroat (three fish, only one over 12 inches) also extend to lakes in the park and Jackson Hole area.
- Snake River tributaries upstream of the West Table boat ramp open to fishing on April 1 and close October 31. These include the Hoback River (downstream from the Elkhorn Store in Bondurant only), Fish Creek, the Gros Ventre River, Buffalo Fork River, and Pacific Creek. Their are some exceptions, most notably sections of Flat Creek, which opens August 1 on the National Elk Refuge, and the Teton and Gros Ventre Wilderness Areas, so be sure to check the full regulations for details. Be aware that the wilderness areas don't open until May 1.

Spawning runs in some restored spring creeks have tripled since the 1970s, according to John Kiefling, former Wyoming Game and Fish's fisheries supervisor in Jackson.

The renovation project started by his predecessor, Jon Erickson, involved a lot of work aided by the cooperation of landowners and volunteer assistance of local sportsmen and organizations such as Trout Unlimited. Hundreds of tons of clean gravel were trucked into the spring creeks to recreate spawning redds and riffles. Silt was removed from key areas and pools, and overhead structures were created to give trout places to hide.

Some of the spring creeks also are being stocked with eggs to restore spawning runs. The trout will imprint on the streams, and future generations will continue to return to their natal waters, Kiefling said.

Funds to assist rejuvenation of the spring creeks and other conservation projects on the river are garnered by Jackson's annual One Fly Contest and other events.

Basically, the department and local anglers are trying to protect what they have left, Kiefling said. The river has radically changed over the years since Jackson Dam was built in 1911, and dikes started going up after a devastating flood in 1950.

Summer-long high flows to funnel irrigation water downstream broke the natural rhythm of the river and disrupted spawning by inundating river channels and creek mouths. The dikes, which now extend 40 miles to protect the expensive homes of Jackson Hole, cause channelization and aggradation, or buildup, of the streambed. In some places the river flows higher than the floodplain behind the dikes. Instream structure has been lost and, by blocking natural meanders through side channels, cottonwood regeneration is prevented in riparian areas.

To address these problems, Teton County signed an agreement in 2003 with the Army Corps of Engineers and Teton Conservation District for a $52 million restoration project along the Snake River to protect and enhance habitat and repair damage caused by levees that constrict river flow.

The multistage project, which may take up to 50 years, will extend more than 20 miles from Grand Teton National Park into South Park, south of Jackson. Among the project planned are a series of structures along the riverbanks and in front of islands to slow the current. The intent is to aid the collection of sediment and create more stable areas of woodlands habitat. Plans also include deepening some river channels to divert currents and hopefully rejuvenate wetlands currently outside the levee system.

Also, Grand Teton National Park and the Bureau of Reclamation, which regulates Jackson Lake Dam releases for downstream irrigators, embarked on a joint study in 2004 to develop science-based recommendations to manage the dam while protecting fish and other natural resources in the river.

Anglers would like to see a return to more natural flows in the Snake. Many complain that high summer irrigation flows from the dam have led to bank erosion and vegetation loss in recent years. Also, there are concerns that low spring releases

Anglers ply the water near Moran Junction.

don't flush sediment adequately and that the naturally braided river is being turned into a single channel.

But while downstream irrigation demands mostly dictate flows below Jackson Lake, Mother Nature still calls the shots.

The highest flows since 1895 were recorded in 1997 along the Snake from the park to Palisades Reservoir at the Idaho–Wyoming state line. The U.S. Geological Survey reported that record flows occurred June 11 and ranged from greater than 24,000 cfs at Moose to about 32,000 cfs near Jackson to over 38,000 cfs upstream of Palisades.

The previous record at Moose was 22,000 cfs on June 16, 1996. Average annual maximum flows are about 16,000 cfs at Jackson and 19,000 cfs upstream of Palisades. Back-to-back high water years, hopefully, caused only temporary setbacks on this great river. In most years, they are much less extreme.

Runoff usually begins in late May, peaks around 15,000 cfs in June, and drops to around 5,000 cfs in July. But even August through September flows can fluctuate between 2,000 and 5,000 cfs. Winter and early spring flows are 1,000 cfs or less, but in high snowpack years, they may be bumped significantly. The minimum winter flow on the river is 280 cfs.

Still, spring runoff may be late, so it's best to plan trips to the Snake in late summer or autumn. And, for hearty anglers, there now is a catch-and-release winter season for trout between November 1 and March 31.

Driftboat on the Snake in Grand Teton National Park.

Floating The Snake

To say the Snake demands respect cannot be overstated. It fishes best from a boat, but it can be dangerous for neophyte rowers or those new to the river. Even people familiar with the Snake need to check on current conditions before setting out. It can change overnight, and flows vary greatly through the summer. Reports posted at the park's boat-launch sites are updated weekly or whenever significant changes occur.

Motorized boats aren't permitted on the river in Grand Teton National Park, and floating is not permitted on other streams in the park. A guide on "Floating the Snake River," as well as permits required for float boats, rafts, and canoes, is available at visitor centers and ranger stations. As of 2011, the fees are $10 for a week permit and $20 for an annual permit. For river information, call 307-739-3602.

As of 2010, all watercraft using Wyoming waters are required to display an Aquatic Invasive Species decal (except for inflatables under 11 feet in length). The cost is $10 for motorized watercraft registered in Wyoming, $30 for motorized watercraft registered in other states, $5 for non-motorized watercraft owned by Wyoming residents and $15 for non-motorized watercraft owned by nonresidents.

For additional information on how to safely float the river, contact the Jackson Game and Fish Office at 307-733-2321 or 1-800-423-4113, or the Bridger Teton National Forest at 307-739-5400. Also consult guides and outfitters at Jackson area fly shops.

The two most dangerous stretches of the river are Deadman's Bar to Moose Landing and Moose to Wilson Bridge. Both park officials and Jackson outfitters stress that only people with advanced boating or rafting skills should enter these runs.

Most of the river's accidents occur on the 10-mile reach from Deadman's Bar to Moose, which is the most challenging stretch of river. The river drops more steeply and has swifter flows than in other sections. "Complex braiding obscures the main channel. Strong current can sweep boaters into side channels blocked by logjams," notes the park's floating guide.

Schwabacher Landing, midway between Deadman's Bar and Moose, requires a tight turn into a narrow channel on the east bank. However, it can't be used during low flows.

The 12-mile Moose to Wilson Bridge run is nearly as difficult as the Deadman's Bar stretch. It also has numerous braided channels and obstructions that require careful consideration by experienced boaters and rafters. The park's south boundary is halfway down this stretch.

Park officials also caution that the 10.5-mile run from Pacific Creek to Deadman's Bar is not for beginners. Intermediate boating or rafting skills are required because this is the first significant drop in the river, and its channel is braided. "Boating experience on lakes has proven to be of little help to river runners on the Snake," states the floating guide.

The only beginner stretch on the river—and one of its prettiest, with Mount Moran in the background—is from Jackson Dam to Pacific Creek. Called the Oxbow Bend for its big looping curve, the 5-mile run is suitable even for canoes. Watercraft also can be launched from Cattleman's Bridge, 2 miles below the dam boat ramp.

The Oxbow Bend run offers the earliest shot at the river. It is less affected by spring runoff and remains clearer. Just downstream, Pacific Creek and the Buffalo Fork River mark the area where the most dramatic runoff effects begin.

Two other runs on the river above Jackson Lake receive much less attention.

The 3-mile stretch from the Yellowstone boundary to Flagg Ranch is an advanced run because it has the only whitewater on the upper river. Its rapids are Class III to IV during spring runoff.

The 10-mile run from Flagg Ranch to Lizard Creek Campground on Jackson Lake is an intermediate run because of the many channels that cut through the marshy flats above the lake. The last 4 miles are a long row or paddle on the lake, which can be made even harder by stiff winds.

Jackson outfitters caution that the channel between Wilson Bridge and the South Park landing (13 miles downstream at the US 26/89 bridge) also was significantly changed by the floods of 1996 and 1997. Below South Park, the river runs through an 8-mile canyon with strong currents and eddies past Hoback to Astoria Hot Springs. The next 8 miles to West Table is flatter but does have some channels and logjams.

West Table is the last pullout for float-fishers. Below it is the famous whitewater run in the Grand Canyon of the Snake. At peak use during the summer, up to 600 boats and 4,000 people per day run the Class III to V rapids in the canyon.

Because the river is so crowded, motorized watercraft, including jet skis and other personal watercraft, are banned on the 8-mile stretch from the West Table launch site to Sheep Gulch.

The author fishing the Snake. (Photo by Mike Retallic)

Wading The Snake

Proceed with caution around the Snake, even when walking the banks. The current is treacherous along undercut banks and where the river spills around logjams and plunges down deep, narrow side channels. Keep back from the river when hiking through heavy brush or deadfall.

Fly casters who wade must stick to quiet, shallow sections and side channels. Take care not to get too far into channels on unstable gravel bars. The Snake is deceptive, and its twisting flows disguise a strong, swift undercurrent.

Unlike the case with boaters, experience as a wader can lull the unwary into a false sense of confidence. A good rule of thumb is to not go in over the knees near the main channel of the river. If the river or a side channel is murky and the bottom can't be seen, stay out of it.

But waders can take advantage of the Snake's meandering runs and quieter backwaters where the floodplain is braided into side channels. Working side channels and the banks essentially reduces the Snake to small-stream fishing. There's more time to pursue rising fish, and fly choices may be more critical. But just as often, tossing out an attractor pattern or generic mayfly is as effective for wading fly casters as it is for those zipping past hotspots in driftboats or rafts.

Don't linger over unproductive waters. Generally, if you're cutthroat fishing and nothing happens within an hour, it is best to move on. When fish start hitting, work the spot fully. Where there's one cutthroat, there's sure to be another.

The best access to the river's east bank from US 26/89 is found near boat ramps, bridges, and the mouths of tributaries—like Pelican Creek and the Buffalo Fork River near Moran Junction and below the dam. An often-overlooked access site to the middle section of the river is Schwabacher Landing. The turnoff down a steep gravel road is just north of the Glacier View scenic turnout on the highway.

Another route to the river not shown on small maps handed out by the Park Service is a dirt road that parallels much of the west bank. It is shown on topographic trail maps and the Buffalo and Jackson Ranger Districts map of the Bridger-Teton National Forest.

The southern turnoff to the road is at a sign for the Bar BC Ranch on Cottonwood Creek, just north of the Taggart Lake parking lot on the park's loop road. The northern turnoff near Jackson Lake is unmarked and easily missed.

The upper river in the Flagg Ranch area also offers good access. It fishes well after runoff subsides through summer into autumn. Large brown trout run upstream from the lake on their fall spawning runs. An excellent tributary on this section is Polecat Creek, which flows out of Yellowstone.

South of the park, the best access sites closest to Jackson are at the Wilson Bridge on WY 22 and at the South Park Bridge on US 26/89. The bonus at South Park is the chance to fish the bottom of Flat Creek.

Below Astoria Hot Springs, the river reenters the national forest. Generally, wherever you can walk to it from the highway it is legal to fish without fear of trespass.

Because of the size of the river and the need to punch flies to the banks and logjams where fish are lurking, a 9-foot, 5- or 6-weight rod is recommended.

Stream Facts: Snake River

Seasons

- The Snake River proper upstream from Palisades Reservoir is open to trout fishing year round. From November 1 through March 31 it is strictly catch and release for trout.
- For a distance of 150 feet below the downstream face of Jackson Lake Dam in Grand Teton National Park is closed all year.

Regulations

- The creel limit on trout is six per day or in possession. However, no more than three may be cutthroat trout and only one can exceed 12 inches. Only one trout can exceed 20 inches. (There are exceptions, such as Flat Creek on the National Elk Refuge, so check the regulations for full details. The three-fish, only one over 12 inches restriction on cutthroat also extends to lakes in the park and Jackson Hole area.)
- Snake River tributaries upstream of the West Table boat ramp open to fishing on April 1 and close October 31. These includes the Hoback River (downstream from the Elkhorn Store in Bondurant only), Fish Creek, the Gros Ventre River, Buffalo Fork River, and Pacific Creek. There are some exceptions, most notably sections of Flat Creek, which opens August 1 on the National Elk Refuge, and the Teton and Gros Ventre Wilderness Areas, which open May 1.
- Artificial flies and lures only from 1,000 feet below Jackson Lake Dam to the WY 22 bridge east of Wilson.

Trout

- Snake River cutthroat trout average 12 to 14 inches, with good numbers in the 16- to 18-inch range, and a rare fish going to 22 inches. Some brown trout are in the river above Jackson Dam in the 14- to 18-inch range, as are some larger fall spawners from the lake.

Miles (the first 32 miles of the upper river are in Yellowstone Park)

- Mile 32: Yellowstone Park boundary
- Mile 40: Jackson Lake
- Mile 57: Jackson Lake Dam
- Mile 62: Pacific Creek
- Mile 73: Deadman's Bar
- Mile 85: Moose Landing
- Mile 95: Wilson Bridge
- Mile 121: Astoria Hot Springs
- Mile 129: West Table landing (last pullout above whitewater canyon)
- Mile 137: Sheep Gulch landing
- Mile 140: Palisades Reservoir (state line)

Character

- Big strong river with treacherous flows and undercurrents; numerous braided channels and logjams in stretch between Deadman's Bar and South Park. Very dangerous to wade around main channel in all parts of the river; waders should stick to shallow side channels or banks. Best suited for float fishing, but should not be attempted without advanced boating skills. Float trips with outfitters or guides recommended for river runners with intermediate or beginner boating skills.

Flows

- Runoff usually begins in late May, peaks around 15,000 cfs in June and drops to around 5,000 cfs in July. August through September flows can fluctuate between 2,000 and 5,000 cfs. In extreme wet years, flows are dramatically higher.

Access

- Grand Teton National Park on upper river
- Wyoming Game and Fish access sites in Jackson Hole
- Bridger-Teton National Forest below Hoback

Camping

- Grand Teton National Park
- Bridger-Teton National Forest
- Jackson

SNAKE RIVER MAJOR HATCHES

Insect	M	A	M	J	J	A	S	O	N	Time	Flies
Stonefly				█						A	Dry: Sofa Pillow, Salmonfly, Chernobyl Ant, Turk's Tarantula, Yellow or Red Double Humpy #2–8; Wet: Black Stone Nymph, Rubberlegs, Woolly Bugger #2–10
Golden Stone					█					A	Dry: Golden Stone, Bird's Stone, Yellow or Orange Stimulator, Yellow Double Humpy #8–10; Wet: Bitch Creek Nymph, JJ's Special, Woolly Bugger #4–12
Little Yellow Stone					█	█				A/E	Yellow Sally, Blonde Humpy, Willow Fly, Yellow Stimulator #10–14; Yellow Wulff, Yellow or Royal Trude #10–12
Caddis							█	█		M/D	Dry: Elk Hair Caddis, Yellow or Royal Humpy, X-Caddis, Goddard Caddis, Renegade #10–14; Wet: Beadhead Prince Nymph, Soft Hackles, Halfback #10–16
Baetis			█				█	█		A/E	Dry: Blue-Winged Olive, Para-BWO, Adams, Para-Adams #14–18; Wet: Beadhead Pheasant Tail, Baetis Emerger #16–18
Pale Morning Dun				█	█					A/E	Dry: PMD, Light Cahill, Rusty Spinner, Sparkle Dun #16–18; Wet: Beadhead Hare's Ear, Beadhead Pheasant Tail #14–18
Gray Drake						█				A	Adams, Para-Adams, Gray Wulff #10–12; Para-BWO, Flav #10–14
Trico						█	█			A	Black and White, Trico Spinner, Para-Adams #18–20
Mahogany Dun								█		A	Mahogany Dun, Sparkle Dun, Mahogany Thorax, Quill CDC #14–18
Midge	█							█		M/E	Griffith's Gnat, Black Midge, Trico Spinner, Para-Adams #18–22
Terrestrials						█	█	█		M/A	Dave's Hopper, Madam X, Turk's Tarantula, Yellow or Red Double Humpy, Chernobyl Ant #6–12; Dave's Cricket, Disc O'Beetle #10–14

M=morning; LM=late morning; A=afternoon; E=evening; D=dark; SF=spinner fall; /=continuation through periods

Rafters run the Lunch Counter Rapids of the Snake.

The Lakes of Grand Teton National Park

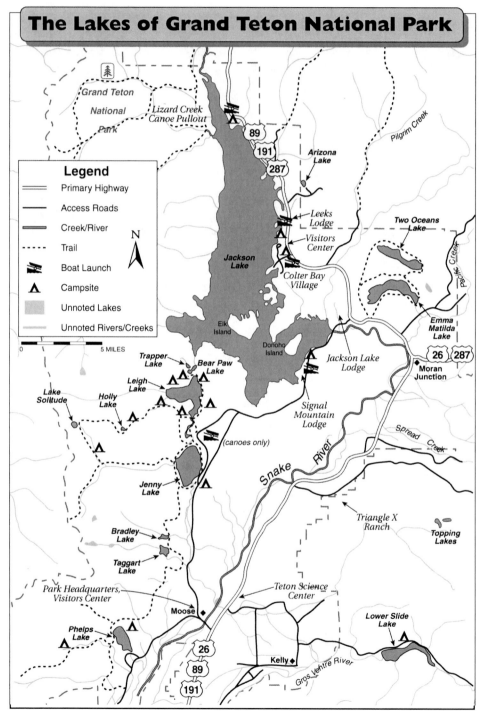

Legend

Primary Highway
Access Roads
Creek/River
Trail
Boat Launch
Campsite
Unnoted Lakes
Unnoted Rivers/Creeks

N

0   5 MILES

Grand Teton
National
Park

Lizard Creek
Canoe Pullout

Pilgrim Creek

89
191
287

Arizona
Lake

Leeks
Lodge

Two Oceans
Lake

Visitors
Center

Jackson
Lake

Colter Bay
Village

Pacific Creek

Elk
Island

Donoho
Island

Emma
Matilda
Lake

26 287

Trapper
Lake

Bear Paw
Lake

Jackson Lake
Lodge

Moran
Junction

Leigh
Lake

Lake
Solitude

Holly
Lake

Signal
Mountain
Lodge

Spread Creek

(canoes only)

Snake River

Jenny
Lake

Bradley
Lake

Triangle X
Ranch

Topping
Lakes

Taggart
Lake

Park Headquarters,
Visitors Center

Teton Science
Center

Moose

Lower Slide
Lake

Phelps
Lake

26
89
191

Kelly

Gros Ventre River

© 2009 Wilderness Adventures Press, Inc.

The Lakes of Grand Teton National Park

A string of deep glacial lakes beneath the towering peaks of Grand Teton National Park are popular with stillwater anglers in Jackson Hole.

The largest, Jackson Lake, is a deep-water fishery best suited for trolling for cutthroat, brown, and lake trout from large watercraft. More intimate waters favored by hikers, canoers, and float-tubers are Jenny and Leigh Lakes. Several lakes on the lower slopes of the Tetons, like Phelps, Taggart, and Bradley, are favorite day hikes. Savvy hikers tote fly rods. High alpine tarns, like Lake Solitude, may or may not hold trout, depending on the last time they were stocked. Check with the Wyoming Game and Fish office in Jackson before packing a rod to the high country.

A quick reminder: a Wyoming fishing license is required in the park. The following waters are closed to fishing: Christian Ponds, Hedrick's Pond, Moose Pond, Sawmill Pond, and Swan Lake.

Boating Permits

Permits, required for motorized and non-motorized watercraft, are available at visitor centers and ranger stations. Non-motorized boat fees are $5 for a week permit or $10 annual permit. Motorized boat fees are $10 for a week permit, and $20 for annual permit.

Backcountry Camping Permits

To obtain reservation forms for backcountry camping permits call 307-739-3602.

JACKSON LAKE

Jackson Lake is a large natural lake in a deep glacial and structural depression at the base of Mount Moran and the northern Tetons. The Snake River flows into the lake from Yellowstone and exits the lake about 30 miles north of Jackson.

Jackson Lake Dam was built at the outlet in 1911, raising the lake level 40 feet. It now covers about 25,730 acres. In 1991, the dam was modified and strengthened against potential damage from earthquakes.

The lake routinely gives up 14- to 18-inch cutthroat and lake trout, and a few browns. Occasional trophy lake trout are caught, and it set the state lake trout record with a 50-pound fish in the 1980s.

Most anglers troll with jigs or bait, or use spinning rods from shore. It gets only moderate attention from fly casters. Deep-water rigs are used when lake trout go deep to escape warm temperatures in summer.

Jackson Lake is closed to fishing in the month of October. The limit on trout is six per day or in possession. Only three may be cutthroat and only one cutthroat may be over 12 inches. Only one trout may exceed 24 inches.

In monitoring fish condition trends over a ten-year period, fisheries biologists found that the body condition for lake trout decreased until they reached 20 inches. Lake trout condition was generally stable from 20 to 24 inches. Body condition increased above 24 inches when lake trout converted to primarily a fish diet.

Since 1988, approximately 36,000 lake trout had been stocked annually. However, it was found that stocked lake trout provided a poor return to anglers (10-20 percent), fisheries biologists report. In addition, the decrease in condition of game fish species, including Snake River finespotted cutthroat trout, raised concerns that the zooplankton resources in Jackson Lake may be over utilized. Therefore, lake trout stocking was systematically reduced for seven years and phased out in 2007. It is anticipated that in the long run natural reproduction will produce more lake trout over 20 inches, the time when they switch to a forage-fish diet. The move also is expected to improve growth rates for cutthroat and brown trout, as well as the lake trout's prey base—red-sided shiners, Utah chubs, and whitefish—since they'll no longer be forced to compete with the yearling lake trout for zooplankton and other food resources.

Mount Moran towers above the nearby water.

THE CANOE LAKES: JENNY, STRING, AND LEIGH

Jenny and Leigh Lakes are popular with canoers as well as flyfishers. Anglers also share Jenny's waters with a shuttle boat that takes hikers to Hidden Falls and the scenic Cascade Canyon. Jenny Lake is most popular with float-tubers because it is directly off the loop road.

In between the two larger lakes is a long, river-like depression called String Lake. It is a marginal fishery because it is shallow and warms early.

In any other mountain range, these would be called foothills lakes. But there are no foothills in the Tetons, and the mountains thrust against the sky right over the glacial ponds. Jenny Lake is at the base of Mount Owen, and Leigh Lake is at the base of Mount Moran. String Lake offers great views of the Grand Teton.

Fishing is good in Jenny and Leigh Lakes for 14- to 18-inch cutthroat and lake trout, and a few small brook trout. Each occasionally gives up a trophy lake trout, a surprise to some float-tubers who may be taken for an unexpected ride.

The limit on trout is six per day or in possession. Only three may be cutthroat and only one cutthroat may be over 12 inches. Only one trout may exceed 20 inches.

Fishing is best after ice-out in spring and again in fall, but both lakes produce in early summer. Float-tube or canoe the shallows for cruising fish in early morning. Also cast to fish lurking around underwater logs and look for fish hanging out at the inlets of mountain streams.

Jenny Lake is fairly deep at the center, but has lots of waterlogged deadfall in the shallows and along the edges of dropoffs. It is circled by trails and has a boat ramp at the mouth of Cottonwood Creek. The inlet from String Lake is at the top of Jenny Lake.

Leigh Lake is reached by a 3-mile trail along String Lake. Canoers must put in at the String Lake parking lot, paddle to the top of the narrow lake and portage about 250 yards to Leigh Lake's landing. Leigh Lake is deep and wide, with incredible views of Mount Moran at its north end. There are a few small islands in the lake and broad shallows along its east shore. A jaunt back into the large bay on the west side can be productive at the inlets of Leigh and Paintbrush Canyons.

Backcountry campsites on Leigh Lake require reservations in advance.

Topwater action on the lakes is basically limited to fly black ants in July and sporadic hatches of large caddis and Callibaetis through the season. Underwater fishing with full-sinking lines is best with Woolly Buggers, leeches, Double Bunnies, Kiwi Muddlers, and other streamers. Beadhead nymphs, emergers, and soft hackles are effective at inlets.

HIKE-IN LAKES

Two low lakes a couple of miles north of Leigh Lake offer a pleasant hike with dramatic scenery and good fishing at the end of the trail.

The lower lake, Bear Paw, holds 10- to 14-inch cutthroat, and Trapper Lake has 8- to 14-inch cutthroat. Backcountry campsites are located at both lakes. The trail to Bear Paw is flat, and there is a moderate climb to Trapper Lake.

The most popular mountain lakes are 2- to 4-mile hikes with moderate climbs on the south end of the park. The lakes are in glacial depressions on the shoulders of the mountains with wide-open views of the Teton Range.

Taggart and Bradley Lakes are reached by the same trailhead a couple miles north of the Moose Visitor Center. Taggart has 8- to 18-inch cutthroat and brook trout, and Bradley's fish are a little smaller.

Phelps Lake is reached from the Death Canyon Trailhead on the Moose-Wilson Road. It offers 14- to 18-inch cutthroat and lake trout.

Fishing is best on the higher lakes in early morning and late in the day for cruising trout in the shallows. The lakes are especially productive when flying black ants are swarming.

Trapper Lake in Grand Teton National Park.

Other Jackson Hole Waters
BRIDGER-TETON NATIONAL FOREST LAKES

Although just beyond the border of Grand Teton National Park, four lakes in the Gros Ventre foothills northeast of Jackson are popular fisheries. A historic landslide blocked the Gros Ventre River to create the aptly named Lower Slide Lake. The Topping Lakes are the only ones in the area with grayling.

The map for the Buffalo and Jackson Ranger Districts of the Bridger-Teton National Forest includes the Teton Wilderness Area.

Lower Slide Lake

This 1,123-acre lake is about 5 miles northwest of Kelly via the Gros Ventre Road, and also is popular with canoers and wind surfers.

It is rated as good fishing for 14- to 18-inch cutthroat and lake trout.

The 1925 landslide that created Lower Slide Lake blocked the river for two years, when it broke during a spring flood. The little town of Kelly, 3.5 miles downstream, was inundated by the torrent rushing down, and six people were killed.

A dam was later constructed at the break to regulate the lower river for irrigation diversions.

Soda Lake

This small lake is about 3 miles southeast of Upper Slide Lake on the Gros Ventre Road. At the lake, take the south fork about 2 miles to the trail. It is a 2-mile hike to the lake.

Fishing is rated as good for 12- to 18-inch cutthroat, and it is managed as a trophy fishery. The limit is one trout per day or in possession. All trout less than 20 inches must be released, and fishing is permitted with flies and lures only.

Toppings Lakes

At the Cunningham Cabin parking lot on US 26/89 in Grand Teton Park, turn east on a Forest Service road. The first lake is an hour's hike from the trailhead, with a steep climb. It is rated as excellent for 8- to 16-inch grayling. The second lake offers tougher fishing for 12- to 16-inch grayling.

TETON WILDERNESS LAKES

There are several small lakes worth fishing in the Teton Wilderness northeast of the park at the end of relatively short hikes.

Gravel Lake

Start at the Pacific Creek Trailhead west of Moran Junction. The small lake is an 8mile hike via Pacific Creek Trail and Gravel Creek Fork. It is rated as good fishing for 10- to 13-inch cutthroat. Both creeks also offer good cutthroat fishing.

Enos Lake

The largest lake in the wilderness, Enos is reached by a 12-mile hike from the Box Creek Trailhead in Buffalo Fork Valley east of Moran Junction on US 26/287. It is rated as good fishing for 12- to 14-inch cutthroat.

Arizona Lake

This is a small lake that drains into Arizona Creek, a tributary of Jackson Lake. It is a 2-mile hike from the trailhead near the picnic site north of Leeks Marina on US 26/89. It is rated as good fishing for 8- to 14-inch cutthroat and brook trout.

Lower Slide Lake on the Gros Ventre River; the scar from the 1925 landslide is visible on the mountain in the background.

UPPER YELLOWSTONE RIVER

Jackson is the southern gateway to the upper Yellowstone River and the best cutthroat fishing in the West. Although located outside the borders of Yellowstone and Grand Teton National Parks, this fishery is inextricably linked to both parks. Located in the Teton Wilderness, the upper river is a long 30-mile hike or horse ride, but fishing is incredible for Yellowstone cutthroat in the 14- to 18-inch range. It's also great in Atlantic and Thorofare creeks in the Hawks Rest area.

Cutthroat spawning runs out of Yellowstone Lake peak with spring runoff in late June or early July, and then taper off. The spawners linger awhile before quickly dropping out of the upper river in August. Some heavy-bodied resident cutthroat stay in the upper river, and fishing is good in nearby Bridger Lake. The window of opportunity is short, but by staying south of Yellowstone's border, anglers can fish earlier than the park's July 15 opener. Also, they don't have to make reservations for designated campsites as is required in the park.

Wilderness trails to the Yellowstone's headwaters are up Pacific Creek west of Moose Junction and up the North Fork of the Buffalo Fork River starting from Turpin Meadows east of Moose Junction. Both trails meet at 8,200-foot Two Ocean Pass to continue down Atlantic Creek to the Yellowstone River. The Forest Service's Buffalo and Jackson Ranger District map and the USGS topographic map for Two Ocean Pass, which shows the meadows and Hawks Rest, are available in Jackson.

A footbridge 2 miles south of the park border is the only crossing on the upper river. The only other access to this section of river is via two Yellowstone Park trails that meet at the river's delta at Yellowstone Lake, 20 miles downstream. One follows the lake's east shore and is 20 miles in reaching the delta. The second starts at the Heart Lake Trail, near the South Entrance, and traverses 35 miles to reach the delta.

The upper Yellowstone in the Teton Wilderness is a classic meadow stream, with riffles and runs, large pools, and long winding glides. The tributaries are tumbling mountain streams with riffles and runs, pools, and pocket waters.

After the spawn, the cutthroat rest in quiet pools and runs meandering through the meadows and feed throughout the day. Good hatches in late June and July are Golden Stones, caddis, and Little Yellow Stones. Pale Morning Duns and Green Drakes also are on the water in mid-July and August. Cutthroat readily take generic mayfly and attractor patterns, too, like Adams, Cahills, Stimulators, Renegades, Humpies, and Elk Hair Caddis.

The best fishing is after runoff wanes, which can vary year to year. Check on conditions before planning a trip. Outfitters and guest ranches based in Jackson specialize in horseback trips into this pristine area. Many anglers also go in on their own horses. There are corrals and a loading ramp at the Turpin Meadows parking lot.

Mosquitoes can be very pesky in marshy meadows, and the region is prime grizzly bear country. Hike in parties of three or more and keep a clean camp.

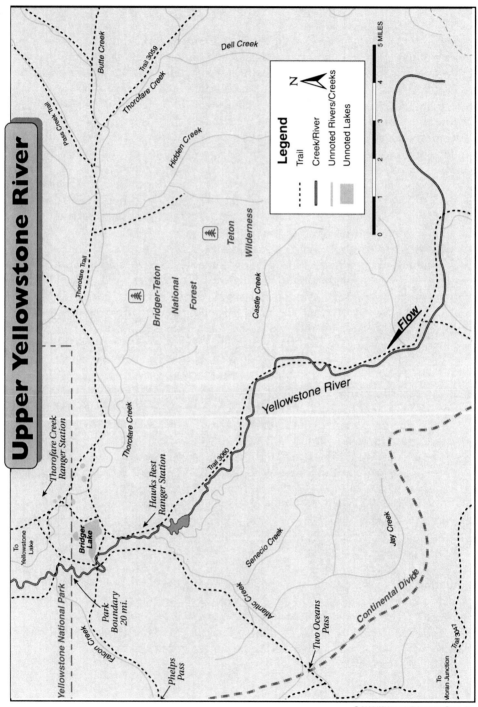

© 2009 Wilderness Adventures Press, Inc.

Pacific Creek on the western access route into the wilderness has good fishing for 10- to 16-inch cutthroat, as well as brook trout. Buffalo Fork River and its North Fork above the Turpin Meadow Campground offer good fishing for 8- to 16-inch cutthroat and rainbows, and they also contain brook trout.

The bag and possession limit in the wilderness is six trout per day or in possession. Only three may be cutthroat and only one cutthroat may be over 12 inches. Only one trout may exceed 20 inches.

SNAKE RIVER TRIBUTARIES

Two Snake River tributaries above and below Jackson offer pleasant day trips. And campgrounds in the Bridger-Teton National Forest invite longer stays. The lower Gros Ventre River shapes the southern border of the park and the northern boundary of the National Elk Refuge. Its name is another Wyoming tongue-twister. Pronounced Gro Vont, it means "big belly" in French. It was the name fur trappers gave to an Indian tribe that often traveled the region with the Blackfeet. The Hoback River is the southern boundary of Teton County just south of Jackson Hole.

Gros Ventre River

The Gros Ventre rises in the Gros Ventre Mountains in the wilderness area behind Jackson and flows about 50 miles to the Snake just below Grand Teton National Park.

Lower Slide Lake on the Gros Ventre was created in 1925 when one of the largest landslides in modern geologic history blocked the river. The dam burst two years later and flooded the little town of Kelly, 3.5 miles downstream. Six people were killed. A dam at the outlet now regulates the lower river for irrigation diversions.

Upper Slide Lake is a string of pools and marshes where the Gros Ventre's headwaters and small tributaries collect to form the main stem of the river. The semiarid terrain is very rugged, with steep ridges and colorful rock outcroppings and sheer cliffs eroded from a variety of formations tinted with layers of red, tan, yellow or graygreen stone.

A road northeast of Kelly hugs the upper river's passage through the steep narrow valley, and up, down, and around a series of short canyons. Rainy weather turns the unpaved portion of the road above Crystal Creek into a muddy mess that can be treacherous. Check the weather forecast before venturing past the two campgrounds near the creek.

Snake River finespotted cutthroat are the dominant fish in this small mountain stream, which also has lesser populations of rainbows. Fishing is good for 10- to 16inch fish, with a few up to 22 inches. Most of the bigger cutthroat are in the upper river because there is less fishing pressure there. Pocket waters in a deep canyon below Lower Slide Lake offer the best rainbow fishing.

The Gros Ventre River was electrofished for the first time in 2004 to obtain a population estimate for Snake River finespotted cutthroat trout. A three-mile reach of the Gros Ventre River in Grand Teton National Park was electrofished. The total estimated cutthroat trout per mile was 229, including an estimated 112 trout per mile greater than 11 inches, fisheries biologists report.

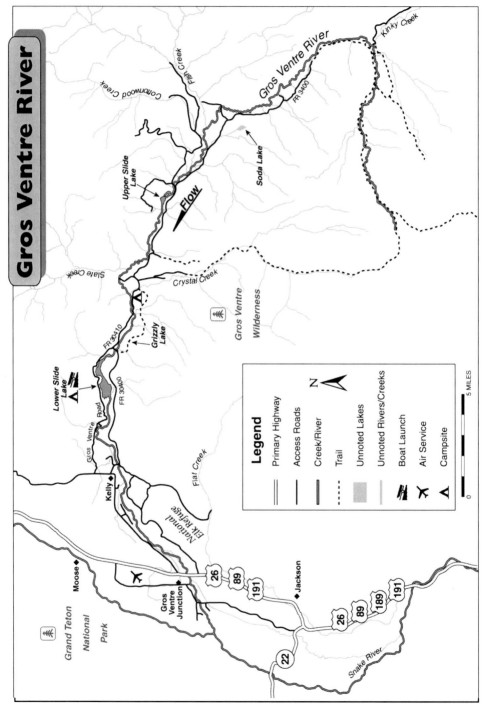

Gros Ventre River

The Gros Ventre is a late summer, early fall fishery that continues fishing well until water flows drop too low. Public access is good throughout the park and the national forest, but there are several ranches on the river where anglers are warned against trespassing. The section running along the north end of the National Elk Refuge is closed to fishing from October 31 to May 20.

The upper river is easily waded in most places after spring runoff subsides, but late summer storms can muddy the water and raise levels temporarily. It descends in a series of riffles and runs, long glides, undercut banks, and deep runs and pools, with some pocket waters on steeper pitches.

In dry years the river below Kelly, where the park's largest campground is located, can be seriously depleted due to irrigation diversions.

A stonefly hatch around the second week of July draws the most attention from local anglers, but the river is rarely crowded above the campgrounds at Crystal Creek and Red Hills. Even though mayfly hatches are sporadic, small generic mayfly patterns work well, as do caddis patterns, attractors, and terrestrials, plus small nymphs and emergers.

Flows in late summer usually are low and clear, which means that you need more delicate leaders and finesse in presentation than on other streams around Jackson Hole.

Where the road loops around the canyons, flyfishers find the best chances for solitude in serene surroundings. The weather during late summer and early fall is often pleasant and mild.

Hoback River

The Hoback River merges with the Snake River 17 miles south of Jackson at Hoback Junction on US 26/89. Public access and good wading opportunities are best along US 191 above the canyon at its mouth. The river is a popular destination during the stonefly hatch in early July, but it fishes better in late summer and fall.

Fishing is good for Snake River finespotted cutthroat in the 8- to 14-inch range. Some larger cutthroat are found in deeper pools and runs, and a few brook trout lurk in the upper river.

And the trout in the Hoback River are wild and feisty--once again.

While the river had been stocked with catchable Snake River finespotted cutthroat trout for many years, in 2005 planting of hatchery fish was discontinued. Biologist established that the estimated number of wild Snake River cutthroat trout was 601 per mile in 2004, well above the recommended mean of 497 Snake River cutthroat trout per mile.

"The biomass of wild Snake River cutthroat trout was estimated at 223 pounds per mile in 2004 - the highest value observed and well above the mean of 188 pounds per mile," reported WGF biologists. "Given the number of wild Snake River cutthroat trout present, further stocking does not seem necessary."

Angler surveys contributed to the decision to let the Hoback "go wild."

"During 2004, the anglers caught an average of 1.7 Snake River cutthroat trout per hour and released 92% of the fish.," reported WGF biologists.

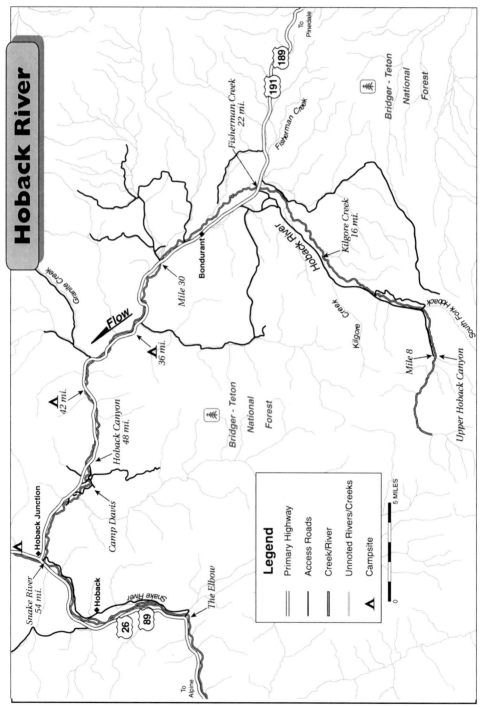

Hoback River

"Catch rates have been high in prior years with harvest remaining low. In 2003, the mean catch rate was 0.93 Snake River cutthroat trout per hour with 95% of the fish released."

Nearly 55 miles long, the Hoback rises in the Wyoming Range southeast of Hoback Junction and almost due south of the village of Bondurant. It emerges from the mountains onto a heavily braided floodplain at US 191 and loops around the village through a marshy flat. Picking up the flows of several tributaries, it returns to the highway and turns sharply northwest on a 20-mile run through a narrow valley to the high-walled canyon above the Snake. The valley descent is mostly riffles and runs, with intermittent pocket waters, cutbank pools, and some deep pools and rock gardens.

A Hoback River angler fishes a riffle.

The canyon and a short stretch above it are private land, and permission is required to cross it. Otherwise, public access is excellent, and there are two Forest Service campgrounds on the highway.

A gravel road to the headwaters climbs about 6 miles through ranchlands and continues another 6 miles into the national forest. Fishing in the headwaters is mostly for pan-sized trout.

Granite Creek enters the Hoback midway between Bondurant and the Snake. A classic small mountain stream, it holds 8- to 12-inch cutthroat and occasional pleasant surprises. It is a principal access route into the south side of the Gros Ventre Wilderness Area. Granite Hot Springs Resort is at the end of the road.

The Hoback's runoff is high and often turbulent from May into July. Summer storms can muddy the water and raise water levels, but late summer and fall flows are mostly gentle and clear.

Both wet and dry stonefly patterns are most effective in early July. Later in the season, traditional high-floating dry flies, grasshoppers, small nymphs, and emergers work best. As on most higher-elevation streams, caddis outnumber mayflies.

Spring Creeks

The clear, cool spring creeks of Jackson Hole are critical spawning grounds for Snake River finespotted cutthroat trout. The majority meander through private property and are closely guarded against trespass.

In recent years, the creeks have been the focus of cooperative projects to return them to their full potential for spawners running out of the Snake River. The landowners opened their gates to Wyoming Game and Fish biologists and local volunteers working on stream renovations crucial to the preservation of the Snake's unique native trout. The rest of the year, most of the spring creeks remain closed.

Unless you are a friend of an owner, the chances of fishing one of these ultraexclusive waters is virtually nil. If you have to ask the cost, you probably can't afford the privilege on a few where limited access is granted. Two in Wilson that advertise accommodations and fishing rights are Fish Creek Ranch on Fish Creek and Crescent H Ranch on Fall Creek. Several other private creeks are available through special arrangements with various Jackson fly shops.

The few public spring creeks in Jackson Hole draw little attention because they are closed most of the year to protect spawning cutthroat. Blacktail Spring Creek, Cottonwood Creek, and Upper Bar BC Spring Creek (in Grand Teton National Park) and Lower Bar BC Spring Creek do not open to fishing until August 1. After the larger spawners return to the Snake River, the creeks hold 6- to 14-inch cutthroat.

But don't despair; Jackson Hole does offer an incredible window of opportunity for quiet water fishing over super wary cutthroat. It's called Flat Creek.

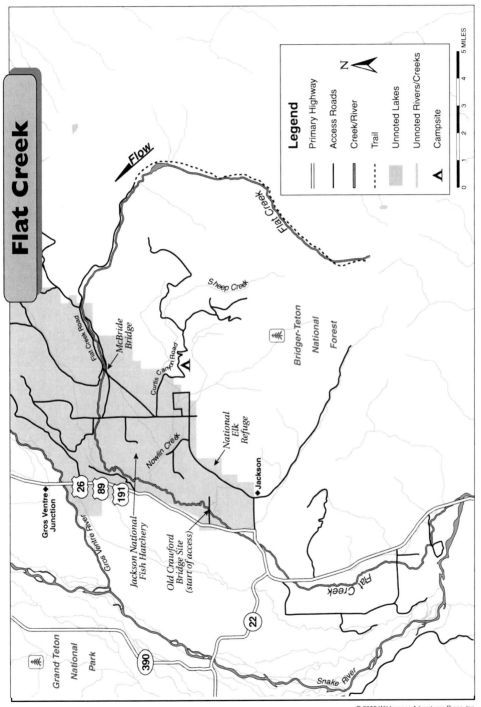

Flat Creek

Flow

Flat Creek

Sheep Creek

Flat Creek Road

McBride Bridge

Curtis Canyon Road

Bridger-Teton National Forest

National Elk Refuge

Nowlin Creek

Jackson

Gros Ventre Junction

Gros Ventre River

Jackson National Fish Hatchery

Old Crawford Bridge Site (start of access)

26 89 191

22

390

Grand Teton National Park

Snake River

Flat Creek

Legend

	Primary Highway
	Access Roads
	Creek/River
	Trail
	Unnoted Lakes
	Unnoted Rivers/Creeks
▲	Campsite

N

0 1 2 3 4 5 MILES

© 2009 Wilderness Adventures Press, Inc.

Lower Flat Creek

While technically not a spring creek, Flat Creek on the National Elk Refuge is the best meadow fishery in western Wyoming. Its special charm is that it really does fish like a spring creek, complete with graduate school lessons from selectively rising trout.

Its fame precedes it, so expect hordes of flyfishers from the August 1 opener through Labor Day. Even then, the numbers of anglers diminish only when bad weather weeds out the less hardy. There is rarely a solitary moment on the creek right up to closing day on October 31.

Flat Creek tumbles out of the Gros Ventre foothills onto the grassy flats of the preserve at Jackson's back door to begin its slow serpentine course to the city line. The remainder of its run down the valley is through private property, except for a short stretch above the Snake River at the South Park access site.

Through spring and most of summer on the refuge below McBride Bridge, Flat Creek is host to spawning Snake River cutthroat and broods of trumpeter swans, ducks, and geese. In winter, it harbors migrating swans and other waterfowl, and the refuge is a sanctuary for the largest elk herd in the world. Coyotes and bald eagles prowl year-round on their own missions of mischief, but only in August, September, and October are people on foot allowed to enter this mystical realm.

Flyfishers are permitted to roam along 3 miles of Flat Creek, but nowhere else on the refuge. Many come looking for a fish of a lifetime—the proverbial 22-inch trout caught on a size 22 dry fly. It may happen, but it won't come easy. The bigger the fish, the smarter the fish is another proverb worth noting on Flat Creek. Its cutthroat range from 14 to 27 inches, with the majority of fish in the 14- to 18-inch class.

But whatever fish you see or hear rising, stalk it with care. The deeply undercut banks of Flat Creek are spongy sounding boards that telegraph the approach of heavyfooted anglers. Also, the water is crystal clear, and the trout flash away to cover at the first hint of danger. Downstream presentations are often the rule.

Long rods with lightweight lines and long, slender leaders and delicate tippets are needed for precise presentations. A good selection of tiny dry flies completes a flyfisher's arsenal. Jackson outfitters recommend typical spring creek fare—thorax patterns, Comparaduns, and hair-wing duns, as well as midges and ants.

Hatches to watch for in August are Pale Morning Duns, size 16-18, and tiny dark caddis, size 18. September is a good month for Mahogany Duns, size 16, and as October begins to huff and puff with hints of winter, tiny fall Baetis, size 20-22, come out to play.

Most of the fishing will be to rising trout, but you don't have to spend all day trying to be a dry fly wizard to catch that one special fish. After all, these are cutthroat and some fish still accommodate less expert tactics and techniques.

There are ample opportunities to prospect opposite banks and have fun with large dries like grasshoppers and craneflies or to search undercut banks with large nymphs and streamers like Woolly Buggers and Muddlers.

Flat Creek is a special place. Savor the angling experience here and leave the trout for the next adventurers.

Fishing regulations:

- Lower Flat Creek is open to fishing August 1 through October 31 from the Old Crawford bridge site upstream to McBride Bridge, and on the mouth of Nowlin Creek up to the closed-area signs a quarter mile upstream.
- Fishing is permitted with flies only on the lower section.
- Fishing at night is not permitted.
- Below Old Crawford Bridge, Flat Creek is closed year-round.
- Above McBride Bridge, the season on Upper Flat Creek is May 1 through October 31.
- The creel limit is six trout per day or in possession.
- The limit on cutthroat in Lower Flat Creek is one per day or in possession. All trout less than 20 inches in length must be returned to the water immediately.
- Kids-only waters: Children under the age of 19 have exclusive rights to fish Flat Creek between the west boundary of the National Elk Refuge and the US 191 bridge adjacent to the Sagebrush Motel and on the Elk Park Pond in Jackson. Persons 19 or older are not permitted to fish these waters.

Grand Teton National Park Hub City
Jackson, Wyoming
Elevation – 6,208 • Population – 9,915

Jackson is the best-known summer and ski resort in Wyoming and, perhaps, the West. Jackson Hole is the home of the Grand Teton National Park and fabulous Snake River. Jackson also is the southern gateway to Yellowstone National Park. In addition to Jackson Hole waters, many local outfitters and guides offer trips to Pinedale's Green River, Swan Valley's Salt and Greys Rivers, Yellowstone's lakes and streams, the Teton Wilderness, and the Wind River Mountains. Jackson's zip code is 83001.

Accommodations

Alpine Motel, 70 South Jean / 307-739-3200 / 18 units / Pets allowed / $

Anglers Inn, 265 North Millward / 307-733-3682 or 800-867-4667 / www.anglersinn.net / 28 units / $$

Anvil Motel, 215 N Cache St. / 307-733-3668 or 800-234-4507 / www.anvilmotel.com / 26 units / $

Lodge at Jackson Hole, 80 Scott Lane / 800-458-3866 / www.lodgeatjh.com / 154 units / $$-$$$

Cowboy Village Resort, 120 South Flat Creek Dr / 307-733-3121 / www.townsquareinns.com / 82 units / $$-$$$

Days Inn of Jackson Hole, 350 S Hwy 89 / 307-733-0033 / www.daysinn.com / 91 units / $$-$$$

Elk Refuge Inn, 1755 North H 89 / 307-733-3582 / www.elkrefugeinn.com / $ / 22 units

Flat Creek Inn, 1935 North Hwy 89/26 / 307-733-1447 / $$ / 46 units / pets allowed / www.flatcreekinn.com

Jackson Hole Lodge, 420 West Broadway / 307-733-2992 / www.jacksonholelodge.com / $$ / 59 units

Snow King Resort, 400 East Snow King Avenue / 307-733-5200 / www.snowking.com / $$$ / 205 units / Pets allowed

Super 8 Motel, 750 South Hwy 89 / 307-733-6833 / $$ / 97 units / www.super8.com

The Alpine House, 285 North Glenwood / 307-739-1570 / www.alpinehouse.com

The Virginian Lodge, 750 West Broadway / 307-733-2792 / $$-$$$ / 170 units / www.virginianlodge.com / Pets allowed

The Wort Hotel, 50 North Glenwood / 307-733-2190 / www.worthotel.com / $$$ / 60 units

Rustic Inn, 475 N Cache / 307-733-2357 / $$$ / 145 rooms / www.rusticinnatjh.com

Red Lion/Wyoming Inn of Jackson, 930 West Broadway / www.wyoming-inn.com / 307-734-0035 / $$$ / 73 units / pets allowed

Teton View Bed and Breakfast, 2136 Coyote Loop, Wilson / 307-733-7954 / www.tetonview.com / $ / 18 units / pets allowed

Spring Creek Resort, 1800 Spirit Dance Road / 307-733-8833/ www.springcreekranch.com /130 units

CAMPGROUNDS AND RV PARKS

Wagon Wheel Campground, 525 North Cache Drive / 307-733-4588 / May 1 - October 1 / 36 RV sites / Full services

Lazy J Corral, 10755 South H 189 / 307-733-1554 / May 1-October 1 / 24 RV sites / Full services

Snake River Park KOA, 10755 South H 89 / 800-562-1878 / June 15 - September 15 / 5 RV sites / www.srpkoa.com

Flagg Ranch Resort, South Entrance of Yellowstone Park; Moran, WY 83013 / 307-543-2861 / www.flaggranch.com / May 15-October 1 / 170 RV sites / Full services

(many campgrounds located in Grand Teton National Park)

RESTAURANTS

Gun Barrel Steakhouse, 862 West Broadway / 307-733-3287 / www.gunbarrel.com

Snake River Brewery & Restaurant, 265 South Millward Street / 307-739-2337 / Pizza, pasta, soup, beer / www.snakeriverbrewing.com

Nani's Genuine Pasta House, 240 North Glenwood Street #229 / 307-733-3888 / www.nanis.com

Blue Lion, 160 North Millward Street / 307-733-3912 / www.bluelionrestaurant.com

The Granary Restaurant at Spring Creek Ranch, 1800 Spirit Dance Road / 307-733-8833 / www.springcreekranch.com

Jedediah's House of Sourdough, 135 East Broadway / 307-733-5671 / Affordable breakfast and lunch

Sweetwater Restaurant, 85 King St / 307-733-3553 / www.sweetwaterjackson.com

Bubba's Bar-B-Que, 100 Flat Creek Drive / 307-733-2288

Snow King Resort: Atrium Restaurant, 400 East Snow King Avenue / 307-733-5200 / www.snowking.com

Rising Sage Cafe, 2820 Rungius Road / 307-733-8649 / Inside the National Museum of Wildlife Art / www.risingsagecafe.com

Billy's Giant Hamburgers, 55 North Cache Street / 307-733-3279 / www.cadillac-grille.com/Billys.html

Snake River Grill, 84 East Broadway / 307-733-0557 / www.snakerivergrill.com

The Bunnery, 130 North Cache Drive / 307-734-0075 / www.bunnery.com

VETERINARIANS

Animal Care Clinic, 415 East Pearl Avenue / 307-733-5590

Jackson Hole Veterinary Clinic, 2950 South Big Trail Drive / 307-733-4279

OUTFITTERS

Jack Dennis Outdoor Shop, 50 East Broadway / 307-733-3270 / www.jackdennis.com

Jack Dennis Fly Fishing, 70 S. King Street / 307-690-0910 / www.jackdennis.com

World Cast Anglers, 485 West Broadway / 307-733-6934 / www.worldcastanglers.com

High Country Flies, 185 North Center Street / 307-733-7210 / www.flyfishingjacksonhole.com

Orvis of Jackson, 485 West Broadway / 307-733-5407 / www.orvis.com/jacksonhole

Westbank Anglers, 3670 North Moose Wilson Road, Teton Village / 307-733-6483 / www.westbank.com

Flagg Ranch, South Entrance of Yellowstone Park; Moran, WY / 307-543-2861 / www.flaggranch.com

Triangle X Float Trips, 2 Triangle X Ranch Road, Grand Teton National Park, Moose, WY / 307-733-5500 / www.triangle-x.com

Turpin Meadows Ranch, P.O. Box 379 Buffalo Valley, Moran WY / 307-543-2496, 800-743-2496 / www.turpinmeadowranch.com

Crescent H Ranch, 1027 S. Fall Creek Road. P.O. Box 730, Wilson WY 83014 / 307-733-3674 / www.crescenthranch.com

The author at Blacktail Creek in Grand Teton National Park. (photo by Mike Retallic)

Mangis Guide Service, P.O. Box 3165 / 307-733-8553 / www.mangisguides.com
Jackson Hole Anglers, 990 Montana Road / 888-45-trout /
www.jacksonholeanglers.com
John Henry Lee Outfitters, Box 8368 Jackson, WY 83001 / 307-733-944 or
800-3-JACKSON / www.johnhenrylee.com

FLY SHOPS AND SPORTING GOODS

Jack Dennis Outdoor Shop, 50 East Broadway / 307-733-3270 /
www.jackdennis.com
Jack Dennis Fly Fishing, 70 S. King Street / 307-690-0910 / www.jackdennis.com
High Country Flies, 185 North Center Street / 307-733-7210 /
www.flyfishingjacksonhole.com
Westbank Anglers, 3670 North Moose Wilson Road, Teton Village / 307-733-6483 /
www.westbank.com
Orvis of Jackson, 485 West Broadway / 307-733-5407 / www.orvis.com/jacksonhole

AUTO REPAIR

Decker's Auto Care, 1525 Berger Lane / 307-733-1608
Rabbit Row Repair, 4280 Leeper Lane, Wilson / 307-733-4331

AUTO RENTAL

Alamo Rent A Car, 1250 East Airport Road / 307-733-0671 / www.alamo.com
Thrifty Car Rental, 220 North Millward Street / 307-739-9300 / www.thrifty.com
Hertz Rent A Car, 1250 East Airport Road / 307-733-2272 / www.hertz.com
Budget Rent A Car, 920 W Broadway, Jackson / 307-733-1736 / www.budget.com

AIR SERVICE

Jackson Hole Airport, 1250 East Airport Road / 307-733-7682 / Services include
Delta Airlines, American Airlines, United Airlines and charter services /
www.jacksonholeairport.com

MEDICAL

St John's Hospital, 625 East Broadway / 307-733-3636 / www.tetonhospital.org

FOR MORE INFORMATION

Jackson Hole Chamber of Commerce
112 Center Street
Jackson, WY 83001
307-733-3316
www.jacksonholechamber.com

Releasing Fish

The following suggestions will ensure that a released fish has the best chance for survival:

- Bring the fish in as quickly as possible; do not play it to total exhaustion.
- Unhook the fish in quiet water such as an eddy or slow spot. Do not drag it across land. Keep fish in water as much as possible when handling and removing hook.
- If you must handle the fish, always make sure your hands are wet. Fish have a protective mucous film sensitive to dry human hands.
- The best way to hold a fish (with wet hands) is with one hand around the tail section and the other beneath the belly just behind the pectoral fins. Never grab or hold a fish through the gills unless it is already dead.
- If you want a photo of the fish, make sure the photographer is ready before you handle the fish. And make it quick.
- Release the fish in quiet water, close to area where it was hooked.
- Remove the hook gently. Don't squeeze the fish. The use of barbless hooks is encouraged to make the release easier.
- Never just throw a fish back into the water. If a fish becomes passive, it is probably close to exhaustion. Gently remove the hook in calm water, then lightly cradle the fish with your hands to see what it does. If it struggles to keep itself upright, release the fish only after its equilibrium is maintained. Gently hold the fish upright around its tail and beneath its belly while pointing it against the current (facing upstream). Move the fish very gently back and forth toward and away from the current. You should notice the gills opening and closing due to the rush of water. This is like giving a fish mouth-to-mouth resuscitation. When the fish has recovered it should swim away on its own.

Game Fish

CUTTHROAT TROUT: NATIVE SONS OF THE WEST

The favorite trout of dry fly purists, the cutthroat's lusty rises to fur-and-feather imitations gladden the hearts of novice and expert flyfishers. Its fight is usually below water and stubborn because it uses stream flows to its advantage, sometimes even rolling with the current and twisting the line around itself. But it is often a short fight if your terminal tackle is not too delicate.

Yellowstone cutthroat, Snake River finespotted cutthroat, and small numbers of westslope cutthroat inhabit Yellowstone and Grand Teton National Parks. The westslope cutthroat is present in only two streams in Yellowstone National Park: Cougar Creek, a tributary of the Madison River, and Specimen Creek, a tributary of the Gallatin River.

Until other species were introduced in the late 1800s, the cutthroat was the only trout in much of the vast interior of the West, from the western slopes of the Sierras in California, up through Utah, Idaho, and Montana, and south to northern Mexico. The rainbow, the other native trout of the West, was historically a Pacific slope fish.

Originally, the cutthroat and rainbow were considered to be descendants of the Atlantic salmon (Salmo salar). Taxonomy specialists agreed in 1990 that western trout are more closely related to the Pacific salmon. Descendants of this genus are described as Oncorhynchus, which means "hooked snout."

Ironically, the taxonomists only recently caught up with the 1804–1806 Corps of Discovery. Meriwether Lewis first recorded the cutthroat for science in 1805 in western Montana. The men of the Lewis and Clark Expedition and later mountain men referred to the fish as the "trout salmon" because of its rich, orange flesh. The Yellowstone, or interior, cutthroat is now known by biologists as Oncorhynchus clarki bouvieri. The westslope cutthroat's scientific name, Oncorhynchus clarki lewisi, honors both captains sent west by President Jefferson to discover a route to the Pacific Ocean.

The Yellowstone cutthroat is a beautiful fish, with rouge-colored gill plates, a rose wash running across its golden flanks, and fins tinted with a translucent salmonorange. Hundreds of round, black spots are sprinkled across it back, with somewhat larger and more heavily concentrated spots on its tail. Its name and fame come from the bright orange-red slashes on the bottom of its jaw. It is the ancestral parent stock of all the many interior subspecies that evolved in the Intermountain West.

It is evident that the Yellowstone cutthroat once had a much broader historical range. Its taxonomic placement is based on the scientific species description made by a U.S. Army officer in 1882 from fish taken from Waha Lake, a now isolated basin in northern Idaho. After Shoshone Falls formed a barrier in the Snake River 50,000 years ago, the rainbow apparently replaced Yellowstone cutthroat in the lower Snake drainage.

During the last Ice Age, it made it across the Continental Divide to the Yellowstone drainage at 8,200-foot Two Ocean Pass north of Jackson. From the pass, Atlantic Creek flows northeast to join the Yellowstone River and Pacific Creek flows southwest to join the Snake River.

Evolving separately, or staying behind, was the Snake River finespotted cutthroat *(Oncorhynchus clarki)* species. It is the predominant trout on the Pacific side of the mountains in western Wyoming. The Yellowstone cutthroat also inhabits some Idaho waters but its realm of dominance is in the park on the Atlantic side of the divide.

Although it is not officially recognized as a separate subspecies, the Snake River finespotted is unique in its ability to coexist with a species of its same genus. Its spotting pattern is heavier and it has many smaller spots than the Yellowstone cutthroat. Many consider it less gullible and a stronger fighter than its cousin.

Healthy Yellowstone cutthroat populations in the park and improving numbers of Snake River finespotted cutthroat in Jackson Hole are largely the success of special regulations to restrict harvest.

Studies show anglers can easily over-exploit the cutthroat. Even with light fishing pressure, up to half the legal-sized cutthroat in a stream are often caught. But Idaho State University studies in Yellowstone show the fish are amazingly hearty. Cutthroat on the upper Yellowstone are caught and released an average of 9.7 times during the river's short fishing season from mid-July to mid-October.

For this reason, the fish responds well to special regulations, such as size or bag limits, or catch-and-release restrictions. Yellowstone Lake's cutthroat population rebounded to historic proportions following tougher regulations in the park.

Cutthroat evolved to spawn on the spring floods common to the northern Rockies. For this reason, some key tributaries with major spawning runs in Yellowstone are off-limits to anglers during the early part of the fishing season. A similar ban extends to late summer on the spring creeks in Grand Teton National Park.

A cutthroat trout comes to net.

Twelve to 17 inches is the average size of Yellowstone cutthroat in the park, with some growing to more than 20 inches and weighing 5 or 6 pounds. But in some lakes outside the park, the fish may exceed 20 pounds. Snake River finespotted cutthroat have a greater size potential since they are more piscivorous. They also are considered to be stronger fighters when hooked.

Cutthroat are most active in water temperatures between 50 and 65 degrees Fahrenheit. They can be found in both fast and slack water, although they are less fond of exceptionally fast waters than rainbows. Like all trout, they take advantage of whatever structural protection a stream provides, from overhanging, willow-lined banks to midstream boulders, logjams, streambed depressions, and deep pools at the base of riffles.

Never pass a logjam or a bankside feeding lane protected by an overhanging tree without working it closely. Riffles also are prime feeding grounds of cutthroat and provide prodigious action, especially at the lip of a deep pool.

Its reputation for eagerly rising to a dry fly remains paramount in most flyfishers' minds. Larger cutthroat will hit a stonefly or hopper pattern with slashing strikes rivaling the ferocity of rainbows or browns. Casting to the feeding frenzy on the lip of a riffle during a heavy caddis or mayfly hatch can bring a host of fish between 8 and 20 inches to the net. At the same time, a hit during selective, sipping rises to tiny mayflies will startle the angler who hooks a lunker lurking beneath the still waters.

A standard set of dry flies to attract cutthroat should include Elk Hair Caddis, Stimulators, Yellow Sallies, Humpies, Adams, Pale Morning Dun, Blue-Winged Olive, Light Cahill, and Parachute Hare's Ear. Nymph and emerger patterns can be equally effective, especially on riffles. Effective sizes for both dry and wet caddis and mayfly patterns can range from No. 10 to 16 in spring and early summer. By late fall, you may have to go as small as No. 18 and 22.

When all else fails, or on big or heavy waters, you can always fall back on standard attractor flies like the Renegade, Royal Wulff, Royal Coachman, Royal Trude, Goddard Caddis, or Irresistible.

Cutthroat also succumb to the usual assortment of small streamers, Muddlers, weighted nymphs, Woolly Buggers, Super Renegades, and rubber-legged patterns. Sizes 8 to 14 generally work best.

Cutthroat can be the least shy of the trout family. Occasionally, you can get amazingly close to feeding fish. On some streams, they may even be right underfoot, feeding on nymphs your boots stir up from the gravel.

But never underestimate the cutthroat. It is not a brown trout with a lobotomy, as some would disparage this remarkable fish. It can be easy to catch, and it can be exactingly selective as it keys in on a specific mayfly or caddis hatch with the resolute intensity of one of its so-called educated brethren.

Either way, it is a joy to catch or to behold.

Cutthroat Trout Identification

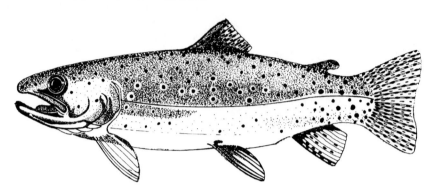

Yellowstone Cutthroat Trout (*Oncorhynchus clarki bouvieri*)

Orange-red slash marks on bottom of jaw are source of its name, and a characteristic common to all cutthroat. The body coloration of Yellowstone species ranges from a silver-gray to olive-green back, with yellow-brown flanks, orange-tinted fins, and reddish gill plates. Spots are spaced out on the body, large and round, and are more closely grouped toward the tail, which is slightly forked. Spotting is less dense than on rainbows, particularly on the tail. A pale crimson wash along the flanks is often bright red during spawning.

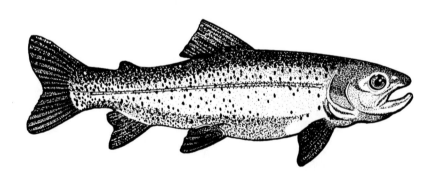

Snake River Finespotted Cutthroat Trout (*Oncorhynchus clarki ssp.*)

The Snake River finespotted is similar to the Yellowstone cutthroat in body conformation and coloration. Its profuse spotting pattern is more similar to coastal species than interior cutthroat. Its many small spots concentrate toward the tail and extend below midline. The tail and lower fins are sometimes darker orange.

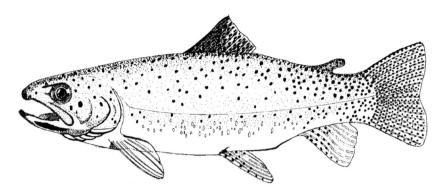

Westslope Cutthroat Trout (*Oncorhynchus clarki lewisi*)

The coloration of westslope cutthroat is richer than the Yellowstone cutthroat, with many small, irregularly shaped black spots across the back, concentrating on the tail and rarely extending below midline. It is generally steel gray on the flanks with an olive back and white belly. Gill plates are dusky red, and a pale crimson swath extends along the flanks; the belly may be bright red during spring spawning season. An oval parr mark is also seen along the midline.

RAINBOW TROUT: MIGHTY LEAPERS

The most exciting fighter of the trout family, the rainbow always pulls something from its bag of tricks, from cartwheeling leaps to reel-sizzling runs to repeated dashes away from the net.

In waters containing other trout species, there's no doubt in an angler's mind when a rainbow is on the end of the line. A rainbow never hesitates in its frenzied quest for freedom. It often leaps more than once in its desperate panic to throw the hook. Even small fish offer a strong and agile fight. Large fish hooked on light tackle or a delicate leader tippet leave the angler one option—give the fish its head and hope the line is long enough for the first run. Your prayers won't always be answered, even on the second or third run. A rainbow rarely comes to the net willingly.

Anglers should use the heaviest terminal tackle conditions permit to make the fight as short as possible and not unduly tire out the fish. Always use a good-sized, soft-meshed net so you aren't inclined to manhandle the fish in attempting to land it.

The feisty rainbow's acrobatic leaps and speckled, multihued beauty—described by a whimsical writer of the past as "sheened like a Kang Shi porcelain vase"—make it one of the most popular game fish in the world. A native of coastal drainages of the northern Pacific, it has been transplanted throughout North America, Europe, and South America.

It gets its name from the crimson to pinkish red band along the midline of its flanks. This reddish band may be absent in lake dwellers, which are generally more silver in appearance. It is marked across its head, back, and upper flanks with many small, irregular black spots that are concentrated most heavily on its squarish tail.

The rainbow trout, Oncorhynchus mykiss, was reclassified as part of the western salmon genus, Oncorhynchus, in 1990. Its former classification was with the Atlantic salmon genus, Salmo. Its former species name, gairdneri irideus, was replaced with mykiss because the Japanese description of the rainbow predated descriptions made in the western United States in the early 1800s.

The rainbow is a spring spawner, like the cutthroat, which leads to hybridization where the species coexist. The rainbow, however, reaches sexual maturity earlier, at ages 2 or 3 years. In hatcheries, they often spawn at 1 year of age. The lifespan of the rainbow is fairly short; few live beyond 5 or 6 years of age.

Rainbow waters can be fast or slow, but chances are more rainbows will be found in faster moving and more turbulent waters than cutthroat or browns. Larger fish are found in the prime holding areas favored by all trout, like overhanging banks, obvious feeding lanes or sheer lines, in front of or behind midstream structures, or at the head of deep pools. While more active in morning or evening, they will move far up into a riffle even at high noon during a prime hatch, using the moving water as cover. Dark, cloudy days will set the fish on the prowl at any hour. The heaviest mayfly hatches regularly occur on these types of days, too.

The rainbow is most active in waters 45 to 75 degrees Fahrenheit. Peak activity is in waters around 60 degrees. It is a highly aggressive fish and will vigorously defend a feeding territory, especially against other salmonids of the same size.

Its food is anything it can catch and swallow. All sizes of rainbows depend heavily on aquatic and terrestrial insects. Larger fish prey on smaller fish, too, and are known to take small mammals like mice or meadow voles. While opportunistic, larger rainbows tend to be very selective and key in on a particular food source, especially during overlapping hatches of mayflies or caddisflies. They also may concentrate on a particular stage of a hatch, keying on the nymph, emerger or adult flying form, or, later, the dead, spinner form. Lake dwellers tend to be more piscivorous.

The selective feeding nature of large rainbows requires more patience and skill by a flyfisher. For those willing to be patient, it boils down to approach and presentation. Approach a feeding fish slowly and quietly to present a fly into its feeding lane. The key is a short-as-possible cast and a drag-free float through that lane. Most rainbows will not move to intercept a fly outside their feeding paths, so keep trying to put your fly right on the mark. Often, presentation is more critical than a perfect hatch-match. If a fish shows an interest, present the fly again immediately. If your first choice doesn't work, rest the fish and try a different pattern. Above all, don't let your expectations cloud your appreciation of the challenge. A day on the stream is valuable, no matter how many fish you net.

Of course, all bets are off during major fly hatches like the Salmonfly or Green Drake. These "Big Macs" of the aquatic insect world bring up trout of all sizes. Wariness is abandoned. This also applies during prime grasshopper activity.

The standard set of dry flies to attract rainbows is much the same as for cutthroat, but, again, presentation is the more important factor. It should include Elk Hair Caddis, Stimulators, Yellow Sallies, Humpies, Adams, Pale Morning Dun, Blue-Winged Olive,

Light Cahill, and Parachute Hare's Ear. Nymph and emerger patterns can be equally effective, especially on riffles. Effective sizes for both dry and wet caddis and mayfly patterns can range from No. 10 to 16 in spring and early summer. By late fall, you may have to go as small as No. 18 and 22. Micro-patterns of midges, Callibaetis, and Tricos also produce amazing results when that's the action on a particular stream. Sometimes small terrestrial patterns, such as ants and beetles, work best, even during an aquatic insect hatch.

Standard attractor flies like the Renegade, Royal Wulff, Royal Coachman, Royal Trude, Goddard Caddis or Irresistible work as well, particularly in faster waters.

Larger streamers, Muddlers, weighted nymphs, Woolly Buggers, Super Renegades, and rubber-legged patterns can be very effective for rainbows. Waders fish them deep, dredging the bottom; float-boaters pound the banks. Leech, dragonfly nymphs, Woolly Bugger, and freshwater shrimp patterns are effective in lakes. Sizes can range from No. 2 to 14.

Nine times out of 10 times, a rainbow will hook itself. Just hang on when a fly scores.

Rainbow Trout Identification

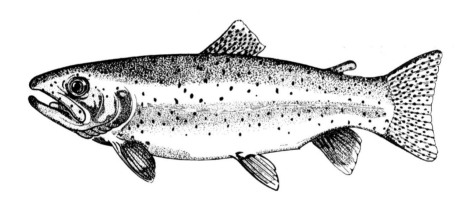

Rainbow Trout (*Oncorhynchus mykiss*)

Its common name comes from the broad swath of crimson to pinkish-red usually seen along the midline of its flanks. Reddish band may be absent in lake dwellers, which are generally more silver in total appearance. River rainbow coloration ranges from olive to greenish-blue on the back, with white to silver on the belly. It is marked with many irregularly shaped black spots on the head, back, and tail, and extending below midline.

BROWN TROUT: CRAFTY BRUTES

The brown trout's well-deserved reputation for wariness demands a dedicated effort on the part of anglers seeking one of these crafty brutes. While most flyfishers pursue browns with large, heavy nymphs or streamers, they rise well to a dry fly when big flies like stoneflies or hoppers are present or a midge, mayfly, or caddis hatch is heavy enough to be profitable.

When hooked, its run is long and deep, although it will jump, especially in shallow-water runs or on riffles. It fights the hook with a bullheaded tenacity that can strip line from a singing reel more than once.

The brown's scientific name, Salmo trutta, declares it as the "true trout." It was first introduced into Yellowstone's Lewis and Shoshone Lakes in 1889 from stocks originating in Scotland and Germany. Many anglers commonly refer to it as a German brown.

Its basic coloration is an overall golden brown, with the back ranging from dark to greenish-brown, and its sides and belly range from light tan to lemon-yellow or white. The back and flanks are marked with many large black or brown spots. The few red spots on the lower flanks are surrounded by light blue-gray halos. There are very few or no spots on its squarish tail.

The older the fish, the bigger and more wary it becomes. Browns normally grow about 4 to 6 inches a year the first three years. Growth then slows to about 2 inches a year, but browns have been known to live up to 15 years. Still, depending on environmental variables such as water temperature and available food, size can range widely. Average fish on some streams may range from 10 to 12 inches and up to 2 pounds, which is still a respectable fish. On others, lunkers over 25 inches and weighing 5 to 10 pounds may be common.

The preferred habitat of the brown is large rivers and lakes at lower elevations, although it can grow to remarkable size in small streams with adequate cover or deep pools. It is generally thought that the brown is able to accept warmer waters than North American species, but the brown's most active periods mirror those of the rainbow. It is active in waters ranging from 45 to 70 degrees Fahrenheit, with activity peaking at 60 degrees. Cold water, in fact, spurs the brown's autumn spawning runs.

Browns first spawn at 3 or 4 years of age. They can spawn in shallow lake waters, but most move up into tributary streams. In rivers, browns are known to make long upstream runs to tributaries, but they will also spawn in shallow waters of their resident streams. In rivers with dams halting their upstream runs, they will go to extraordinary lengths to spawn, even to the extent of turning over cobble-sized rocks to create redds.

A large spawning male can be distinguished from a female by its hooked lower jaw. This morphological adaptation is called a kype.

Browns rarely hybridize with brook trout, which also spawn in fall. It has, however, happened. One case was reported in California on a tributary to Lake Tahoe. The hybrids are called "tiger fish" and are sterile.

The typical realm of larger browns can be summed up in a single phrase: "Under the cover of darkness."

Small browns can be found in most waters common to other trout species. Larger fish prefer quieter waters than cutthroat or rainbows, and they are more likely to hole up in areas where they feel safest and don't have to expend undue energy to feed.

By day, they hide out in the darker cover provided by deep pools, overhanging banks, and bankside or midstream structure such as logjams and large boulders. The other essential element of a good brown hiding place is that it has a steady supply of food streaming into it or close by.

A big brown will lay claim to the same prime spot for years. When it succumbs to old age or an angler, another large brown fills the vacancy.

Older browns are nocturnal feeders, as well as being very active during early morning or evening hours and on heavily overcast days. At these times, they'll move out of the deeper waters of lakes and cruise the shallows or come out of their streamside haunts on feeding excursions.

Browns are known for their piscivorous nature, which contributes to their ability to obtain massive body weight. They even eat their own kind, but they also feed on a large variety of other organisms, including aquatic and terrestrial insects, mollusks, and crawfish.

To entice them from their deeper hiding places, a lot of anglers resort to the chuckand-duck technique of casting large nymphs to large trout. These heavy patterns in sizes 2 to 6 include large stonefly nymphs, Woolly Buggers, Zug Bugs, and Super Renegades. They are bounced off the bottom or drifted just above it. Also effective in similar sizes are streamers such as Marabou Muddlers, Zonkers, and Spruce Flies that imitate sculpin or other baitfish.

Both styles of wet flies can be used to pound the banks, too, by both drift boat and wading anglers. The same goes for large, buggy styles of dry fly patterns. In either case, hit the places with the thickest cover the hardest.

Stonefly hatches bring large browns up just like other trout in spring. In midsummer, a hopper bounced off a grassy bank or tossed up under an overhanging tree can be deadly. Smaller dry flies, including large drakes, caddis patterns, and Stimulators in No. 10 to 14 occasionally bring up a good-sized fish if floated directly through a feeding lane. Browns will move the least of all the trout to intercept a fly. Still, under the right conditions, they will move up into a riffle to grub for nymphs or take emergers. And when there's a carpet hatch, they will slurp down huge quantities of micro-flies, such as midges, Tricos, and *Callibaetis*. Western anglers pursuing these cruisers call them gulpers and revel in the experience of taking a 20- to 25-inch fish on a No. 20 or 22 hook.

Whether you use wet or dry patterns, you can expect to lose more than a few if you are getting them into the haunts where large browns reside. That is one of the costs of going after these hiders. Also expect to spend more time on the water. Studies show that for every five rainbow or brook trout taken, one brown is caught.

It is sometimes easier to tie into one during the fall spawning season, but some anglers frown on this practice because the fish are more vulnerable at this time, and their redds can be damaged by waders. Other trophy hunters attempt to intercept large browns in long, deep runs on their upstream migrations and in the tailwaters of dams blocking spawning runs. Autumn weather plays a major role in this pursuit. You can encounter conditions commonly associated with steelhead fishing, when days of spitting rain or snow prove to be the most rewarding.

Any time of the year, a brown in the net is a flyfisher's reward earned the hard way.

Brown Trout Identification

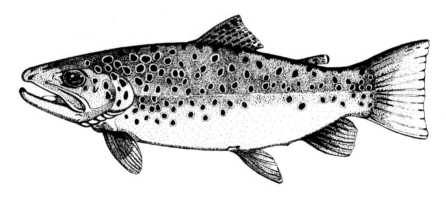

Brown Trout (*Salmo trutta*)

The coloration is generally golden brown; the back is dark- to greenish-brown, with the sides and belly ranging from light brown to lemon yellow. Spaced out, large black or brown spots are mixed with a few red spots on the sides. These spots have light blue-gray halos. The adipose fin usually has an orange border. Very few or no spots can be seen on its squarish tail.

Brook Trout: High Country Brawlers

The flamboyant brook trout is the painted porcelain doll of the trout world. A beautiful fish, it is almost birdlike in the brilliance of its colors. Brookies offer stubborn, scrappy fights, with leaps rivaling the rainbow's, and frantic, line-tugging runs.

Native to East Coast and Canadian waters, the brook trout (Salvelinus fontinalis) is actually a char, like the lake trout, bull trout, Dolly Varden, and Arctic char. Both trout and char belong to the same family, Salmonidae. The main difference between the two is that char have light spots on dark backgrounds and trout have dark spots on light backgrounds. Both prefer cold water environments, but char seek out the coldest.

Introduced into the West in the 1880s, the brook trout is a resident of pure, cold waters of headwater mountain streams and alpine lakes.

Unfortunately, its eastern reputation as a scrappy fighter is lost to most western anglers because it tends to overpopulate the waters it occurs in, which stunts its growth. The short growing seasons of alpine lakes also contribute to its diminutive size. But many high country hikers don't mind. They love to catch pan-sized brookies because they are excellent table fare, often rated as the best among the trout species.

Average size in most western waters is 8 to 12 inches, although its potential is much greater. Brook trout sometimes take up residence in lower lakes, reservoirs, and beaver ponds, where they may grow to a substantial size and provide a tussle worthy of their renown as excellent game fish. A 2- or 3-pounder taken from one of these waters is considered a good-sized fish.

The brook trout's most distinctive markings are white and black edges on the fronts of its lower fins. It is dark green or blue-black on its back, fading to white on the belly. Numerous wavy wormlike lines, or vermiculations, cover its back and dorsal fin. Scattered red spots surrounded by blue halos are seen on its flanks. The belly and lower fins of a spawning male are brilliant red in autumn.

Brook trout reach sexual maturity in 2 or 3 years. Their life span ranges from 6 to 10 years, although a fish over 5 is rare. It is a fall spawner and breeds in both streams and lakes.

The brook hybridizes with other trout species and its introduction into the West, along with habitat loss and pollution, are the main contributors to the demise of the native bull trout throughout much of its former range.

There is at least one record in California of brook trout naturally crossbreeding with the fall-spawning brown trout, an introduced European species. The two also are crossbred in hatcheries. The hybrids are called "tiger trout," due to their yellowish coloration marked with dark, wavy stripes. Some states, like Wyoming, also cross brook trout with lake trout in hatcheries for introduction into a few lakes. These hybrids are called "splake."

The brook trout is the classic coldwater fish. Anglers who like to fish small waters can do well seeking it out in the churning pocket waters and small pools of cascading mountain streams. In quieter waters, it can be found lurking under overhanging stream banks and under logjams. Beaver pond and lake haunts include the edges of weed beds near deep pools and along bushy banks. As summer heats up, they often hang out in the cooler water at the mouths of tributary streams or spring inflows.

Rarely found in waters with prolonged temperatures above 65 degrees Fahrenheit, the brook trout is most active in waters ranging from 45 to 65 degrees. Activity peaks at 58 degrees.

Its primary food base is aquatic insects and other small aquatic invertebrates, but it also attacks terrestrial insects with abandon. Larger brook trout eat small fish, including their own kind.

In fast waters, high-floating buggy patterns, such as the Goddard Caddis or Humpy, and easily seen attractor patterns, such as the Royal Wulff or Royal Trude, work best. Standard nymphs can include the Gold-Ribbed Hare's Ear and caddis emergers. Beadhead patterns eliminate the bother of dealing with split shot. Streamers also can be effective in streams and lakes. Leech and freshwater shrimp patterns, dragonfly nymphs, and Woolly Buggers are good producers in lakes and ponds.

Some consider the brook trout only slightly less gullible than the cutthroat. On small streams or alpine lakes where populations are profuse, brookies offer a good chance for young anglers to practice their fly-fishing skills.

At times, brook trout can be over-exploited like the cutthroat, particularly by hotspotting anglers going after big fish in a lake or pond. Most often, though, larger fish are more cautious, usually active only in the early morning or evening hours or on heavily overcast days. On quiet waters, such as smooth flowing streams and beaver ponds, they should be approached slowly and quietly, using available cover.

Many flyfishers like to pursue brook trout with light tackle, like a 2-weight rod or one of the smaller backpacking models. A substantial brookie taken on one of these is a true challenge.

Large or small, a brook trout in the hand is a portrait of beauty taken in a picturepostcard setting.

Brook Trout Identification

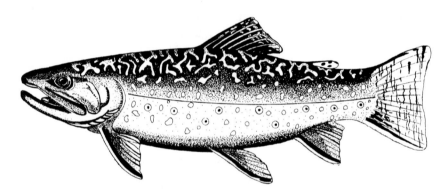

Brook Trout (Salvelinus fontinalis)

The most distinctive markings are the white and black edges on the fronts of lower fins; it also has wavy or wormlike markings on its back and scattered red spots surrounded by blue halos on its flanks. It is dark green or blue-black on the back to white on the belly. In fall, the belly and lower fins turn brilliant red in spawning males. The tail is square.

LAKE TROUT: WOLVES OF THE DEEP

Native to the Northeast, the Great Lakes area, and Canadian waters, the lake trout *(Salvelinus namaychush)* is a char like the brook trout. Its overall coloration is gray, and it has no colored spots like the brook trout. The lake trout's tail is deeply forked; the brook trout's is square.

Lake trout planted in Yellowstone Park's Lewis Lake in 1889 are the Bear Island strain from the northwest shore of Lake Michigan. They then migrated to Shoshone and to Heart Lakes. Eventually they made their way down the Snake River to Jackson Lake, and since then they have been stocked in numerous Wyoming waters. In 1994, lakers were discovered in Yellowstone Lake, the progeny of an illegal introduction that may have occurred in the 1970s.

Also called Mackinaws, lake trout inhabit large, deep lakes, but occasionally they are washed through dams or over waterfalls into the rivers below. They are very sensitive to warm temperatures and in summer may go as deep as 300 feet to find cool water. They spawn in fall over rocky shoals in lakes rather than in moving water like other trout.

Once it reaches 20 inches, a lake trout's diet is almost exclusively fish, including other trout, chubs, suckers, whitefish, and kokanee.

Flyfishers get their best shot at lakers in shallow waters after ice-out on lakes in spring and again in fall when cool weather reduces shoreline water temperatures. Lakers also follow spawning rainbow and brown trout out of lakes into streams like the Lewis River in Yellowstone Park. Large nymphs, streamers, Woolly Buggers, and egg patterns are the most effective flies.

Illegal introduction of lake trout in Yellowstone Lake has caused great dismay because the predator could seriously harm the foremost inland cutthroat sport fishery in North America. In addition to destruction of the lake's fishery, a lake trout takeover would ravage the fabled fishery in the Yellowstone River between the lake and Upper Falls. The threat is real since lakers are credited with virtually eliminating cutthroat from Jackson Lake.

Anglers are required by the park to kill all lake trout taken from Yellowstone Lake and Heart Lake. On other park waters, regulations for harvest are still in place.

Growth potential for lake trout in Yellowstone Lake is phenomenal, considering the histories of the other lakes. Unofficial trophy fish records range from 50 pounds in Heart Lake to 40 pounds in Shoshone Lake and 30 pounds in Lewis Lake.

The record angler catch was a 63-pound, 51.5-inch lake trout from Lake Superior in 1952. The largest one ever netted was a 121-pound gargantuan from a Canadian lake.

Ironically, eggs collected in Lewis Lake have been used to establish brood stocks to return lake trout to Lake Michigan.

Lake Trout Identification

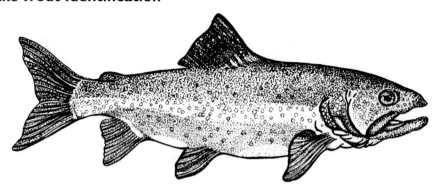

Lake Trout (*Salvelinus namaychush*)

Colors are dark gray or gray-green on the head and upper flanks, slightly gray to white on the belly. Irregularly shaped gray spots are found on the back, sides, dorsal fin, and tail. There are no pink or blue spots. White borders on the fins are less distinct than on brook trout. The tail is deeply forked.

MOUNTAIN WHITEFISH: UNHERALDED GAME FISH

The whitefish gets little respect from flyfishers on trout-rich waters. There is almost a social stigma against taking one, but it is an excellent food species. Part of the scorn for whitefish is a presumption that it competes with trout. In fact, the two species evolved to occupy separate niches in a shared habitat. There is no biological evidence that high whitefish numbers harm trout populations.

While it is in the same family as trout, salmon, and char—Salmonidae—the whitefish's silvery body is slender and almost round in cross-section. It has a small head and tiny mouth, with a slightly overhanging snout. Its scales are large and coarse. Like its cousins, it has an adipose fin.

The most common species in the northern Rockies, the mountain whitefish (Prosopium williamsoni) prefers clear, cool streams. It is also found in some lakes. The Lewis and Clark Expedition first recorded the species for science.

A similar species is the rare Arctic grayling, whose trademark is its huge, colorful sail-like dorsal fin.

Mountain whitefish average 10 to 12 inches, but on nutrient-rich streams, 18- to 20-inch fish are relatively common.

Whitefish hang out in deep pools and shallow, slow-water runs. They feed actively in riffles on mayfly nymphs and caddis larvae. Surface feeding on adult insects occurs most often toward evening.

Among the best wet flies for whitefish are small green-colored nymphs, caddis larvae, and emergers. Beadhead patterns are very effective. Perhaps because of their small mouths, many whitefish fail to take a dry fly when they strike. These misses can be frustrating, but they are also a sign that actively rising fish aren't trout.

Whitefish Identification

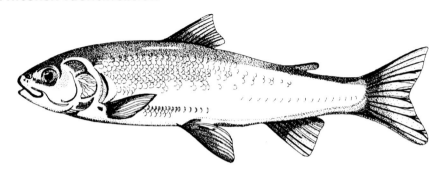

Mountain Whitefish *(Prosopium williamsoni)*

The color is light grayish blue on the back, silver on the sides, and dull white on the belly. Scales are large, and it has a small mouth without teeth. The body is almost round in cross-section.

ARCTIC GRAYLING: SILVERY SAILFISH

The first trademark of the arctic grayling *(Thymallus arcticus)* is its huge, colorful sail-like dorsal fin. The second is its characteristic leap to take floating flies on the returning dive into the water.

The grayling is a popular game fish, both because of its beauty and its rarity. A native of Wyoming in Yellowstone National Park's Madison drainage, it was exterminated by the early 1900s due to introduction of nonnative species, primarily brook trout. It was reintroduced to the park in 1921 and then transplanted to other waters.

Grebe Lake in the park was for many years its hatchery source for grayling after reintroduction of the Montana subspecies. Both Wyoming and Yellowstone have shared grayling eggs with other states and Canadian provinces. The park is attempting to reestablish fluvial, or river-running, grayling in tributaries of the Madison River.

It spawns in spring by migrating into tributaries or outlets of lakes. After high water years, Grebe Lake grayling often show up in the Gibbon and Madison Rivers. The fish is also present in Wolf and Cascade Lakes in the park.

Though they are coldwater fish, grayling generally do best in shallow mountain lakes with longer growing seasons than in alpine lakes. They sometimes become stunted from overpopulation.

Grayling, while suckers for small dry flies, particularly terrestrial patterns like ants and beetles, rise eagerly to most any small dry fly or attractor pattern. And they take small nymphs with even more abandon.

Grayling in Yellowstone are catch-and-release. Wyoming permits inclusion of grayling in its aggregate trout bag limit. Think twice; it's almost too easy to catch one of these relics of the past. Their distinctive lavender sheen quickly fades, and it's not the same fish in a creel.

Grayling Identification

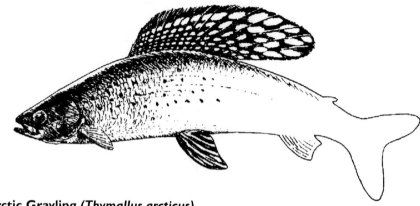

Arctic Grayling *(Thymallus arcticus)*

The dorsal fin is large, sail-like, and colorful. Dark spots are on the front half with purple-silver sides; scales are more pronounced than on trout. The mouth is troutlike. The adipose fin is very small and slender. The forked tail has rounded tips.

Equipment Checklist and Travel Tips

When setting off on a fishing trip, make your travel list and check it twice. Nothing ruins a vacation faster than forgetting to bring a key piece of equipment. Be paranoid; check off your rods, reels, and fishing vest a third time.

Come prepared for inclement weather and be physically fit to handle highelevation trekking.

SUMMER EQUIPMENT CHECKLIST

☐ Selection of rods and reels, such as a 7- or 6-weight, 8½- or 9-foot graphite rod and a 4- or 5-weight, 8½- or 9-foot graphite rod. For alpine hiking trips, a 3- or 4piece backpack rod is recommended. Optional: extra reel spool(s) equipped with shooting-head floating line or sinking line.

☐ Fishing vest or fannypack to hold tackle.

☐ Forceps to remove hooks from fish; line nippers or fingernail clippers to trim leader tippets or flies.

☐ Selection of tapered leaders and tippet material, 2X to 6X; selection of sinking tips.

☐ Selection of standard fly patterns.

☐ Fly floatant.

☐ Nontoxic split shot.

☐ Fishing net.

☐ Stocking-foot chest waders and wading boots.

☐ Wading staff if you plan to wade rocky or swift waters.

☐ Polarized sunglasses.

☐ Stout fishing hat to protect neck and ears.

☐ Lightweight rain jacket.

☐ Wool or fleece sweater, windbreaker jacket, fingerless gloves for cool mornings and evenings.

☐ Water bottle or canteen.

☐ Sunscreen.

☐ Insect repellent.

☐ Camera, extra film, and batteries.

FALL AND WINTER EQUIPMENT CHECKLIST

- ❑ In addition to the above items, pack the following:
- ❑ Neoprene chest waders.
- ❑ Extra warm clothing to wear in layers.
- ❑ Warm hat or wool ski cap that covers ears.
- ❑ Neoprene gloves, wool gloves.
- ❑ Heavy wool socks and polypropylene foot liners.
- ❑ Cigarette lighter in waterproof pouch to start fire.
- ❑ High-energy snacks to munch on.
- ❑ Full change of clothing in vehicle in case you get wet.
- ❑ Parka and down vest for campwear, gloves or mittens.

TRAVEL TIPS

Flyfishers embarking for Yellowstone Country via commercial airlines should plan on transfers at one or more service hubs, some with layovers. So take precautions to protect your equipment.

Pack rods in aluminum or plastic rod holders or a rod-holder caddy, securely sealed and clearly labeled with name and home address. Make sure flight destination tags are firmly attached.

Never ship cameras or telephoto lenses as cargo in recognizable photography equipment containers. If you don't plan to take them as carry-on luggage, stuff them into your suitcases.

Travel light; don't be a clotheshorse. Your fishing equipment is most important.

Be in Shape

Remember that as soon as your plane lands you're already almost a mile above sea level. Your next destination in the park may be even higher.

Don't overextend yourself while wading; appreciate the volume of the bigger rivers. One cubic foot per second of water, the standard measurement of flow, is roughly equivalent to one foot of water continually flooding a football field. A football field is flat and rock-free. Yellowstone area rivers are not, and their waters are almost always frigid.

Traditional Dry Flies Endure the Test of Time

No dedicated flyfisher's vest seems to be complete without 10 to 30 boxes capable of holding several hundred flies. Many also pack containers in their car trunks filled with additional fly boxes. Truly rabid flyfishers even pack along fly-tying vices and materials.

This obsession with being prepared for all situations makes fly shop cash registers sing the Star Spangled Banner year-round. For those who tie their own flies, numerous magazine articles send them scurrying to their fly-tying benches.

But what if you are only recently learning to wet a line, or just want to have fun without all the hassle? For newcomers and fun seekers alike, it's a good idea to stick to traditional fly patterns. There's a lot to be said for tradition.

Sure, spring creeks and other selectively feeding trout situations present challenges requiring more finesse in fly selection. Don't worry; you'll evolve to that plateau. On less demanding waters, fly pattern anxiety is unnecessary. Newcomers can perform reasonably well with tried-and-true patterns. Catching a trout on a No. 14 Old Fashion attractor pattern is just as much fun as catching one on a No. 22 High Tech modern concoction.

Common aquatic choices are generalized imitations of mayflies, caddisflies, and stoneflies. Terrestrial imitations include grasshoppers, ants, beetles, and crickets. With those options in mind, consider the following as a quick course in Basic Dry Fly Patterns 101.

DRY FLY ATTRACTOR PATTERNS

Attractor patterns that float like corks are steadfast producers on the pocket waters of the West's fast-flowing, cascading mountain streams. When in doubt (or if there is no obvious mayfly or caddis hatch), start with a high-riding attractor pattern. These patterns are not intended to represent any single species of aquatic insect. Instead, their colors and characteristics mimic the essential ingredients of mayflies and caddis, as well as those of some terrestrial insects. Stepped down a size or two, the same flies perform admirably on quiet waters, especially during masking hatches of more than one species.

Mayfly attractor patterns rely on glossy colors to mimic key strike factors presumed to attract fish. More numerous in number, variety, and down-to-earth colors are the prolific caddisfly families and the smaller species of the stonefly families. Most caddis attractor patterns employ simple tufts of hair for wings and earth-tone body materials. Still, vivid colors cannot be denied a role, and some caddis attractors rival mayfly versions.

COLORFUL ATTRACTORS

The Renegade is a classic dry fly attractor that replicates key characteristics of caddisflies. Hackle wraps at the front and back make it float better than a cork. Its peacock body is the main ingredient of numerous other productive attractor patterns. The white hackle in front gives it visibility; the brown hackle at the rear provides natural stimulation for fish strikes.

The Renegade's greatest charm is that it often saves the day for novices and pros alike. Play it safe. Don't go afield without a selection in sizes ranging from No. 10 to No. 18.

The Royal Wulff is perhaps the best known and most popular mayfly attractor pattern. Its principal asset, for both fly casters and fish, is the addition of red. The fly's peacock body is divided in the middle with wraps of scarlet. Its divided, white calf-tail wings are visible to even the most myopic of anglers. Sizes can range from No. 6 to No. 20.

Since it is more mayfly-like in appearance, the Royal Wulff is often the preferred attractor pattern of most fly casters. An excellent substitute is the Coachman Trude. Its white calf-tail wing is slanted back at a 45-degree angle. Also, many Idaho anglers are partial to it because the Trude series originated at the old Trude Ranch in Island Park.

All these patterns can be fished underwater. Large Royal Wulffs and Royal Trudes are fished wet as streamers or minnow imitations. Renegades, and color variations on its theme, can be fished wet in all sizes to imitate mayfly and stonefly nymphs.

CADDISFLY ATTRACTORS

The Elk Hair Caddis is the ultimate dry fly attractor pattern, especially since its many variations represent such a great number of choices in productive patterns. Caddisfly species far exceed the ever-popular mayfly species. Minor differences between caddisflies and small stoneflies boggle the minds of flyfishers and biologists.

Yet the basic shape and dimensions of the Elk Hair Caddis—a simple tent-like hair wing flared at a 45-degree angle over a thinly wrapped body—fits the bill for the legions it imitates. Adding wraps of hackle over the body or in front of the wing is a personal choice. Body color sometimes adds to the success ratio, although wing color and hook size are often the deciding factors. Also, wing hair selection is not limited to different colors of elk hair. Many productive patterns employ color and texture variations in the hair of deer, moose, and antelope.

An assortment of basic Elk Hair Caddis patterns is perhaps the one guarantee to success anywhere on mountain streams and lakes, West or East, Midwest or Southwest. Adding a few modern variations—like the Stimulator series—certainly ups the ante for a good day. Size selections range from No. 10 to No. 22. Patterns on the same theme, in size No. 8 and larger, mimic various stoneflies.

An equal rival of the elk hair pattern as a caddis attractor is the Humpy. This uniquely western pattern also gained fame as the Goofus Bug, but don't be turned off by either name. The fly's ability to pop back to the surface after being submerged makes it as unsinkable as the West's best known Titanic survivor, Molly Brown.

The Humpy's great flotation qualities are derived from the best feature of both mayfly and caddis patterns. Elk or deer hair is drawn humpback-style over a full body and flared or divided as wings. In front and behind the wings, thick wraps of dry fly quality hackle further guarantee a high-riding fly.

Hands down, the premier producer among Humpies is the Yellow Humpy, mainly because it is also a handy substitute for a small grasshopper. But hair and body colors can be mixed to create numerous variations of the Humpy. The Royal Humpy, of course, incorporates a red body and white wings to increase visibility. Small Humpy sizes are the same as for the Elk Hair Caddis. Similarly, large Double Humpy patterns are intended to simulate various stoneflies like Golden Stones.

GENERIC MAYFLY ATTRACTORS

Although outnumbered by caddis species, the popularity of mayflies prevails among dry fly anglers. Generic patterns developed to meet this demand, like the Adams and Light Cahill, rely more on size and shape than color. Both have the classic silhouette of mayfly patterns, but their bodies and hackle colors are generalized or muted. Sizes for both run the gamut from No. 10 to No. 22.

Of the two, the Adams is definitely the single fly pattern no fly caster should leave home without, in a full complement of sizes. Its gray body, grizzly hackle tip wings, and grizzly and brown hackles perform under all light conditions on streams or lakes. Match the size, and you'll usually match the hatch with this versatile pattern. This is especially true on overcast days when overlapping mayfly hatches often occur. Better yet, the Adams is a prime prospecting fly for testing slipstreams, foam lines, and eddies when action is slow. On lakes it is a handy substitute for both Callibaetis and caddis hatches.

Also, the Para-Adams is establishing high standards for the many water-hugging parachute styles. The parachute concept was developed by wrapping a fly's hackle around the base of its wings (or a stub) parallel to the water.

The Light Cahill is another generic mayfly pattern that often saves the day when prospecting on new waters or fishing less demanding streams. Its light cream body, wood duck wings, and ginger tail and hackle mimic characteristics of Pale Morning Duns, Sulfurs, and other light-colored species.

While the Light Cahill usually isn't tied as a parachute pattern, a good substitute in this style is the Parachute Hare's Ear. The natural, soft tans of this new pattern ensure its future representation among the traditional patterns. The same goes for its companion pattern, the Parachute Olive Hare's Ear.

Prime Terrestrial Patterns

A distinct advantage of terrestrial dry fly patterns is that they play to the opportunistic nature of fish. Grasshoppers, ants, beetles, and crickets are out of their element when they land on water. They are extremely vulnerable. Trout know this, and few can resist an opportunity to gobble one.

When prospecting for trout, a grasshopper pattern is one of the most effective options in an angler's arsenal. It produces an adrenaline rush exceeded only by savage strikes on stoneflies. The bonus is the extended season of the grasshopper, compared to the short duration and sometimes fickle timing of stonefly hatches.

Most years, grasshopper patterns are productive from late July to October. They'll produce even after the first frost because the fish are still tuned into these juicy morsels. The best grasshopper prospecting time is late afternoon. If it's windy, all the better.

Patterns come in many colors and styles. Yellow predominates for body dubbing, although green and brown work, depending on the stream. Closed-seal foam bodies of newer patterns are good low-riding floaters. Most patterns have turkey tail or primary wing feathers as the fly's wings. Pheasant tails are another good source of wing material. The head is usually clipped deer or elk hair, but the drawn back, bullethead style is effective, too.

Most often, size is more critical than color. Choices range from No. 2 to No. 14. Patterns that have stood the test of time include the flared-wing, clipped deer hair head of the Joe's Hopper or Letort Hopper for fast waters and the more realistic Whitlock's Hopper or Henry's Fork Hopper for slow waters. And, again, several new parachute patterns are attracting a lot of attention, from both anglers and fish.

Many anglers also routinely carry a selection of ant patterns, No. 16 to No. 20, for quiet spells on streams or when they give up trying to match the hatch for a super-selective trout. But anglers packing the right stuff when a swarm of flying ants descends on a stream will think they died and went to heaven.

However, generally more productive as a secondary terrestrial pattern is a small black beetle. Patterns tied with black foam float better and are more durable than older versions tied with deer hair. A few wraps of grizzly around the neck should be clipped at the bottom so the fly floats snug to the water. Sizes can range from No. 12 to No. 16.

The Disc O'Beetle offers a simple solution to determining the size and shape of foam beetles. Cut the foam in the shape of a circle with a diameter the length of the hook shank. Then place the disc on top of the hook shank, fold it down and tie it off about one-fourth the way back from the head. The pattern also calls for a peacock body, and short thin legs or a clipped-bottom hackle wing. Harrison Steeves, inventor of the pattern, notes that foam sheets come in many colors in addition to black.

Food for Thought:
Aquatic Insect Prey of Trout

I was standing on the boardwalk of a little western resort town a few years ago when I overheard two women behind me discussing the slogan on the back of my T-shirt. Its words of wisdom circled a large colorful drawing of a Royal Wulff.

"The way to a man's heart is through his fly," the first woman read aloud.

Her companion chuckled. "Isn't that the truth."

They laughed again, and one of them tapped me on the shoulder. "I like your Tshirt," she declared.

The double entendre is intended to draw a chuckle. Some also might claim the message is that the many colorful fur, feather, chenille and wool imitations, tied in newer and better patterns each year, catch more flyfishers than trout. But the record is clear. The way to a trout's heart is through a well-presented fly.

The dry fly angler's task is determining the Blue Plate Special of the day. Most know, though, that 90 percent of a trout's daily grub is consumed underwater. So a working knowledge about the life histories and habitats of aquatic insects can add significantly to bringing more fish to the net.

Aquatic insect forms are available to trout in two basic groups, depending on how they metamorphose after their eggs hatch. Caddisflies and midges, which have a complete metamorphosis, are food sources for trout as larvae, pupae, and adult flying insects. Mayflies, stoneflies, and dragonflies have an incomplete metamorphosis and are fed on by trout as nymphs and adults.

Each type of insect is in a biological classification known as an order. An order is divided into families, genera, and species. Aquatic insects of most interest to Yellowstone area flyfishers include:

Ephemeroptera / Mayflies

Adult mayflies rest with their large wings in an upright position and their long, slender bodies curved in a graceful arc, front to back. When floating on water they look like miniature sailboats. They usually are quiet and docile on the water, rarely fluttering except for emergers that failed to shuck their nymphal casings. Mating swarms can be very busy and thick. The adults are literally ephemeral. Few species live longer than a day.

The newly emerged adult is known as a subimago, or dun. Large mayflies are called drakes. The body color is dull, nonreflective, and the wings are dark or grayish. After molting into the imago, or reproductive form, the body color is bright, and the wings are clear or transparent. Spent females that have completed laying eggs fall to the water with outspread wings and are called spinners.

Nymphs can live one to three years underwater, although a few species have two or three generations in a single season. The nymphs go through growth stages, called instars, where they shuck their exoskeletons each time they outgrow them. As they approach the emerger stage, the dark wing pad on the back of the thorax becomes more prominent.

The four categories of nymphs—swimmers, crawlers, clingers, and burrowers—reflect their habitats and habits. When it is time to emerge into adults, the nymphs of most species float or swim to the surface as they shuck their exoskeleton and unfold their wings. Most fly off immediately. On cold or rainy days their float on the water can be quite a bit longer. The nymphs of a few species crawl ashore or up the stems of aquatic vegetation to emerge.

Trout will grub for nymphs in their hiding places, move up into riffles to snatch nymphs or emergers, or wait in their feeding lanes to snare dislodged nymphs. Emergers and floating adults are taken as they pass down a feeding lane, flow over the lip of a riffle, or are swirled together in the backwaters of an eddy. When a multiple hatches occur, trout will often key on a single species—and not always the larger one.

Characteristics of mayfly species are reflected by the colors and other descriptive terms assigned to their common names and popular dry fly patterns.

Major mayfly hatches in the Yellowstone region include:

Siphlonuridae

This family has only one major genus in most of the West. A large fly, the Gray Drake is somewhat rare but very important on streams where it occurs. Key hatches begin in late summer and go into fall.

Siphlonurus / Gray Drake

Habitat:
Swimming nymphs prefer quiet pools and slack waters in streams, and the edges and shallow waters of lakes and ponds. Nymphs find food and shelter in weed beds and around stems of aquatic vegetation. They emerge by crawling up stems of plants or onto logs.

Nymphs:
Gray Drake, Black Drake, No. 10 to 14.

Hatch/dry flies:
Siphlonurus occidentalis—Gray Drake Dun, Gray Drake Spinner, Gray Wulff, Adams, No. 10 to 12; mid-July to mid-October.

Baetidae

One of the most abundant and hardy families in the West, its many important species guarantee blue-ribbon action. Carpet hatches of Blue-Winged Olive (BWO) are common. Baetis hatches overlap through fishing season, from early spring into late fall.

Baetis / Blue-Winged Olives

Habitat:
Swimming nymphs prefer flowing waters. They are mostly found in shallow riffles but are also in rapids and eddies. They feed and find shelter in crevices and rock cobble of a streambed, sometimes in weed beds. They emerge by floating or swimming to surface to shed nymphal casing. Present adults downstream and across.

Nymphs:
Soft hackle and emerger patterns tied sparsely in olive, brown/olive or tan, No. 14 to 24.

Hatches/dry flies:
Baetis tricaudatus—Blue-Winged Olive, Iron Blue Quill and Adams; late March through mid-May, No. 16 or 18, and October through November, No. 18 to 22.
Baetis bicaudatus—Tiny Blue-Winged Olive, No. 22 or 24; July through August.
Baetis parvus—Tiny Brown Dun and tiny Blue Quill, No. 20 or 22; mid-July through October.
Pseudocloeon edmundsi—Tiny Blue-Winged Olive, No. 22 or 24; mid-July through October.

Callibaetis / Speckle-Winged Dun

Habitat:
A very important species on lakes, ponds, and reservoirs; it is also found in slow, quiet waters of some mountain streams and spring creeks. Sporadic hatches occur throughout the season, spring to autumn, but emergers and spinners offer most action. Swimming nymphs find food and shelter in weed beds, stands of aquatic vegetation, and in the debris of stream and lakebeds. Nymphs are very active prior to emergence and rise swiftly to the surface.

Nymphs:
Callibaetis nymph, Sheep Creek Special, and Gold-Ribbed Hare's Ear, No. 12 to 18. Sizes become smaller as season progresses; usually weighted and fished as rising emergers.

Hatches/dry flies:
Callibaetis coloradensis—Speckled Dun, Speckled Spinner, Speckled Biot Spinner, No. 14 or 16, also Light Cahill, Comparadun or Parachute Adams; mid-July to mid-August.
Callibaetis nigritus—Speckled Spinner, No. 14 or 16; July through September.

Ephemerellidae

This family offers perhaps the two most productive patterns on western streams. Tiny Pale Morning Duns (PMD) are a class act throughout the summer, and giant Green Drakes elicit exciting early season action.

Drunella / Green Drakes

Habitat:

This genus marks the beginning of the season on many streams for anglers who seek big fish on big flies. Crawling nymphs are poor swimmers and prefer to find food and hide in haunts of streams with weedy, silty bottoms. Emergers are very vulnerable as they crawl to quiet waters or rise slowly to the surface. Adults are equally vulnerable because of long floats after emerging.

Nymphs:

Charles Brooks's Ida Mae, Green Drake Nymph, Lead-Wing Olive Nymph, Zug Bug, No. 8 to 10.

Hatches/dry flies:

Drunella grandis—Western Green Drake, Green Paradrake, Green Drake Wulff, Green Drake Comparadun, Extended-Body Drake, Great Red Spinner, No. 8 to 12; late June to mid-July.

Drunella flavilinea—Flavs, Small Western Drake, Slate-Winged Olive, Parachute Olive Hare's Ear, No. 14 to 16; July.

Drunella coloradensis—Slate-Winged Olive, Parachute Olive Hare's Ear, No. 14 to 16; August.

Ephemerella / Pale Morning Dun

Habitat:

Crawling nymphs are poor swimmers and prefer to find food and hide in haunts of streams with weedy, silty bottoms. Emergers are very vulnerable as they crawl to quiet waters or haphazardly rise slowly to the surface. Small size of adults requires downstream or down-and-across presentations.

Nymphs:

PMD Nymph, Hare's Ear, Yellow Soft Hackle, No. 16 to 20.

Hatches/dry flies:

Ephemerella infrequens—PMD, Hair-Wing Dun, Comparadun PMD, Parachute PMD, Rusty Spinner, No. 14 to 18; June and early July.

Ephemerella inermis—PMD, Hair-Wing Dun, Comparadun PMD, Parachute PMD, No. 16 to 20; July through September.

Ephemeridae

The principal fly in this family is the Brown Drake, a large, slow-water species that may overlap with the Green Drake hatch on some streams. It usually hatches at night in early summer.

Ephemera / Brown Drake

Habitat:

Nymphs burrow into silty sand bottoms of streams and lakes and feed at night. The hatch occurs at twilight or at night, with the emerger rapidly rising to the surface.

Nymphs:
Brown Drake Nymph, No. 10 to 12.

Hatch/dry flies:
Ephemera simulans—Brown Drake, Brown Drake Parachute, Brown Drake Spinner, No. 10 to 12; mid-June to early July.

Leptophlebiidae

The principal fly in this family is the Mahogany Dun, a tiny, fast-water species with a relatively long season. Late summer hatches are common.

Paraleptophlebia / Mahogany Dun

Habitat:
Crawling nymphs prefer flowing waters, like fast riffles; they hide and feed in debris and gravel of the streambed. Poor swimmers, they move to quieter waters prior to emerging.

Nymphs:
Hare's Ear Nymph, No. 14 to 18.

Hatch/dry flies:
Paraleptophlebia bicornuta—Mahogany Dun, Mahogany Spinner, No. 16 or 18; late August through September.

Tricorythodidae

The very tiny flies of this family are a major feeding source for selective trout, mostly on streams but also on some lakes. Late summer hatches are common.

Tricorythodes / White-Winged Black

Habitat:
Nymphs prefer slow waters of streams and hide in bottom debris. Floating emerger and dun patterns work, but spent female spinners are most vulnerable to slurping trout.

Nymphs:
Poxy-White-Black Nymphs, black or olive midge pupa, Pheasant Tail Nymph, No. 20 to 24.

Hatch/dry flies:
Tricorythodes minutus—White-Wing Black, Parachute Trico, black or olive midges, Griffith's Gnat, Trico Spinner, No. 20 to 24; August into September.

Heptageniidae

Common to fast mountain streams, the species of this family prefers clear, cold water. The midsummer hatch continues into fall.

Eperous / Pink Albert

Habitat:
Nymphs cling to the substrate of tumbling riffles and fast runs. Emergers and floating duns are most vulnerable to quick-acting trout.

Nymphs:
Soft hackle patterns and Hare's Ear Nymph, No. 10 to 16.

Hatch/dry flies:
Eperous albertea—Pink Albert Cahill, Pink Lady, Cream Dun, No. 14 to 16; July to September.

TRICHOPTERA / CADDISFLIES

Few anglers bother to learn the Latin names of caddisflies. Few have common names, although on many streams they are more prolific than mayflies. Popular caddis patterns are impressionistic but take tons of trout. Larval patterns are effective year-round because caddis are so common. Emerger patterns generally are more productive during a hatch than dry flies. A dry fly produces best when females return to deposit their eggs. But a dry fly is a good attractor pattern in spring and summer because caddis are on the water throughout their adult stage.

The two pairs of wings of the caddisfly slant back over the body in a tent-like position when it is resting. In the air, caddis have an erratic, bouncing flight pattern. On the water, they often continue fluttering or swimming about. Their wings are not transparent, and coloration tends toward earth tones in shades of tan, brown, gray, or black. The body color can match the wings or be in shades of green or yellow. Adult caddisflies may live one to two weeks.

In the larval stage, most caddis live in cases built from small grains of sand, sticks, strands of vegetation, or a combination of materials. Some live in a free-swimming form or construct a silken retreat with a web.

Caddis hibernate a week or more during pupation, like caterpillars, as they change into winged adults in their cases. When the transformation is complete, the pupae shuck their casings as they soar to the surface in a dash to freedom. Most adults fly off as soon as they hit the surface.

Trout chasing caddis emergers often rocket fully out of the water in their pursuit. Their next best shot at caddis is when the females return to deposit their eggs. It is a busy affair, with lots of buzzing wings and swimming about, although a few dive straight to the bottom. With all that activity, trout hit caddis hard. Fishing strategies should follow suit.

The two most common families in the West are Brachycentridae, dark-gray and dark-brown caddis with wood-case larvae, and Rhyacophilidae, green caddis with free swimming larvae.

The most effective dry fly to cover the bases is the Elk Hair Caddis in No. 12 to 20 with a green, tan, brown, or gray body. Other popular patterns include the Colorado King, Goddard Caddis, Humpy, Henryville Special, Hemingway Caddis, Bucktail Caddis, X-Caddis, and Stimulator.

Larvae and pupae patterns in No. 10 to 18 include the Peacock Herl Caddis and Latex Caddis, or soft-hackle patterns like the Green Partridge, Charles Brooks's Little Green Caddis, and the Sparkle Pupa, Little Gray Caddis and Moss's Caddis Emerger.

PLECOPTERA / STONEFLIES

These prehistoric monsters of the aquatic insect world incite slashing, explosive rises by trophy trout during early season hatches. But for wet flyfishers, the 2- to 3-inch nymphs of the largest species, Pteronarcys californica, are a standard pattern yearround. The Salmonfly feeding frenzy often peaks around the Fourth of July in the Yellowstone River's canyon. But nature doesn't always make it easy. Local weather or spring runoff conditions can speed up or slow a hatch dramatically. Elsewhere, hatches can be very sporadic, and nymph patterns often perform better than dry flies.

Stoneflies look a lot like giant caddisflies, although their two pairs of heavily veined wings lie flat over their backs. Their flight is helicopter-like, with the long body hanging below the whirling wings. Nymphs follow the same life history as mayflies and live underwater one to four years. All species are found in swift, rocky waters rich in oxygen.

Members of the P. californica species were dubbed Salmonflies because of the bright orange highlights on dark brown bodies of nymphs and adult flying insects. A smaller species, the Golden Stonefly (Acroneuria pacifica) is highlighted by golden yellow markings on its light brown body. Golden Stones typically hatch toward the end of a Salmonfly hatch. They also come in a wider variety of sizes and can be an effective dry fly pattern for a longer duration.

Stoneflies do not emerge in midstream. The nymphs crawl across the streambed to water's edge, climb a rock or bush, and shuck their shells as they metamorphose into short-lived, airborne insects.

The key to fishing Salmonflies is staying at the front of the hatch as it moves upstream, usually about 5 miles a day. The point at which only a few flying insects or nymph casings can be found determines a hatch's head. The best bet is to cast nymphs toward the shoreline from a boat or parallel to shore when wading.

Behind the vanguard of the emerging nymphs, dry flies come into play. Late afternoon flights of Salmonflies occur when egg-laying females ride the up-swells of hot air flowing up the canyons cut by the rivers. The large, black egg sacs are deposited like bombs in rocky, fast-water stretches of the stream to begin the cycle anew. Many females fall exhausted onto the water, and the bugs are often blown off streamside bushes by high winds.

There are hundreds of patterns, ranging from super realistic to plain buggy looking impressions, and new ones are being created annually. Check with local fly tackle shops on what's hot.

A variety of Salmonflies, No. 2 to 8, is highly recommended. Golden Stone patterns range from No. 8 to 14. Popular dry flies include the Sofa Pillow, Bird's Stonefly, Golden Stonefly, large Yellow or Orange Stimulators, and Double Humpies. Traditional nymph patterns include the Brooks's Stone, tied in the round, Box Canyon Stone, Montana Stone, Bitch Creek Nymph, orange or black Girdlebug, black Rubber Legs, Super Renegade, and Woolly Bugger.

Small caddis-like insects on the water with wings resting flat over orange or yellow bodies are small species of brown or golden stoneflies. These are often called Little Yellow Stoneflies or Yellow Sallies. Smaller yellow or orange Stimulators and Yellow Sally patterns are very effective, along with Humpies, Bucktail Caddis, and yellow Elk Hair Caddis, No. 10 to 14.

Little Yellow Stonefly hatches may overlap Salmonfly and Golden Stone hatches, and typically last through July into August.

Diptera / True Flies

Midges and mosquitoes are the two families in this order of most interest to flyfishers.

Chironomidae / Midges

Midges can be a dry fly fisher's best friend in winter and early spring on streams open year-round. Float-tubers often count on Chironomid emergers to ensure a good day on lakes and ponds.

Midge larva and pupa patterns are tied very sparsely with green, olive, light olive, tan, brown, or black dubbing on No. 18 to 28 hooks. Peacock or ostrich herl is used on the thorax of pupa patterns.

Flying midge patterns are tied very sparsely in colors to match a variety of hatches with only two or three turns of the same colored hackle for wings, No. 14 to 26. The Griffith's Gnat, tied with a grizzly hackle palmered over a peacock herl body, No. 18 to 28, represents a clump of midges on the water.

Culicidae / Mosquitoes

This is the one fly everyone can identify. Both larva and pupa patterns are tied to float in the surface film. Stripped hackle stems or peacock herls are used for the thin body, in No. 14 to 18. The Mosquito Dry Fly and Adams also work in No. 14 to 18.

Odonata / Dragonflies

Dragonfly and damselfly hatches on lakes and ponds can rival the excitement of stonefly hatches on mountain streams. But even without a hatch, Damsel Nymphs, Assam Dragons, Woolly Worms, Krystal Buggers, and Carey Specials, No. 4 to 12, should be part of a stillwater flyfisher's arsenal year-round.

Long-bodied dry flies also are available at many fly shops.

Yellowstone National Park
GENERAL INFORMATION AND REGULATIONS

Yellowstone National Park
Visitor's Service
P.O. Box 168
Yellowstone National Park, WY 82190-0168
307-344-7381; 307-344-2386
www.nps.gov/YELL/

Operating Hours, Seasons

- **Summer:** Season runs from mid-April to late October. Once a road/entrance opens, it is open 24 hours. (Exceptions: road construction and weather-caused restrictions.)
- **Winter:** Season runs from mid-December to mid-March. The road from the North Entrance at Gardiner, Montana, to the Northeast Entrance and Cooke City, Montana, is open to wheeled vehicle use year round.

Entrance Fees and Permits Costs

The entrance fee is $25 for a private, noncommercial vehicle; $20 for each snowmobile or motorcycle; or $12 for each visitor 16 and older entering by foot, bike, ski, etc. This fee provides the visitor with a 7-day entrance permit for both Yellowstone and Grand Teton National Parks. Remember to keep your admission receipt in order to re-enter the parks. Snowmobile operators must possess a valid motor vehicle operator's license.

Advance reservations are not needed to enter the park. Annual or Lifetime Passes are possible alternatives to the above fees.

Park Annual Pass: The $50 park annual pass provides entrance to pass holder and accompanying passengers in a single private non-commercial vehicle at Yellowstone and Grand Teton National Parks. Pass is valid for 12 months from date of purchase. Purchase your pass at one of the park's entrances.

Interagency Annual Pass: The $80 Interagency Annual Pass provides entrance or access to pass holder and accompanying passengers in a single, private non-commercial vehicle at most federal recreation sites across the country. Pass is valid for 12 months from date of purchase. The pass is not valid for Expanded Amenity fees such as camping or parking at Mt Rushmore. Purchase your pass at one of Yellowstone's entrance stations or online at http://store.usgs.gov/pass.

Interagency Senior Pass: The $10 Interagency Senior Pass (62 and older) is a lifetime pass available to U.S. citizens or permanent residents. Pass is available only in-person at entrances or visitor centers.

Interagency Access Pass: Free lifetime pass available to citizens or permanent residents of the U.S. who have been determined to be blind or permanently disabled. Pass is available only in-person at entrances or visitor centers.

The above passes replace the Golden Eagle, Golden Age and Golden Access Passports as well as the National Parks Pass. These passes will remain valid until they expire or are lost or stolen.

Required Permits and Fees for Fishing

A Yellowstone National Park Fishing Permit is required to fish in the park. Anglers 16 years of age and older are required to purchase a $15 three-day permit, a $20 seven-day permit or a $35 season permit.

Anglers 15 and younger have two options:

1) Children 15 and younger may fish without a permit if they are fishing under the direct supervision of an adult who has a valid park fishing permit, or
2) Children 15 and younger may obtain a free permit that must be signed by a responsible adult; with this permit, a child can fish without direct adult supervision.

Fishing permits are available at all ranger stations, visitor centers, and Yellowstone Park General Stores. Fishing permits are also available at many businesses in the Greater Yellowstone Area. No state fishing license is required in Yellowstone National Park.

Obtain and closely read the park's Fishing Regulations brochure. A PDF copy is available online at: http://www.nps.gov/yell/planyourvisit/fishdates.htm

Medical Services

In the summer season, outpatient medical services are offered at Lake, Mammoth, and Old Faithful. Ambulances, 24-hour emergency service, laboratory, pharmacy, and radiology services are available. Mammoth Clinic is open year round.

Chambers of Commerce near Yellowstone National Park

- Big Sky, MT: 406-995-3000
- Billings, MT: 406-245-4111
- Bozeman, MT: 406-586-5421
- Cooke City/Silver Gate, MT: 406-838-2495
- Gardiner, MT: 406-848-7971
- Livingston, MT: 406-222-0850
- Red Lodge, MT: 406-446-1718
- West Yellowstone, MT: 406-646-7701
- Cody, WY: 307-587-2297
- Dubois, WY: 307-455-2556
- East Yellowstone–Wapiti Valley, WY: 307-587-9595
- Jackson, WY: 307-733-3316
- Idaho Falls, ID: 208-523-1010
- Eastern Idaho Visitor Information Center, Idaho Falls, ID: 1-800-634-3246

Private Boat Permits and Fees

A permit is required for all vessels (motorized and non-motorized, including float tubes) and must be obtained in person at any of the following locations: South Entrance, Lewis Lake Campground, Grant Village Backcountry Office, and Bridge Bay Ranger Station. Non-motorized boating permits are available at West Entrance, Northeast Entrance, Mammoth Backcountry Office, Old Faithful Backcountry Office, Canyon Backcountry Office, Bechler Ranger Station, West Contact Station, West Yellowstone Chamber of Commerce and locations where motorized permits are sold.

- The fee is $20 (annual) or $10 (7 day) for motorized vessels and $10 (annual) or $5 (7 day) for non-motorized vessels. A Coast Guard approved wearable personal flotation device is required for each person boating.
- Boat permits issued in Grand Teton National Park are honored in Yellowstone, but owners must register their vessel in Yellowstone and obtain a no-charge Yellowstone validation sticker from a permit issuing station.
- Jet skis, personal watercraft, airboats, submersibles, and similar vessels are prohibited in Yellowstone National Park.
- All vessels are prohibited on the park's rivers and streams except the channel between Lewis and Shoshone Lakes, where only hand-propelled vessels are permitted.
- Obtain and closely read the park's Boating Regulations brochure. A PDF copy is available online at: http://www.nps.gov/yell/planyourvisit/upload/boating_regs.pdf

Rentals and Guided Boat Trips

Outboard-motorized boats and rowboats may be rented (first come, first served) from Xanterra Parks & Resorts at Bridge Bay Marina on Yellowstone Lake.

- Xanterra also provides guided fishing boats that may be reserved in advance by calling (307) 344-7311 or 1-866-GEYSERLAND (439-7375).
- Other commercial businesses are permitted to offer guided services for canoeing, kayaking, and motorized boating.
- See appendix for list of all outfitters licensed to operate in the park.

Lodging in Yellowstone

Lodging in Yellowstone National Park is operated by Xanterra Parks & Resorts. Visit their website (www.xanterra.com) for information about accommodations or phone 307-344-7311 or 1-866-GEYSERLAND (439-7375) for reservation information. Accommodations range from rustic cabins to luxury suites.

Campgrounds in Yellowstone

Campsite availability is first-come, first serve at the following seven campgrounds in Yellowstone National Park: Indian Creek, Lewis Lake, Mammoth, Norris, Pebble Creek, Slough Creek, and Tower Fall. Campgrounds may be filled by 11 a.m.; arrive early to obtain a site. Overnight camping of any type (tent, vehicle, or RV) outside designated campgrounds is not permitted.

Some campsite reservations area available through Xanterra Parks & Resorts, which operates campgrounds at Bridge Bay, Canyon, Fishing Bridge RV Park, Grant Village, and Madison. Same-day reservations can be made by calling: 307-344-7901. Advance reservations can be made by calling: 307-344-7311 or 1-866-GEYSERLAND (439-7375), or by writing: Yellowstone National Park Lodges, PO Box 165, Yellowstone National Park, WY 82190.

Fishing Bridge RV Park is the only campground offering water, sewer, and electrical hookups, and it is for hard-sided vehicles only (no tents or tent-trailers are allowed).

It is recommended that people driving recreational vehicles over 30′ make a reservation since there are a limited number of campsites over 30′ available in Yellowstone. Large RV sites are located at Flagg Ranch, Fishing Bridge RV Park, West Yellowstone and Gardiner.

Yellowstone Trip Planner

For more information, check out the park's web site's Trip Planner tips and internet links for services in the park and contacts for chambers of commerce of surrounding communities: http://www.nps.gov/yell/planyourvisit/index.htm

Backcountry Camping

Yellowstone has a designated backcountry campsite system, and a Backcountry Use Permit is required for all overnight stays. Permits may be obtained only in person and no more than 48 hours in advance of your trip. Backcountry campsites still may be reserved in advance. Requests for reservations must be submitted by mail or in person. They cannot be made over the phone or by fax. Reservations are booked on a first-come, first-served basis. A confirmation notice, not a permit, is given or mailed to the camper. This confirmation notice must then be converted to the actual permit not more than 48 hours in advance of the first camping date. Details are provided on the confirmation notice. The reservation fee is $20 regardless of the number of nights out or the number of people involved. The fee is not refundable. Forms for making an advance reservation are available to download online at www.nps.gov/yell or by writing to: Backcountry Office, P.O. Box 168, Yellowstone National Park, WY 82190l or call 307-344-2160.

Because only a portion of the approximately three hundred backcountry campsites are available for advance reservations, you may choose to wait until you arrive in the park to reserve your site(s) and obtain your permit. The $20 fee applies only to reservations made more than 48 hours in advance of the start of your trip.

Where to Get Your Permit

During the summer season (June–August), permits are available 7 days a week between 8:00 a.m. and 4:30 p.m. at the following locations:
• Bechler Ranger Station

- Canyon Ranger Station/Visitor Center
- Grant Village Visitor Center
- Lake Ranger Station
- Mammoth Ranger Station/Visitor Center
- Old Faithful Ranger Station
- South Entrance Ranger Station
- Tower Ranger Station
- West Entrance Ranger Station

Licensed Outfitters Serving Yellowstone Park
(alphabetical by town)

Yellowstone Outfitters
  Box 1149
  Afton, WY 83110
  800-447-4711
  www.yellowstoneoutfitters.com

Three Rivers Ranch
  1662 Idaho 47
  Ashton, ID 83420
  208-652-3750
  www.threeriversranch.com

East Slope Anglers
  47855 Gallatin Road
  Big Sky, MT 59716
  406-995-4369
  www.eastslopeoutdoors.com

Gallatin Riverguides
  47430 Gallatin Road
  Big Sky, MT 59716
  406-995-2290
  www.montanaflyfishing.com

Lone Mountain Ranch, Inc.
  750 Lone Mountain Ranch Road
  Big Sky, MT 59716
  406-995-4644
  www.lmranch.com

Wild Trout Outfitters
  Hwy 191
  Big Sky, MT 59716
  406-995-4895
  www.wildtroutoutfitters.com

Adventure Yellowstone Inc.
  P.O. Box 746
  Bozeman MT 59771
  406-585-904

Dave Corcoran Outfitters
  3400 Water Hole Trail
  Bozeman, MT 59715
  406-587-7214

Eagle Creek Outfitters
  12255 Skunk Creek Road
  Bozeman, MT 59715
  406-686-4789

Greater Yellowstone Flyfishers
  31 Spanish Peak Drive
  Bozeman, MT 59718
  406-586-2489
  www.gyflyfishers.com

Hawkridge Outfitters
  8000 Trail Creek Road
  Bozeman, MT 59715
  406-585-9608

Montana Outdoor Adventures, Inc.
2201 Milwaukee Road
Bozeman, MT 59715
406-586-8524
www.montanaoutdooradventures.com

Yellowstone/Glacier Adventures
65 Hidden Valley Drive
Bozeman, MT 59771
406-585-9041

Grub Steak Expeditions
P.O. Box 1013
Cody, WY 82414
307-527-6316
www.grubsteaktours.com

North Fork Anglers
1107 Sheridan Avenue
Cody, WY 82414-3627
307-527-7274
www.northforkanglers.com

John Henry Lee Outfitters, Inc.
P.O. Box 990
Dubois, WY 82513
307-733-9441
www.johnhenrylee.com

Headwaters Guide Service
611 Garnet Mountain Way
Gallatin Gateway, MT 59730
406-763-4761
www.headwatersguideservice.com

Parks' Fly Shop
202 South 2nd Street
Gardiner, MT 59030
406-848-7314
www.parksflyshop.com

Rendezvous Outfitters
232 Park Street
Gardiner, MT 59030
406-848-7967

Henry's Fork Anglers, Inc.
3340 Hwy 20
Island Park, ID 83429
208-558-7525
www.henrysforkanglers.com

Trouthunter
3427 North Highway 20
Island Park, ID 83429
208-558-9900
www.trouthunt.com

Fish the Fly
P.O. Box 42
Jackson, WY 83001
307-690-1139
www.fishthefly.com

High Country Flies
185 North Center Street
Jackson, WY 83001
307-733-7210
www.flyfishingjacksonhole.com

Jack Dennis Fly Fishing
70 S. King Street
Jackson, WY 83001
307-690-0910
www.jackdennis.com

Jackson Hole Anglers
990 Montana Road
Jackson, WY 83001
888-45-trout
www.jacksonholeanglers.com

Mangis Guide Service
P.O. Box 3165
307-733-8553
Jackson, WY 83001
www.mangisguides.com

Orvis of Jackson
485 West Broadway
307-733-5407
Jackson, WY 83001
www.orvis.com/jacksonhole

Snake River Angler
490 South Highway 89
Jackson, WY 83001
307-733-3699
www.snakeriverangler.com

World Cast Anglers
485 West Broadway
Jackson, WY 83001
307-733-6934
www.worldcastanglers.com

Lost River Outfitters
171 N. Main
Ketchum, ID 83340
208-726-1706
www.lostriveroutfitters.com

Blue Ribbon Fishing Tours
209 Blue Heron Drive
Livingston, MT 59047
406-222-7714

Hatch Finders
113 #3 West Park Street
Livingston, MT 59047
406-222-0989

www.hatchfinders.com
Montana Fly Fishing Guides
417 South 12th Street
Livingston, MT 59047
406-223-2488
www.montanaflyfishingguides.com

Montana's Master Angler
602 S. 12th Street
Livingston, MT 59047
406-222-2273

Slough Creek Outfitters
136 Deep Creek Road
Livingston, Montana 59047
406-222-6642
www.sloughcreek.com

Williams Guide Service
P.O. Box 2
Livingston, MT 59047
406-222-1386

Yellowstone Angler
Highway 89 South
Livingston, MT 59047
406-222-7130
www.yellowstoneangler.com

Triangle X Ranch
2 Triangle X Ranch Road
Moose, WY 83012
307-733-2183
www.triangle-x.com

Beartooth Plateau Outfitters
819 Clear Creek Road
Roberts, MT 59070-9537
406-445-2293
www.beartoothoutfitters.com

Far and Away Adventures
P.O. Box 54
Sun Valley, ID 83353
208-726-8888
www.far-away.com

Westbank Anglers
3670 North Moose Wilson Road
Teton Village, WY 83025
307-733-6483
www.westbank.com

Arrick's Fishing Flies
37 North Canyon Street
West Yellowstone, MT 59758
406-646-7290
www.arricks.com

Blue Ribbon Flies
305 Canyon Street
West Yellowstone, MT 59758
406-646-9365
www.blue-ribbon-flies.com

Bud Lilly's Trout Shop
39 Madison Avenue
West Yellowstone, MT 59758
406-646-7801
www.budlillys.com

Firehole Ranch
Denny Creek Road (On the northwest
    shore of Hebgen Lake)
West Yellowstone, MT 59758
406-646-7294
www.fireholeranch.com

Jacklin's Fly Shop
105 Yellowstone Avenue
West Yellowstone, MT 59758
406-646-7336
www.jacklinsflyshop.com

Lost Fork Outfitters
PO Box 1896
West Yellowstone MT 59758
406 581-9113
www.lostforkoutfitters.com

Madison River Outfitters
117 Canyon Street
West Yellowstone, MT 59758
406-646-9644
www.madisonriveroutfitters.com

West Yellowstone Fly Shop
140 Madison Ave
406-646-1181
West Yellowstone, MT 59758
www.wyflyshop.com

Fatboy Fishing Company
5455 W Highway 22
Wilson, WY 83014
307-733-3061

Teton Troutfitters
P.O. Box 536
Wilson, WY 83014
307-733-5360
www.tetontroutfitters.com

Grand Teton National Park
GENERAL INFORMATION AND REGULATIONS

Grand Teton National Park
P.O. Drawer 170
Moose, WY 83012
307-739-3300 / Visitor Information: 307-739-3399
www.nps.gov/grte

Fees

- The entrance fee is $20 per car, good for both Grand Teton and Yellowstone National Parks; $12 per night per site camping fee. Fees are also charged for watercraft.

Season

- The park is open every day; visitor centers are closed on Christmas Day.

Campgrounds

- Reservations through AMFac Parks & Resorts: 307-344-7311
- Gros Ventre Campground, open late April to early October
- Jenny Lake Campground, open late May to late September, fills by 8AM
- Signal Mountain Campground, open early May to mid-October, fills by 10AM
- Colter Bay Campground, open late May to late September
- Lizard Creek Campground, open early June to early September

Lodging and Reservations

- Jackson Lake Lodge, Jenny Lake Lodge, and Colter Bay Village: contact Grand Teton Lodge Co., Box 240, Moran, WY 83013 / Reservations: 307-543-2855 or 800-628-9988 / Nonreservation calls: 307-543-2811
- Flagg Ranch, Box 187, Moran, WY 83013, 800-443-2311
- Signal Mountain Lodge Co., Box 50, Moran, WY 83013, 307-543-2831
- Dornan's Spur Ranch Cabins, Box 39, Moose, WY 83012, 307-733-2415

Backcountry Camping Permits

- Overnight stays in the backcountry require a free backcountry permit available at the Moose or Colter Bay Visitor Centers and the Jenny Lake Ranger Station. Reservations may be made for backcountry campsites between January 1 and May 15, or up to 30 days ahead of your first night's stay. For information or copy of permit application call 307-739-3309 or 739-3397, or write Permits Office in care of the above address.
- River and backcountry permit information (recorded): 307-739-3602

Fishing

- A Wyoming fishing license is required for fishing in the park, and regulations are set by the Wyoming Game and Fish Department. Licenses may be purchased in fishing tackle stores in Jackson, Dornan's, and at park marinas.

Boating

- Permits required for motorized and nonmotorized watercraft are available at visitor centers and ranger stations. Nonmotorized boat fees are $5 for a week permit or $10 for an annual permit. Motorized boat fees are $10 for a week permit and $20 for an annual permit.

Additional Information

Jackson Hole Chamber of Commerce
Box E
Jackson, Wyoming 83001
307-733-3316 or 307-733-5585
www.jacksonholechamber.com

Fly Shops and Sporting Good Stores

BOZEMAN, MT

Bob Ward and Sons, 3011 Max Ave., Bozeman, MT 59718 / 406-586-4381 /
www.bobwards.com

Bozeman Angler, 23 East Main, Bozeman, MT 59715 / 406-587-9111 or
800-886-9111 / www.bozemanangler.com

Fins `n' Feathers, SW Corner of 4 Corners, 81801 Gallatin Rd Bozeman, MT 59718 /
406-585-2917 / www.finsandfeathersonline.com

Greater Yellowstone Flyfishers, 31 Spanish Peak Drive, Bozeman, MT 59718 /
406-585-5321 / www.gyflyfishers.com

Montana Troutfitters, 1716 West Main, Bozeman, MT 59718 / 406-587-4707 /
www.troutfitters.com

Powder Horn Sportsman's Supply, 35 East Main, Bozeman, MT 59715 /
406-587-7373 / www.schnees.com

The River's Edge, 2012 North 7th Avenue, Bozeman, MT 59715 / 406-586-5373 /
www.theriversedge.com

Wholesale Sports, 2214 Tschache Street, Bozeman, MT 59718 / 406-586-0100 /
www.wholesalesports.com

Yellowstone Gateway Sports, 21 Fork Horn Trail, Bozeman, MT 59718 / 406-586-2076

BIG SKY, MT

East Slope Outdoors, Hwy. 191 / 406-995-4369 / www.eastslopeoutdoors.com

Gallatin River Guides, Hwy. 191 / 406-995-2290 / www.montanaflyfishing.com

Wild Trout Outfitters, Hwy 191 / 800-423-4742 / www.wildtroutoutfitters.com

CODY, WY

North Fork Anglers, 1438 Sheridan Avenue / 307-527-7274 /
www.northforkanglers.com

Outdoor Sports Center, 1138 12th Street / 307-587-9526

Rocky Mountain Discount Sports, 1526 Rumsey Ave / 307-527-6071

The Humble Fly Shop, 1183 Sheridan Ave / 307-587-2757 / www.thehumblefly.com

COOKE CITY, MT

Beartooth Plateau Outfitters, Main Street (P.O. Box 1127), Cooke City, MT 59020 /
406-838-2328 or 800-253-8545 / www.beartoothoutfitters.com

EMIGRANT, MT

Angler's West Flyfishing Outfitters, P.O. Box 4, Emigrant, MT 59027 / 406-333-4401
/ www.montanaflyfishers.com

Hubbard's Yellowstone Lodge, Miner Basin, Emigrant, MT 59027/406-848-7755

River's Bend Lodge, Hwy 89 just south of Emigrant / 800-541-4113 /
www.riversbendlodge.com

GARDINER, MT

Park's Fly Shop, PO Box 196, 202 Second Street South (US-89) Gardiner, MT 59030 / 406-848-7314 / Licenses / Flyfishing guides and instructors / Full service fly shop / www.parksflyshop.com

Tank N Tackle, Park Ave & 2nd Street / 406-848-7501

IDAHO FALLS, ID

Hyde Outfitters & Last Chance Lodge, 1520 Pancheri Drive, Idaho Falls / 800-428-8338 / www.hydeoutdoors.com

Jimmy's All Seasons Angler, 275 A St. / 208-524-7160 / www.jimmysflyshop.com

Sportsman's Warehouse, 2909 S. 25th E. / Ammon / 208-542-1900 / www.sportsmanswarehouse.com

ISLAND PARK, ID

BS Flies Shop, 3757 N. Hwy 20 (in Pond's Lodge) / 208-390-2177 / www.bsflies.com

Henry's Fork Anglers, 3340 Highway 20 / 208-558-7525 / Mike Lawson / www.henrysforkanglers.com

Trout Hunter, 3327 N. Highway 20 / 208-558-9900 / www.trouthunt.com

Three Rivers Ranch, 3386 N Hwy 20 / 208-558-7501 / www.threeriversranch.com

JACKSON, WY

Crescent H Ranch, 1027 S. Fall Creek Road. P.O. Box 730, Wilson WY 83014 / 307-733-3674 / www.crescenthranch.com

Flagg Ranch, South Entrance of Yellowstone Park; Moran, WY / 307-543-2861 / www.flaggranch.com

High Country Flies, 185 North Center Street / 307-733-7210 / www.flyfishingjacksonhole.com

Jack Dennis Outdoor Shop, 50 East Broadway / 307-733-3270 / www.jackdennis.com

Jack Dennis Fly Fishing, 70 S. King Street / 307-690-0910 / www.jackdennis.com

Jackson Hole Anglers, 990 Montana Road / 888-45-trout / www.jacksonholeanglers.com

John Henry Lee Outfitters, Box 8368 Jackson, WY 83001 / 307-733-944 or 800-3-JACKSON / www.johnhenrylee.com

Mangis Guide Service, P.O. Box 3165 / 307-733-8553 / www.mangisguides.com

Orvis of Jackson, 485 West Broadway / 307-733-5407 / www.orvis.com/jacksonhole

Turpin Meadows Ranch, P.O. Box 379 Buffalo Valley, Moran WY / 307 543-2496,800-743-2496 / www.turpinmeadowranch.com

World Cast Anglers, 485 West Broadway / 307-733-6934 / www.worldcastanglers.com

LIVINGSTON, MT

Dan Bailey Fly Shop, 209 West Park Street / 800-356-4052 / Flies, tying material, fishing equipment, clothing, and accessories / www.dan-bailey.com

George Anderson's Yellowstone Angler, 5256 Highway 89 South / 406-222-7130 / Flyfishing specialties, outdoor clothing / www.yellowstoneangler.com

Hatch Finders Fly Shop, 113 West Park #3 / 406-222-0989 / www.hatchfinders.com

Sweetwater Fly Shop, 5082 US Highway 89 S / 406-222-9393 / www.sweetwaterflyshop.com

MOOSE, WY

Triangle X Ranch / Harold Turner / 2 Triangle Ranch Road / 307-733-2183 / www.trianglex.com

PRAY, MT

Knoll's Yellowstone Hackle, 104 Chicory Road / 406-333-4848 / www.knolls.us / hackle specialists

RIVERTON, WY

Rocky Mountain Discount Sports, 709 N Federal Boulevard / 307-856-7687

SHERIDAN, WY

Big Horn Mountain Sports, 176 North Main Street / 307-672-6866 / www.bighornmountainsports.com

Fly Shop of the Big Horns, 227 North Main Street / 307-672-5866 / www.troutangler.com

Rocky Mountain Discount Sports, 440 Broadway Street / 307-672-3418

TETON VILLAGE, WY

Westbank Anglers, 3670 North Moose Wilson Road, Teton Village / 307-733-6483 / www.westbank.com

WEST YELLOWSTONE, MT

Arrick's Fly Shop, 37 North Canyon Street / 406-646-7290 / www.arricks.com

Bud Lilly's Trout Shop, 39 Madison Avenue / 406-646-7801 / www.budlillys.com

Madison River Outfitters, 117 Canyon Street / 406-646-9644 / www.madisonriveroutfitters.com

Blue Ribbon Flies, 305 Canyon Street / 406-646-7642 / www.blue-ribbon-flies.com

Jacklin's Fly Shop, 105 Yellowstone Avenue / 406-646-7336 / www.jacklinsflyshop.com

West Yellowstone Fly Shop, 140 Madison Ave / 406-646-1181 / www.wyflyshop.com

WILSON, WY

Fatboy Fishing, 5455 W. Highway 22 / 307-733-3061

Index

NOTES

NOTES

NOTES

NOTES